JOURNAL FOR THE STUDY OF THE OLD TESTAMENT
SUPPLEMENT SERIES
149

JSOT Press
Sheffield

PRIESTS, PROPHETS AND SCRIBES

Essays on the Formation and Heritage
of Second Temple Judaism in Honour
of Joseph Blenkinsopp

edited by

**Eugene Ulrich, John W. Wright,
Robert P. Carroll and Philip R. Davies**

Journal for the Study of the Old Testament
Supplement Series 149

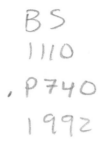
Copyright © 1992 Sheffield Academic Press

Published by JSOT Press
JSOT Press is an imprint of
Sheffield Academic Press Ltd
343 Fulwood Road
Sheffield S10 3BP
England

Typeset by Sheffield Academic Press
and
Printed on acid-free paper in Great Britain
by Biddles Limited
Guildford

British Library Cataloguing in Publication Data

Priests, Prophets and Scribes: Essays on
the Formation and Heritage of Second
Temple Judaism in Honour of Joseph
Blenkinsopp.- (JSOT Supplement Series,
ISSN 0309-0787; No. 149)
I Ulrich, Eugene II. Series,
296.8

ISBN 1-85075-375-X

CONTENTS

PART IV
THE THEOLOGY OF THE HEBREW BIBLE

Acknowledgments

The editors wish to thank several people for their contributions to the completion of this volume. Alan Krieger, Bibliographer for Philosophy and Theology at the University of Notre Dame, assisted in compiling Professor Blenkinsopp's bibliography. Professor James Vanderkam aided in editing the Ethiopic. Margaret Jasiewicz and her staff at Notre Dame helped with the computerization of a number of the articles. Robert A. Kugler, Peter W. Flint and Catherine Murphy provided research assistance to complete the editing. To Irene Blenkinsopp also thanks are due for help in initiating this project. The contributors to this volume want to thank Joseph Blenkinsopp for all that he has taught us through his writings on the priests, prophets and scribes of ancient Israel.

University of Notre Dame
University of Sheffield
24 June 1992

ABBREVIATIONS

AB	Anchor Bible
AfO	*Archiv für Orientforschung*
AnBib	Analecta biblica
ANET	J.B. Pritchard (ed.), *Ancient Near Eastern Texts*
BASOR	*Bulletin of the American Schools of Oriental Research*
BDB	F. Brown, S.R. Driver and C.A. Briggs, *Hebrew and English Lexicon of the Old Testament*
BETL	Bibliotheca ephemeridum theologicarum lovaniensium
BHK	R. Kittel (ed.), *Biblia hebraica*
BHS	*Biblia hebraica stuttgartensia*
Bib	*Biblica*
BKAT	Biblischer Kommentar: Altes Testament
BZAW	Beihefte zur *ZAW*
CAD	*The Assyrian Dictionary of the Oriental Institute of the University of Chicago*
CBQ	*Catholic Biblical Quarterly*
CBQMS	*Catholic Biblical Quarterly* Monograph Series
CChr	Corpus Christianorum
ConBOT	Coniectanea biblica, Old Testament
DJD	Discoveries in the Judaean Desert
HAT	Handbuch zum Alten Testament
HBT	*Horizons in Biblical Theology*
HeyJ	*Heythrop Journal*
HSM	Harvard Semitic Monographs
HTR	*Harvard Theological Review*
IB	*Interpreter's Bible*
ICC	International Critical Commentary
IDB	G.A. Buttrick (ed.), *Interpreter's Dictionary of the Bible*
IDBSup	*IDB*, Supplementary Volume
Int	*Interpretation*
JAOS	*Journal of the American Oriental Society*
JBL	*Journal of Biblical Literature*
JJS	*Journal of Jewish Studies*
JPSV	Jewish Publication Society Version
JSHRZ	Jüdische Schriften aus hellenistisch-römischer Zeit
JSOT	*Journal for the Study of the Old Testament*
JSOTSup	*Journal for the Study of the Old Testament*, Supplement Series
JTS	*Journal of Theological Studies*

KJV	King James Version
LUÅ	Lunds universitets årsskrift
NASB	New American Standard Bible
NCB	New Century Bible
NEB	New English Bible
NICOT	New International Commentary on the Old Testament
NRSV	New Revised Standard Version
NTS	*New Testament Studies*
OBO	Orbis biblicus et orientalis
OLP	Orientalia lovaniensia periodica
OTG	Old Testament Guides
OTL	Old Testament Library
OTS	*Oudtestamentische Studiën*
PEQ	*Palestine Exploration Quarterly*
RA	*Revue d'assyriologie et d'archéologie orientale*
RSV	Revised Standard Version
SANT	Studien zum Alten und Neuen Testament
SBLDS	SBL Dissertation Series
SBLMS	SBL Monograph Series
SBLSCS	SBL Septuagint and Cognate Studies
SBLTT	SBL Texts and Translations
SBT	Studies in Biblical Theology
Scr	*Scripture*
SJOT	*Scandinavian Journal of the Old Testament*
SOTSMS	Society for Old Testament Study Monograph Series
STDJ	Studies on the Texts of the Desert of Judah
TBü	Theologische Bücherei
TS	*Theological Studies*
VT	*Vetus Testamentum*
VTSup	*Vetus Testamentum*, Supplements
WBC	Word Biblical Commentary
WMANT	Wissenschaftliche Monographien zum Alten und Neuen Testament
ZAW	*Zeitschrift für die alttestamentliche Wissenschaft*
ZDPV	*Zeitschrift des deutschen Palästina-Vereins*
ZTK	*Zeitschrift für Theologie und Kirche*

LIST OF CONTRIBUTORS

James Barr
Vanderbilt Divinity School, Nashville, Tennessee

Robert P. Carroll
Department of Biblical Studies, University of Glasgow

James L. Crenshaw
Duke University Divinity School, Durham, North Carolina

Philip R. Davies
Department of Biblical Studies, University of Sheffield

David Noel Freedman
University of Michigan, Ann Arbor, Michigan

Walter Harrelson
Vanderbilt Divinity School, Nashville, Tennessee

Neils Peter Lemche
Department of Old Testament Studies, University of Aarhus, Denmark

Rolf Rendtorff
Karben, Germany

Judson R. Shaver
Regis College, Denver, Colorado

Vassilios Tzaferis
Israel Antiquities Authority, Jerusalem

Eugene Ulrich
Department of Theology, University of Notre Dame, Indiana

James C. VanderKam
Department of Theology, University of Notre Dame, Indiana

Christiana de Groot van Houten
Calvin College, Grand Rapids, Michigan

Joel P. Weinberg
Daugavpils, Republic of Latvia

Moshe Weinfeld
Department of Bible, The Hebrew University, Jerusalem

R.N. Whybray
Ely, Cambridgeshire

Robert L. Wilken
Department of Religious Studies and History, University of Virginia,
Charlottesville, Virginia

John W. Wright
Winamac, Indiana

Introduction

Robert L. Wilken

I first met Joe Blenkinsopp in the winter of 1971 during my interview
for a position in the Department of Theology at the University of
Notre Dame. I remember walking across the campus with him from
O'Shaughnessy Hall to the University Club, talking about the university, the department, and the prospects it offered for theological scholarship. As we made our way through the snowdrifts, the conversation
drifted from topic to topic. Gradually, however, we found ourselves
talking about Judaism, the Hebrew language, and Christian biblical
and historical scholarship. Years later I realized that we had hit upon
a common love which kindled our friendship and would forge a
lasting intellectual and spiritual bond. In those few minutes it became
clear that Joe was as much interested in Jewish history and thought as
he was in his chosen field of Hebrew Bible scholarship.

I do not know how Joe came to combine scholarship on the Hebrew
Bible with the study of Judaism. If one looks back at his earlier
writings it is not clear what planted the seed for this development.
Those who know only his later scholarly works may not realize that in
1968 he published a book with the imposing title, *Celibacy, Ministry,
Church: An Enquiry into the Possibility of Reform in the Present
Self-Understanding of the Roman Catholic Church and its Practice
of Ministry.* After that book appeared, Jim O'Gara, editor of
Commonweal, asked him to write a book on sex which appeared a
year later under the title, *Sexuality and the Christian Tradition*.
Apparently O'Gara felt that someone who could write a book on
celibacy was an ideal choice to write on sexuality. His judgment was
sound; the book sold out. During those years Blenkinsopp also did
extensive translating from German, for example a work of
Schnackenburg's and some 150,000 words for a German theological
lexicon. His high devotion to German scholarship was, I understand,

surpassed only by the need to pay his bills.

Blenkinsopp's first degree was an Honors in history at London University in 1948. During the next decade he studied theology, chiefly in Italy, where he took the Licentiate in Turin in 1956 and his first degree in Scripture, the LSS at the Biblical Institute in Rome in 1958. From 1958–1962 he taught at the International College, Romsey, England, and in 1963–1964 at Landivar University, Guatemala City, Guatemala. His doctoral studies were at Oxford where he received the D. Phil. in Old Testament studies in 1967 with a dissertation on Gibeon published several years later as *Gibeon and Israel: The Role of Gibeon and the Gibeonites in the Political and Religious History of Early Israel.*[1] He came to the United States in 1968, teaching at Vanderbilt, at Chicago Theological Seminary, and the Hartford Seminary Foundation before settling at Notre Dame in 1970.

When Blenkinsopp first came to Notre Dame, interest in Judaism on campus was, as he once noted, 'initially slight to nonexistent'. But the university had received a gift from the Rosenstiel family that allowed the department to bring Jewish scholars to the campus, and the department chairperson, David Burrell, warmly supported Blenkinsopp's interest in fostering serious study of Judaism at Notre Dame. Already Blenkinsopp had many friends in Jewish studies and he was able to attract them to lecture at Notre Dame. The University of Notre Dame has become so familiar to Jewish scholars all over the world that it is well to remember that in 1970 Jews were a bit wary of visiting this quintessential Catholic institution named after 'Our Lady'. At one point we had to remind the administration that remembering the names of Jewish donors in the Mass was hardly an ecumenical gesture and giving Jewish scholars tickets to Saturday afternoon Notre Dame football games was not a token of gracious hospitality.

Joe was the first Christian Old Testament scholar I had met who thought that Jewish thought and interpretation should become an integral part of the study of the Old Testament. He was not, of course, unique in this regard. Brevard Childs had recently published his commentary on Exodus in which he had drawn on the medieval Jewish exegetical tradition. But few consulted Jewish sources in their research and even fewer read modern Hebrew scholarship. In the main, Christian Old Testament scholarship was carried on then, as

1   Cambridge: Cambridge University Press, 1972.

now, as a branch of Near Eastern languages and literature or the history of the ancient Near East or as a subsection of biblical theology, which of course meant reading the Hebrew Bible in light of its appropriation by the Christian tradition.

Like all good scholars Blenkinsopp realized that the study of the history of one's discipline is a way not only of gaining a perspective on current scholarship, but also of generating fresh ideas. In an article published in 1984, he surveyed the history of Old Testment scholarship in light of its attitudes toward Judaism and one can see here the line of thinking that has shaped his scholarship.[2] One of his initial discoveries, as he wryly observes in a discussion of the work of Georg Lorenz Bauer in 1796, was that Bauer had the dubious distinction of being the first to write an Old Testament Theology 'while dismissing as...unworthy of serious attention about four-fifths of the content of the Old Testament'.[3] In the name of critical scholarship (Bauer had accepted the new theories concerning the 'Jehovist' and 'Elohist' sources and the late date of Isa. 40–66), he passed on without examination traditional Christian anti-Jewish biases. The God presented in the Pentateuch was a 'narrow nationalistic deity' and the vision of Daniel 'manifests all the illiberality which characterized the opinions of the later Jews'.[4] These ideas became the basis for later reconstructions of Israelite religion, namely that of Julius Wellhausen. As Wellhausen put it in his article on 'Israel' in the Encyclopaedia Britannica:

> Jesus casts ridicule on the works of the law, the washing of hands and vessels, the tithing of mint and cummin, the abstinence even from doing good on the Sabbath. Against unfruitful self-sanctification He sets up another principle of morality, that of the service of one's neighbour.[5]

With characteristic understatement Blenkinsopp notes that these developments in biblical scholarship 'were not shaped exclusively by exegetical considerations'.[6]

Paradoxically Christian Old Testament studies, a discipline devoted to the study of the Hebrew language and to the history and literature

---

2. Joseph Blenkinsopp, 'Old Testament Theology and the Jewish–Christian Connection', *JSOT* 28 (1984), pp. 3-15.
3. Blenkinsopp, 'Old Testament Theology', p. 3.
4. Quoted in Blenkinsopp, 'Old Testament Theology', p. 4.
5. Quoted in Blenkinsopp, 'Old Testament Theology', p. 8.
6. Blenkinsopp, 'Old Testament Theology', p. 10.

of ancient Israel, became an 'instrument in Jewish–Christian alienation'. It had helped to create among Christian scholars an artificial
world called 'Spätjudentum', that is, the period of the Second Jewish
Commonwealth, or in Christian parlance, the intertestamental literature, which served chiefly as a foil to the study of Jesus and the New
Testament. Ultimately the intellectual developments in Old Testament
scholarship helped to isolate the New Testament from its Jewish
world, just as preoccupation with origins and background blinded
New Testament scholars to the insights that could be gained by reading texts *after* the New Testament, namely rabbinic literature and
early Christian literature. As a consequence rabbinical literature has
contributed little to the interpretation of the New Testament.

Blenkinsopp has pointed out that Old Testament theologies have not
only neglected the legal sections of the Pentateuch, they also gave
scant attention to the wisdom literature, especially when the organiz-
ing motif was *Heilsgeschichte*.

> Leaving aside this curious idea of a *Heilsgeschichte* which comes to an
> end at a certain point or (even more curious) which stops and starts again,
> we may note the irony involved in a Theology of the Old Testament which
> cannot accommodate those writings which, in theme and procedure, most
> closely approximate theology as we recognize it today. Issues such as free
> will, divine providence and the destiny of the individual after death, were
> certainly raised by the sages [that is, the wisdom literature].[7]

In Blenkinsopp's view the wisdom tradition provides a link that joins
together classical rabbinical Judaism and early Christianity. The earli-
est attributions in both extend back into the biblical period, and the
Alexandrian school of Christian theology has its roots in Israel's
scribal tradition. It might also be observed that when Clement of
Alexandria wrote his *Paidagogos*, the first Christian treatise on morals
and manners, he had the text of Sirach and Proverbs before him.
Origen's first efforts to forge a Trinitarian theology depend heavily
on the Wisdom of Solomon. In *First Principles* (1.2.5) Origen noted
the remarkable similarity between the language used of Sophia in the
Wisdom of Solomon, 'she is the breath of the power of God and a
pure emanation of the glory of the Almighty...for she is a reflection
(ἀπαύγασμα) of eternal light', (7.25-26) and in Hebrews, 'his is the
reflection (ἀπαύγασμα) of God's glory and the exact imprint of

---

7.   Blenkinsopp, 'Old Testament Theology', p. 6.

God's very being' (Heb. 1.3). In his *Commentary on the Gospel of John* Origen identifies wisdom as the first great title for the Logos.

Shortly before Blenkinsopp arrived at the University of Notre Dame, the Department of Theology, in the wake of Vatican II, had begun a doctoral program. By the early seventies, as the faculty grew and became more diverse, the department began to discuss how they might structure the program to respond to the burgeoning interest in theology and the study of religion in American colleges and universities. The influential Welch report had concluded that many doctoral programs had similar or identical specializations and urged that departments attempt to break out of the model provided by traditional seminary education. In response to this situation the theology department at Notre Dame devoted a year to study and debate the matter and in 1976 adopted the following divisions for doctoral study in theology: Theological Inquiry, embracing systematic theology, philosophical theology, and ethics; Liturgical Studies, Notre Dame's oldest graduate program; and Christianity and Judaism in Antiquity.

Christianity and Judaism in Antiquity, or CJA as it came to be called, was made possible by the interest in Judaism that had developed within the department since Blenkinsopp had joined the faculty. Many factors went into its formation, but the key idea was to bring Christian scholarship on the Hebrew Bible as well as the New Testament and early Christianity (patristics) in relation to the history, literature and thought of Judaism. This meant, of course, that the department shifted the emphasis from pre-Christian Jewish literature, the so-called intertestamental literature, to the post-biblical literature, that is, to the classical texts of rabbinical Judaism. The program was designed, as Blenkinsopp wrote, to 'counter scholarly apartheid'. What it accomplished was deceptively simple, but historically and theologically profound. It taught students (and no less important, faculty) to see Judaism as a living religion that took its distinctive shape during the same period that Christianity was being formed. In this way the new program called CJA echoed the decree on non-Christian religions of Vatican II. In *Nostra Aetate* the council fathers, citing the words of St Paul in Rom. 11.18, 'remember that it is not you that support the root, but the root that supports you', emphasized that Judaism continues to play a role in the divine economy: 'Nor can [the Church] forget that she *draws* [present tense!] sustenance from the root of that good olive tree onto which have been grafted the wild olive branches of the Gentiles'.

During the formative years of CJA, Blenkinsopp continued his scholarship on the Hebrew Bible and on Judaism in the period of the Second Temple. In 1977 he published *Prophecy and Canon* with the subtitle, *A Contribution to the Study of Jewish Origins*. Here Blenkinsopp was interested in the question of how the 'canon' was established by juxtaposing the Torah and the prophets, and the movement from the prophets as oral speakers to the codification of their oracles as a fixed body of prophetic literature included in the 'canon' of Scripture. In 1983 he published *A History of Prophecy in Israel*, the first full scale history of the development of prophecy written in English, as well as *Wisdom and Law in the Old Testament: The Order of Life in Israel and Early Judaism*. More recently he has published a commentary on Ezra and Nehemiah.

But Joe is not only a scholar. He has been a faithful friend and a stimulating colleague to many in the academic community all over the world: in the United States, in Israel, in France, Germany, and Italy, and in England, his native country which he loves without, however, the romanticism of American academics. Blenkinsopp's England is not Oxbridge, but the north (he was born in Durham) and he reminds American colleagues that on their visits to England, they seldom make their way to the real England. His father, Joseph William Blenkinsopp (1897–1931) to whom he dedicated his most mature book, *A History of Prophecy in Israel*, was a coal miner who died in an accident when Joe was a child. One of the small debts I owe to Joe is that he once suggested I read Emile Zola's *Germinal*, a grim but compassionate novel of the life of coal mining families in northern France in the nineteenth century.

It is a great pleasure to join others in this volume in honoring our esteemed colleague and friend Joseph Blenkinsopp, the John A. O'Brien Professor of Biblical Studies at the University of Notre Dame.

Part I
CHRONICLES, EZRA, NEHEMIAH

FROM CENTER TO PERIPHERY:
1 CHRONICLES 23–27 AND THE INTERPRETATION OF CHRONICLES
IN THE NINETEENTH CENTURY

John W. Wright

The interpretation of Chronicles in the nineteenth century has significant implications for the history of modern Hebrew Bible studies—a
fact often overlooked by the historians of the field.[1] Sara Japhet has
even asserted that Chronicles research moved against the current of
nineteenth-century Hebrew Bible studies.[2] The recent work of
M. Patrick Graham, however, has ably documented the nineteenth
century's preoccupation with Chronicles.[3] Yet Graham's encyclopedic
approach merely establishes a typology of Chronicles scholarship,
moving from individual scholar to individual scholar, categorizing

1. For instance, H.-J. Kraus, *Geschichte der historish-kritischen Erforschung
des Alten Testaments* (Neukirchen: Kreis Moers, 1956) mentions Chronicles only
twice—both in reference to Wellhausen's work. L. Diestel (*Geschichte des Alten
Testaments in der christlichen Kirche* [Jena: Mauke's Verlag, 1869]), T.K. Cheyne
(*Founders of Old Testament Criticism* [London: Methuen, 1893]), R.E. Clements
(*One Hundred Years of Old Testament Interpretation* [Philadelphia: Westminster
Press, 1976]) and A. Duff (*History of Old Testament Criticism* [New York: The
Knickerbocker Press, 1910]) ignore the significance of Chronicles in the development of nineteenth-century scholarship. Only John Rogerson's *Old Testament
Criticism in the Nineteenth Century* (Philadelphia: Fortress Press, 1986) among
general treatments of nineteenth-century Hebrew Bible scholarship stresses the role
of Chronicles in the field's development.
2. 'The focus of interest in Chronicles, from the beginning of research into it
and for a long time afterwards, centred upon questions of historical reliability and not
upon matters of literary and theological concerns, which were at the heart of the
attention of biblical scholarship at the time.' Sara Japhet, 'The Historical Reliability
of Chronicles', *JSOT* 33 (1985), pp. 83-107.
3. M.P. Graham, *The Utilization of 1 and 2 Chronicles in the Reconstruction of
Israelite History in the Nineteenth Century* (SBLDS, 116; Atlanta: Scholars Press,
1990).

them according to their view of the pre-exilic historical reliability of Chronicles. He thereby obscures lines of development within the nineteenth-century debate over Chronicles. It is the purpose of this article to document those lines of development and show how conservative reactions against de Wette's challenge to the historicity of Chronicles altered the nature of scholarship and ultimately set the agenda for mainline twentieth-century Chronicles scholarship.

In order to analyze the development within nineteenth-century interpretations of Chronicles, I will focus on the history of interpetation of one particular passage: 1 Chronicles 23–27. Not only does the interpetation of this passage represent the whole of nineteenth-century Chronicles interpetation, but it also intersects with key developments in nineteenth-century Hebrew Bible scholarship. By carefully examining the history of interpretation of 1 Chronicles 23–27, one can watch the process whereby Chronicles moved from the center of Hebrew Bible scholarship to its periphery in the course of the nineteenth century.

1. *Chronicles in the Center: From de Wette to Ewald*

Julius Wellhausen's *Prolegomena to the History of Israel* is often recognized as beginning an era—the era of the general acceptance of the documentary hypothesis. Indeed, Wellhausen's brilliant synthesis established a broad consensus regarding the compositional history of the Pentateuch and consequently regarding the history of Israelite religion. Viewed from the perspective of the history of interpretation of Chronicles, however, Wellhausen ended an intense debate concerning the role of Chronicles in the reconstruction of the history of Israelite religion. Wellhausen's work, therefore, represents the closure of an era and the marginalization of Chronicles in Hebrew Bible scholarship.

In contrast, Wilhelm de Wette's *Beiträge zur Einleitung in das Alte Testament* began the debate by placing the interpretation of Chronicles in the center of nineteenth-century Hebrew Bible scholarship on the history of the religion of Israel. The work of Heinrich Ewald, while differing markedly from de Wette's historical conclusions concerning Chronicles, fulfilled de Wette's agenda by placing Chronicles squarely in the middle of his reconstruction of the history of Israel. Yet despite the apparent historical confidence that scholars had developed in

Chronicles, the conservative response to de Wette had eroded the compositional integrity of Chronicles, paving the way to later literary criticism that would move Chronicles to the periphery of Hebrew Bible scholarship and discredit further the historicity of its narrative.[4]

a. *De Wette and his* Beiträge
Fully cognizant of the dangers of overstatement, John Rogerson has convincingly argued 'that the work of W.M.L. de Wette (1780–1849) inaugurated a new era in critical Old Testament scholarship, and. . . his two-volume *Contributions to Old Testament Introduction* (Halle, 1806–07) was his most significant contribution to this end'.[5] Since the first volume of de Wette's work dealt exclusively with Chronicles, scholars have recognized the pivotal and foundational character of his interpretation of Chronicles. Indeed, his *Beiträge* began the modern interpretation of Chronicles and created the framework for future discussions.

De Wette read Chronicles as a coherent narrative. For instance, he interpreted 1 Chronicles 23–27 within the context of 1 Chronicles 22–29, the end of David's reign. He did not separate the passage from the broader narrative, but read it as part of the succession narrative from David to Solomon. This reading enabled him to compare the Chronicler's account with the succession narrative of 2 Samuel–1 Kings. Naturally, he found the general differences striking. The discrepancy between the 'court intrigues' in Samuel–Kings and the smooth transference of power from David to Solomon in Chronicles suggested to de Wette that the two accounts could not both provide an accurate depiction of the history of Israel.[6] He concluded that 'This whole narrative [of 1 Chron. 22–29] has the character of a legend'[7]

---

4.   I use the term 'literary criticism' in the traditional sense within Hebrew Bible studies as the study of literary features in order 'to establish the literary integrity or compositeness of a text unit. . . . In the case of composite texts, the task is to separate the layers from one another and to establish their relative chronology.' R. Knierim, 'Criticism of Literary Features, Form, Tradition, and Redaction', in D.A. Knight and G.M. Tucker (eds.), *The Hebrew Bible and its Modern Interpreters* (Philadelphia: Fortress Press; Chico, CA: Scholars Press, 1985), p. 130.

5.   Rogerson, *Old Testament Criticism*, p. 28.

6.   W.M.L. de Wette, *Beiträge zur Einleitung in das Alte Testament* (Halle: Schimmelpfennig und Compagnie, 1806; New York: Georg Olms Verlag, 1971), I, p. 120.

7.   De Wette, *Beiträge*, I, p. 122.

and possessed no historical value for the reign of David.

This conclusion was very significant for de Wette's broader agenda. His chief interest in the *Beiträge* was the history of the religion of Israel, especially the history of Israel's cult.[8] De Wette therefore examined Chronicles in general, and 1 Chronicles 23–27 in particular, in order to determine the historicity of that portrayal of Israel's cult. The Chronicler's picture of an operative 'Mosaic-Levitical' cult in the time of David, however, clashed with 'an unpriestly freedom of the cult' ('einer unpriesterlichen Freiheit des Cultus') and the absence of Levitical ceremony in Samuel–Kings.[9] A historical evaluation of Chronicles was an essential first step in his argument, for Samuel–Kings did not depict the cult or the law operating in the period of the united monarchy as described in the Pentateuch. The historical inaccuracy of Chronicles, therefore, implied a postexilic date for the Pentateuchal legislation. De Wette's historical evaluation of 1 Chronicles 22–29 as legendary occupied a central position in his overall perspective on the history of Israelite religion. Only after he had discredited Chronicles' portrayal of the pre-exilic cult could he suggest a postexilic date for the cultic system as detailed in the Pentateuch.

For de Wette, this history of Israel's cult transcended mere antiquarian interests. Underlying the historical development of the cult was its theological significance.[10] By 1869, Ludwig Diestel had

---

8. 'Das wichtigste Augenmerk für den Forscher der israelitischen Geschichte muß die Geschichte der Religion und des Gottesdienstes seyn', de Wette, *Beiträge*, I, p. 4.

9. De Wette, *Beiträge*, I, p. 5.

10. Japhet ('Historical Reliability', p. 84) makes a category error at this point that pervades her essay: 'The main question which engaged all biblical scholars of the time and which was the focus of protracted and lively debate, was the question of the authorship of the Pentateuch in its various aspects'. The problem of the historical reliability of Chronicles, however, was not directly the problem of the authorship of the Pentateuch, but rather the problem of the history of the religion of Israel—the real central historical and theological concern of the nineteenth century. As Rogerson (*Old Testament Criticism*, p. 43) notes,

> De Wette's youthful works achieved a breakthrough in critical studies because they shifted attention away from preoccupation with the authorship of the Old Testament books and the sources or fragments used in the compilations. They raised the question 'is the Old Testament read uncritically a true guide to the history of Israelite religion?'

By seeing the authorship of the Pentateuch as the central concern of the nineteenth

already recognized the merging of the historical and theological in his *Geschichte des Alten Testaments in der christlichen Kirchen*. He observed that the history of Old Testament religion had developed both an antiquarian and a theological dimension. This theological significance of the history of Israelite religion contributed to the development of a new field—Old Testament theology:

> Here [also] the religious and theological understanding of the OT develops most clearly; differing positions group themselves according to the viewpoint under which they understand the religion of Israel and, to some extent, are reflected again in the multifaceted treatment of that new discipline, the biblical theology of the OT.[11]

Read from this perspective, de Wette's research represented a sympathetic theological advance, rather than a destructive attack on the biblical writings. As Rogerson states,

> Judged by the criterion that the truth of Old Testament narratives is their *historical* truth, de Wette's *Contributions* of 1806–1807 looked very negative indeed. Judged by his own criterion, that theology is concerned to study *religion*, the *Contributions* were meant to be positive.[12]

De Wette's work was not interpreted by all in such a sympathetic manner. His conclusions evoked apologetic responses, centering largely on his interpretation of Chronicles. Yet he had framed the terms of the discussion: to what extent, if any, did 1 Chronicles 23–27 accurately depict events or personages in the time of David? De Wette had quickly dismissed the historical reliability of 1 Chronicles 23–27. The apologetic response centered on literary arguments for the presence of authentic source material in Chronicles, especially 1 Chronicles 23–27. As a result, literary-critical questions isolated 1 Chronicles 23–27 from the narrative context of 1 Chronicles 22–29. The narrative of Chronicles soon became little more than the topsoil for literary-critical excavations.

---

century, rather than as a debate within the construction of the history of Israelite religion, Japhet does not sufficiently frame the issues involved in the interpretation of Chronicles, and thus is not able to evaluate its development properly.

    11. L. Diestel, *Geschichte des Alten Testamentes in der christlichen Kirchen* (repr. Leipzig: Zentralantiquariat der Deutschen Demokratischen Republik, 1981 [1869]), p. 563.

    12. Rogerson, *Old Testament Criticism*, p. 43.

b. *The Aftermath of de Wette*

J.G. Dahler was the first to produce a response to de Wette's work.[13] Though not as influential as the later work by Keil and especially Movers, Dahler mapped out the basic strategy of those who defended the historical accuracy of Chronicles: he argued that the Chronicler employed accurate sources. Dahler responded to de Wette mechanically, briefly summarizing each section in Chronicles and suggesting the presence of independent sources or other indications of authenticity which would 'refute' de Wette. He also believed that genealogies and census tables were carried into exile and brought back in the return, appealing to the written document that David gives Solomon (1 Chron. 28.13) as evidence that such documents lay behind the narrative of Chronicles.[14] Whereas de Wette had read the chapters as a narrative account of the end of David's reign, Dahler isolated the chapters from their narrative context, seeing them as void of any narrative function. While his historical conclusions had little or no impact, Dahler established the consensus interpretation that sees 1 Chronicles 23–27 as a separate unit within the Chronicler's David narrative. While 1 Chronicles 23–27 had been placed in Chronicles, internal literary evidence suggested that its origin—and significance—lay outside its current narrative context. By refocusing the issue of Chronicles' historicity from its narrative content to a search for its literary beginnings, Dahler successfully altered the nature of future scholarship by sacrificing the literary coherence of the narrative of Chronicles.

C.P.W. Gramberg's *Die Chronik nach ihrem geschichtlichen Character und ihrer Glaubwürdigkeit neu geprüft*[15] extended de Wette's arguments in response to the work of Dahler. Like de Wette, Gramberg initially evaluated the historical plausibility of 1 Chronicles 23–27 not as a separate unit, but as an account of the end of David's reign. Like de Wette, his method was historical-critical, comparing Chronicles with 2 Samuel and applying the criterion of historical analogy. For instance, Gramberg argued that we cannot hold the depiction of a Judaean standing army of 288,000 soldiers in 1 Chronicles 27 as historical. Not only are such figures absent from

---

13. J.G. Dahler, *De librorum paralipomenon auctoritate atque fide historica* (Leipzig: Argentorati, 1819).

14. Dahler, *De librorum*, p. 72.

15. Halle: Anton, 1823.

2 Samuel, but the size of David's standing army would have exceeded that maintained by the Prussian state—a highly unlikely event in light of the fact that Prussia's population was ten million![16]

Unlike de Wette, Gramberg introduced a typology based on the supposed priestly nature of the unit. He argued that David in 1 Chronicles 23–27 becomes a servant of priests. David brings the spoils of his battles to 'greedy priests' ('gierigen Priestern') and concerns himself only to prepare Solomon for the establishment of the Temple. This priestly picture had little to do with history.[17] Gramberg's association of 1 Chronicles 23–27 with a specifically priestly interest foreshadowed, and most likely directly influenced, Wellhausen's association of Chronicles and the Priestly Codex as representing 'late Judaism'.

While Gramberg incorporated de Wette's method and thesis, he altered his interpretation of Chronicles through his engagement with Dahler's arguments. In order to refute Dahler's hypothesis that authentic sources lay behind 1 Chronicles 23–26 and 27, Gramberg divided these chapters from each other within the context of 1 Chronicles 22–29. He argued against the historicity of 1 Chronicles 23–26 separately from the military lists of ch. 27.[18] Thus Gramberg subtly accepted the literary-critical perspective of Dahler even though he denied Dahler's view of the historicity of Chronicles.

Gramberg also began a significant trend by incorporating his arguments for the historical status of Chronicles into a developmental schema of the religious ideas of the Old Testament.[19] He developed de Wette's perspective on the relation between the history of the Israelite cult and the theological significance of the Hebrew Bible. In particular, Gramberg incorporated his earlier study of Chronicles into a larger, synthetic project.[20] Chronicles was firmly established at the heart of the historical and theological investigation of the Hebrew Bible in the nineteenth century.

16. Gramberg, *Die Chronik*, p. 194.
17. Gramberg, *Die Chronik*, p. 75.
18. See Gramberg, *Die Chronik*, pp. 130 and 194.
19. C.P.W. Gramberg, *Kritische Geschichte der Religionsideen des Alten Testaments* (2 vols.; Berlin: Duncker und Humbolt, 1829–30). This work was left incomplete by Gramberg's premature death at the age of 33.
20. Gramberg, *Kritische Geschichte*, I, pp. xxiii-xxiv, 252-54.

As de Wette's work formed the impetus for Dahler's, and Dahler's for Gramberg, Gramberg's work led to C.F. Keil's *Apologetischer Versuch über die Bücher der Chronik und über die Integrität des Buches Esra.*[21] Keil combined the perspectives of Dahler, de Wette and Gramberg in his attempt to defend the historicity of 1 Chronicles 23–27. First, he recognized that the late date of Chronicles demanded that he could defend its historical accuracy only by appealing to hypothetical earlier sources embedded within the narrative.[22] He fundamentally reasserted the position of Eichhorn that Samuel–Kings and Chronicles arose from a common source, which each compiler used according to his interests.[23]

Keil did not argue his case, however, on the merits of Eichhorn alone. He met de Wette and Gramberg on their own ground of critical historical plausibility, gathering data that he thought indicated the historicity of 1 Chronicles 23–26. Keil argued that the specificity of the names and asides within the lists and the allusions to the genealogies by 1 Macc. 2.1 and Lk. 1.5 prove that David actually did establish this cultic order at the end of his reign. Only the most obstinate skeptic would not accept such evidence as persuasive![24]

Keil thus attempted to defend the historicity of Chronicles on critical grounds. The criteria he used, however, differed from those of Gramberg. Whereas Gramberg depended on the criterion of analogy, Keil employed literary criteria, the precision of the lists and references in later works, as evidence for the passage's historicity. While we could and should criticize Keil's criteria, we should also recognize that the mode and goal of his argumentation were identical with those of de Wette and Gramberg. De Wette had established the main issue as the historicity of Chronicles. Literary arguments for the presence of sources in Chronicles, however, had removed 1 Chronicles 23–27 from its context within the narrative of David's reign. Chronicles as a

21. Berlin: Oehmigke, 1833, p. ix. Keil's investigation into Chronicles continued for the next forty years, culminating in his commentary. Yet his basic view remained unchanged from the positions he endorsed in *Apologetischer Versuch.*

22. 'Von diesen Quellen also und der treuen Benutzung derselben hängt die Glaubwürdigkeit unsers Buchs ab' (Keil, *Apologetischer Versuch*, p. 149).

23. See Keil, *Apologetischer Versuch*, pp. 149-55, 268.

24. 'Wer daher seine grenzenlose Zweifelsucht so weit treibt, diese Nachrichten zu verwerfen, der muss als pyrrhonischer Skeptiker, wenn er sich nicht grössten Willkühr schuldig machen will, alle Geschichte ohne Ausnahme verwerfen', Keil, *Apologetischer Versuch*, pp. 402-403.

coherent narrative disintegrated under the apologetic search to find historical sources embedded within the text.

Keil saw the basic import of the historical accuracy of Chronicles as directly related to the origins of the Pentateuch, and not directly as a matter of the history of the development of the cult.[25] This realignment of the issue (and misunderstanding of de Wette's and Gramberg's agenda) reveals a basic division that existed in nineteenth-century Old Testament scholarship. The theological significance of the Hebrew Scriptures for critical scholars lay in its reflection of the 'religious life' of the people of Israel; for the orthodox apologists, the significance was found in the 'historical truth' preserved in the biblical writings. Both sides were committed to the history behind the biblical writings, but their radically different presuppositions influenced not only the results of their studies, but also the way they saw the issues. The claim by the 'critical school' that the 'apologists' were not truly interested in the historical criticism of the biblical writings was false, as we have seen in Keil:[26] but so was the apologist's claim that the critical scholars, or 'Rationalists', destroyed the theological significance of the Scriptures. The critical scholars redefined this theological significance in terms of the religious development of Israel, a vastly different position from Protestant orthodoxy.

The last participant in the initial furor created by de Wette's work was F.C. Movers in his *Kritische Untersuchungen über biblische Chronik*. Movers' work basically won the day in the mid-nineteenth century and his influence lingers today.[27] For our purposes, however, the significance of Movers' work lay in his detailed literary-critical arguments that presented the Chronicler as a compiler of older sources. While Dahler and Keil merely attempted to refute de Wette

25. 'Nächst dem Pentateuche haben in neuerer Zeit besonders die Bücher der Chronik die Aufmerksamkeit vieler gelehrten Forscher auf sich gezogen. Doch war es bei beiden nicht sowohl die gründliche Verforschung ihres Entstehung, Echtheit, und Glaubwürdigkeit, die in den meisten darüber erschienenen Schriften behandelt wurde', Keil, *Apologetischer Versuch*, p. 1.

26. We may see the importance of 'critical history' as a theological construct on the 'orthodox' side, as Movers attacks Gramberg's work, not as rationalistic, but as 'ein so frivoles, unkritisches Machwerk'. F.C. Movers, *Kritische Untersuchungen über biblische Chronik* (Bonn: Habicht, 1834), p. vi.

27. Compare Movers' categories with the categories of exegesis used by the Chronicler proposed by T. Willi, *Die Chronik als Auslegung* (Göttingen: Vandenhoeck & Ruprecht, 1972), pp. 66-69.

by referring to names of supposed sources contained in the narrative of Chronicles and historical-critical arguments, Movers compiled internal literary-critical data to arrive at the same conclusion.[28] His discussion of 1 Chronicles 23–27 is thus highly representative of his whole work and significant for the later literary-critical arguments for the origins of 1 Chronicles 23–27:

> The compilatory manner [of the Chronicler] is especially noticeable when the author begins with the words of his first source, interpolates from a second source for augmentation, and then continues with a repetition of the first, interrupted sentence. [So] mentioning the leaders, and the priests and the Levites [1 Chronicles 23–27] provides an occasion to insert the divisions made by David, which are known to him [the Chronicler] from another source. When he comes back to his first source in 28.1 he resumes the narrative again with the same interrupted sentence.[29]

Movers isolated 1 Chronicles 23–27 by an internal literary-critical analysis on the basis of a supposed doublet in 1 Chron. 23.1 and 28.1, and, in turn, used this to support the general historical reliability of Chronicles.[30]

c. *Chronicles within the History of Israelite Religion*
After the initial debate caused by de Wette's work, Chronicles, and 1 Chronicles 23–27 in particular, were absorbed into the center of de Wette's larger agenda—the theological significance of the history of Israelite religion. Even in this respect, the field remained divided. Wilhelm Vatke and Heinrich Ewald represent two positions that emerged. Each scholar's interpretation of Chronicles played an important role in his reconstruction of the chronological and developmental features of Israelite religion, Vatke within the tradition of de Wette and Ewald within the critical, but conservative, response.

Wilhelm Vatke divided his developmental schema of the history of Israel into eight historical eras, stretching from Mosaic times to the

---

28. 'Der Chronik nicht unsern BB. Sam. u. Kön., sondern ein anderes, zum Theile minder vollständiges Geschichtsbuch benutzt habe', Movers, *Kritische Untersuchungen*, p. 100.

29. Movers, *Kritische Untersuchungen*, p. 102.

30. Ironically, his argument ultimately led to Martin Noth's argument that 1 Chronicles 23–27 was a later addition to Chronicles, and thus even further removed the passage from the Davidic period. See M. Noth, *The Chronicler's History* (Sheffield: JSOT Press, 1987), p. 149, n. 1.

Hellenistic era. He discussed Chronicles in two of these eras. First, he attempted to justify his exclusion of Chronicles from his depiction of Israelite religion in the time of David. Vatke used the standard de Wette–Gramberg approach, but overstated the degree of scholarly acceptance of this position.[31] Yet Vatke changed the role of Chronicles within his reconstruction of the history of Israelite religion. Chronicles functioned as an illustration rather than as an essential ingredient in his overall chronology for Israel's religion. He first argued, based on an internal analysis of the Pentateuch and without reference to Chronicles, that the Pentateuchal legal material generally had been projected back into the Mosaic era from a later time. He then extended the analogy of the Pentateuch to Chronicles: 'Just as the Pentateuch places the institution of the priestly laws in the Mosaic period, these books, in similar fashion, place the later, postexilic cultus in the Davidic-Solomonic period'.[32] Vatke based his rejection of the historicity of Chronicles on the basis of the lateness of the Pentateuchal legislation, whereas de Wette had argued in the opposite direction. No longer did the postexilic dating of Pentateuchal legislation logically necessitate the denial of the historicity of Chronicles. Rather, Chronicles illustrated a process similar to that which produced the Pentateuchal legislation. Yet the comparison that Vatke drew introduced a significant typology into the interpretation of Chronicles: as the Pentateuch depicts the Law originating with Moses, so 1 Chronicles 23–27 depicts the cult originating with David. Like much of the Pentateuchal legislation, Chronicles illustrated postexilic priestly interests. The way was opened to Wellhausen's formulation.

Secondly, Vatke, following Gramberg, briefly discussed Chronicles as a product of the Hellenistic era, although Ezra–Nehemiah formed

---

31. He asserted that the unhistorical nature of Chronicles was 'commonly recognized', when, in fact, this was the minority position:

> Bei den Büchern der Chronik ist der theilweise unhistorische Charakter ziemlich allgemein anerkannt. . . Denkt man sich z.B. den Cultus, dessen Stiftung die Bücher der Chronik schon David beilegen, im Zeitalter der Könige herrschend, so gewinnt man keinen Raum für dem Götzendienst, begreift nicht mehr die Ausprüche der Propheten und die Satzungen des Pentateuchs. . . (W. Vatke, *Die biblische Theologie* [Berlin: Bethge, 1835], I, p. 290).

32. Vatke, *Die biblische Theologie*, p. 291.

his chief interest. Vatke referred to 1 Chronicles 23–26 in his attempt to solve the problem of the history of the Levites, a problem highlighted by the uncertainty of the relationship between the priests, Levites, the singers, gatekeepers and temple servants in Ezra–Nehemiah.[33] In Vatke's interpretation, influenced perhaps by the arguments of Movers and Keil, 1 Chronicles 23–26 formed a fixed reference point in the relationship between these Temple offices under the Hasmoneans.[34]

Although his historical conclusions followed the perspective of de Wette, Vatke tacitly accepted the literary arguments of Dahler, Keil and Movers by abstracting the lists from their narrative context. Vatke's dating of the lists to the time of the Hasmoneans, then, exerted influence on later critics. When subsequent scholars dated Chronicles to the late Persian period, they preserved the Hasmonean date for 1 Chronicles 23–27 and argued that the unit was added to the book at that date. The apologetic response to de Wette, therefore, ultimately forced a date later than that posited by de Wette for some of the materials in Chronicles.

Vatke completed the project begun by de Wette, incorporating a claim for the non-historicity of Chronicles in order to understand the theological development of the history of the cult. Yet until Wellhausen, this aspect of his work had little impact. Instead, the critical, yet conservative, view of Heinrich Ewald carried the day.

In Ewald's reconstruction of Israelite history and religion 1 Chronicles 23–27 plays an important supportive role. Ewald adopted the position of Eichhorn towards Chronicles, arguing that Chronicles reflects essentially two different periods: the era of David and Solomon, and a much later age that remembered the glory of these years:

> As in that [late] age the nation as a whole lived upon the memory of the earlier glory and power of its religion, so the individual historian [the Chronicler] dwells with marked exultation and scarcely concealed regret on the glories of the earlier ages only of the Holy City, on those kings and

33. Vatke, *Die biblische Theologie*, p. 568, n. 1.

34. 'Freilich ist die Genauigkeit der Listen, welche durch die Hand des Chronisten gegangen sind, nicht recht verbürgt, namentlich in den Zahlenangaben; indaß darf man wenigstens die Ordnung der Priester und Leviten, welche der Chronik in's davidsche Zeitalter zurückverlegt (1 Chr. 23–26.), von den Zeiten der ersten Colonie andatiern', Vatke, *Die biblische Theologie*, p. 568.

heroes whose acts on behalf of the Temple and its ordinances, as well as
on behalf of the ordination and elevation of the Levites, had been
conspicuously meritorious, and on such historical events as appeared to
teach the power and inviolability of the sanctuary at Jerusalem. Wherever
anything of this kind enters into the narrative, the historian's heart
expands with joy, and he retains unabridged the fullest details given by
his authorities.[35]

Ewald believed that much of 1 Chronicles 23–27 originated in tax
records which had 'already passed into various historical works and
were only taken by him [the Chronicler] from these'.[36] Later he
identifies this historical work as a biography of David, which the
Chronicler refers to in 1 Chron. 23.27 and 26.31.[37] The original
source of 1 Chronicles 23–27 is embedded in two later works: a
biography of David (a view endorsed by Eichhorn) and the narrative
of Chronicles itself. From Ewald's perspective, 1 Chronicles 23–27
contains important data concerning the establishment of the theocracy
in the last days of David.

This time of the united monarchy was a significant era for Ewald.
The last years of David and the rule of Solomon represented the high
point of Israelite history when

the laws and institutions of the Theocracy could expand to their full
extent. . . Ancient Israel was for the first time firmly established in the
country, and the finer manifestations of its life under the Theocracy now
also first assumed the forms which they ever after essentially retained.

This fact is confirmed by their literature. The important remains of the
Book of Origins, dating from just this exalted period, supply us with the
most complete and vivid descriptions of the laws of the Theocracy which
we possess.[38]

The complete historical synthesis of Ewald centered around this 'Book
of Origins'. According to him, the book originated in the same exalted
era that produced the sources for the Chronicler's history of David.
1 Chronicles 23–27 played an important supportive role in detailing
Israel's history at a crucial point in Ewald's reconstruction. He

35. H. Ewald, *History of Israel* (London: Longmans, Green & Co., 1883),
pp. 176-77.
36. Ewald, *History*, p. 182.
37. Ewald, *History*, p. 186.
38. Heinrich Ewald, *The Antiquities of Israel* (London: Longmans, Green &
Co., 1876), pp. 1-2.

supplemented the information of the Book of Origins with the precise
Levitical arrangement provided by 1 Chronicles 23–26:

> Now, if the two high-priestly houses were thus put on an equal footing
> under the monarchy, this arrangement itself would lay the foundation of a
> fresh organisation of the whole tribe of Levi; and the Book of Chronicles
> gives a more detailed description of the manner in which this was worked
> out, at all events in the last years of David.[39]

While Ewald later inconsistently attributed the organization of the
priests described in 1 Chronicles 23–26 to the reign of Solomon,[40]
Chronicles still reveals the same view of religion as that reflected in
the Book of Origins.

This close relationship between the Book of Origins and Chronicles,
especially 1 Chronicles 23–27, also functioned in the work of Ewald's
most prominent student, Julius Wellhausen. While Wellhausen
accepted the arguments of de Wette and Graf for the non-historicity
of the Chronicler's account of Israelite religion, he maintained
Ewald's argument concerning the relationship between the Book of
Origins (known to Wellhausen as the Priestly Codex) and Chronicles.
Rather than combining P and Chronicles to describe the high point of
Israelite religion, Wellhausen transposed both to the postexilic period
as the beginning of Judaism. Together, the Priestly Codex and
Chronicles combined to give the portrayal of postexilic Judaism con-
tained in chapter 11 of the *Prolegomena*, 'The Theocracy as Idea and
as Institution'. The history of the interpretation of Chronicles reveals

39. Ewald, *History*, III, p. 134.
40. 'Their [the Levites'] duties and occupations, moreover, increased to such an
extent, that they were certainly in need now of more thorough reorganisation and in
part of more complete transformation than had been previously effected by David.
Some of the particulars of this new organisation in the case of the Levites who were
to be employed at Jerusalem, are known to us chiefly through the Chronicles. It is
true the Chronicler really describes everything appertaining to it only in the shape to
which it had been developed towards the conclusion of the whole history of the
monarchy at Jerusalem, because his sources supplied him with only such materials;
while he refers the origin of the organisation to the precepts of David—nay, even of
Samuel. But as this is only the result of his general view. . . of Solomon's career,
we have no ground for doubting that the basis of the whole of his new organisation
of the Priesthood was laid in the age of Solomon, which omitted nothing from its
creative arrangements'. Ewald, *History*, III, pp. 247-48. Ewald does not seem to be
aware that this attribution to the time of Solomon calls into question his source
arguments asserted earlier.

the background of significant shifts within the history of Old
Testament scholarship.

With the publication of Ewald's work, the apologetic response had
seemingly won the day. While the political machinations of
Hengstenberg assured that German professorships fell into the hands
of his sympathizers, Keil had engaged de Wette and Gramberg on
their own terms, and Movers had developed previous arguments and
thereby initiated the modern literary criticism of Chronicles. Thus,
the first modern commentary on Chronicles by Ernst Berteau (1854)
presupposed the view that the Chronicler had drawn upon the same
source as that used for Samuel–Kings, and therefore contained
authentic historical material.[41] On the eve, then, of the work of Graf
and Wellhausen, the interpretation of Chronicles occupied a central
point in Hebrew Bible scholarship. Critical scholarship, however, had
seemingly lost the fray. The historical arguments of Keil and especially the literary arguments of Movers had replaced the de Wettian
view of the non-historicity of Chronicles. Ewald had absorbed the
de Wettian agenda for a history of the religion of Israel. Now,
however, Chronicles served to detail pre-exilic, rather than postexilic,
Israel. It was Graf who reintroduced the de Wettian view in 1866.
Even he, however, accepted in a modified form the literary-critical
conclusions of the apologetic response.

2. Towards the Periphery: Graf and Wellhausen

Karl Graf has rightfully received credit for 're-awakening'[42] the
interest in Chronicles, the date of the Priestly Code, and the incorporation of de Wette's position into the history of Israelite religion.[43]
From the perspective of the history of the interpretation of Chronicles,

41. E. Berteau, *Die Bücher der Chronik* (Leipzig: Verlag von S. Hirzel, 1854),
p. xxxiii. Berteau explicitly refers to Movers, Ewald and Keil.

42. 'The fact was, that it had been merely put to sleep, and Graf has the credit of
having, after a considerable interval, awakened it again', J. Wellhausen, *Prolegomena
to the History of Ancient Israel* (New York: Meridian Books, 1973), p. 10.

43. 'Die Hauptschwierigkeit. . . zu einer klaren geschichtlichen Anschauung des
Entwicklungsganges der israelitisch-jüdischen Geschichte zu gelangen, liegt vielmehr
in der eigenthümlichen Beschaffenheit eben der Quellen dieser Geschichte selbst,
über welche sie noch keineswegs überall ein sicheres Urtheil erlangt hat',
K.H. Graf, *Die geschichtlichen Bücher des Alten Testaments* (Leipzig: Weigel,
1866), p. vi.

Graf represents the merging of de Wette's negative assessment of the historicity of Chronicles with the source-critical arguments of Movers.[44] He thus foreshadows the late nineteenth- and twentieth-century discussion of Chronicles.

Structurally, the place of Chronicles in Graf's argument differed from that in de Wette's. Whereas de Wette had argued, on the basis of the non-historicity of Chronicles, that the Mosaic law was a later development, Graf argued the postexilic date of P on the basis of a comparative study of legislation, independent of the historicity of Chronicles.[45] It was still necessary, however, to argue that the 'Mosaic-levitical' perspective of Chronicles reflected a postexilic date, rather than an accurate account of the Davidic and pre-exilic age. While de Wette began his work with an examination of Chronicles in order to argue against the antiquity of the Mosaic law, Graf analyzed Chronicles in the second part of his book after his discussion of the Pentateuch. After Wellhausen's *Prolegomena*, it became unnecessary to examine Chronicles at all in order to discuss the age of the Priestly legislation. Graf and Wellhausen moved Chronicles from the center towards the periphery of Hebrew Bible scholarship.

Graf's exegesis of Chronicles was, if anything, more sophisticated than Wellhausen's. Graf took up a position in relation to the work of earlier scholars, especially the position of Movers. His treatment of 1 Chronicles 23–27 was typical of his work as a whole. He argued on literary-critical grounds that 1 Chronicles 23–27 fundamentally originated with the Chronicler, although it incorporated older lists:

44. Rogerson neglects to mention the significance of Graf's work from the perspective of Chronicles, focusing merely on the Pentateuchal contributions of his work. Rogerson also overemphasizes the continuities between Graf's *Geschichtlichen Bücher* and de Wette's *Beiträge*, and ignores significant differences in the mode of argumentation between the two. See Rogerson, *Old Testament Criticism*, p. 258 and below.

45. 'Sie besteht aus zwei eng zusammengehörenden Theilen, einer Untersuchung der geschichtlichen Bücher. . . vom Deuteronomium ausgehend den verschiedenen Theilen der mosaischen Gesetzgebung ihren Platz in der Geschichte anzuweisen und im Zusammenhang damit darzulegen. . .und zweitens einer Vergleichung des Buches der Chronik in Inhalt und Darstellung mit diesen Büchern zu dem Zwecke, sein Verhältniss zu denselben und seinen Werth als Quelle der Geschichte ihnen gegenüber in ein klareres Licht zu setzen', Graf, *Geschichtlichen Bücher*, p. viii.

This insertion was neither included later, nor already part of a pre-existing narrative, but was taken up by him [the Chronicler] in his own account. Hence it follows that, by the resumption of 23.2 in the continuation of the narrative in 28.1, [the Chronicler] sought to relate [ch. 28] to the immediately preceding lists. One recognizes his freely composing hand in the enormous numbers of 23.4, 5; 27.1ff and in the imitative nature and artificiality of the. . . overall symmetrical arrangement according to the numbers 12 and 24. Moreover, this arrangement is based upon a very uncertain foundation, in that the differing classifications of priests and Levites must be determined, on the one hand, through lineage, and on the other, through the lottery mandated by David, which contradicts itself. . . In part the historian used for his presentation older lists, which he crafted and treated according to his own manner to which he. . . added from his own.[46]

Graf compiled evidence for the redaction of the section by the Chronicler, and attempted to delineate the older source that he used. While Graf constructed his argument chiefly on literary grounds, he also employed critical analysis in the tradition of de Wette and Gramberg.[47] He concluded that Chronicles indeed contained material from older sources, but that these sources were still postexilic.[48]

Graf thereby incorporated the literary methods of the conservative 'apologists' into a denial of the historicity of Chronicles. This position was very influential in the commentaries of the late nineteenth and early twentieth centuries, and remains so today. The crucial difference

---

46. Graf, *Geschichtlichen Bücher*, pp. 232-33.
47. Thus he wrote concerning 1 Chron. 27:

Wenn irgendwo, so tritt es in diesem Stücke klar hervor, dass wir es, trotz der scheinbar so genauen Namen, mit reiner Dichtung zu thun haben. Nicht nur erscheinen die Zahlen an und für sich als phantastische, sondern das 2te B. Sam. u. 1 Kön. c. 1 weiss nichts von einer solchen Leibwache; wie bescheiden erscheint dagegen die kleine Schaar der Krethi u. Plethi und der 600 Gathiter, als David auf Flucht vor Absalom bei dem letzten Hause von Jerusalem sie an sich vorbeiziehen lässt 2 Sam. 15,18! (Graf, *Geschichtlichen Bücher*, p. 242).

48. 'Wie viel in den vorliegenden Verzeichnissen dem Chronisten selbst angehört, wie viel er aus ältern Verzeichnissen entlehnt hat, lässt sich nicht überall genau bestimmen; klar ist aber, dass auch die von ihm benutzten nachexilische sind und dass seiner Bearbeitung das Streben zu Gründe liegt, die Verhältnisse der Priester und Leviten seiner Zeit als von jeher da gewesen und schon in der Zeit der Gründung des Tempels gestiftet, aber auch dieselben der Mangelhaftigkeit der Gegenwart gegenüber in idealer vorbildlicher Gestalt darzustellen', Graf, *Geschichtlichen Bücher*, pp. 244-45.

is that the evidence for literary sources employed by the Chronicler eventually came to be interpreted as evidence for later literary accretions to the text.

Following Graf's work, Julius Wellhausen's *Prolegomena* provides a decisive point in the nineteenth-century discussion relating the history of the religion of Israel to Chronicles. Wellhausen's book continued to move the debate over the history of the Israelite cult from the issue of the historicity of Chronicles. Like Vatke and Graf, Wellhausen did not argue against the historicity of Chronicles in order to disprove the antiquity of the Priestly code; this he accomplished in the first section of the work by a comparative analysis of Pentateuchal legislative material. Wellhausen examined Chronicles in the second part, which,

> in many respects dependent upon the first, traces the influence of the successively prevailing ideas and tendencies upon the shaping of historical tradition, and follows the various phases in which that was conceived and set forth. It contains, so to speak, a history of tradition.[49]

Within the structure of his argument, Wellhausen established the postexilic date of P independently from Chronicles. Wellhausen did not use Chronicles to prove the lateness of the Priestly Code, but to show the Priestly Code's effect on the historical traditions of Israel:

> The Books of Samuel and of Kings were edited in the Babylonian exile; Chronicles on the other hand, was composed fully three hundred years later, after the downfall of the Persian empire, out of the very midst of fully developed Judaism. We shall now proceed to show that the mere difference of date fully accounts for the varying ways in which the two histories represent the same facts and events, and the difference of spirit arises from the influence of the Priestly Code, which came into existence in the interval.[50]

Wellhausen's dating of the Priestly Code grounded his argument for the lateness of Chronicles, rather than vice versa, as was the case for de Wette. This further isolated Chronicles from the issue of the development of Israelite religion and represented a complete shift from the structure of de Wette's argument. In consequence, the post-Wellhausen discussion of the Pentateuch no longer entailed an

49. J. Wellhausen, *Prolegomena to the History of Israel* (New York: Meridian Books, 1957), p. 13.

50. Wellhausen, *Prolegomena*, pp. 171-72.

examination of Chronicles, a central element in the previous debate.

Despite this important structural difference from de Wette, Wellhausen asserted de Wette's direct influence on his examination of Chronicles:

> De Wette's 'Critical Essay on the Credibility of the Books of Chronicles'...is throughout taken as the basis of the discussion: that essay has not been improved upon by Graf...for here the difficulty, better grappled with by the former, is not to collect the details of evidence, but so to shape the superabundant material as to convey a right total impression.[51]

Indeed, Wellhausen conducted his review of Chronicles using de Wette's method: the historical discrediting of Chronicles through a narrative reading, historical analogy, and comparison with Samuel–Kings. The chief difference between de Wette and Wellhausen is the latter's spectacular rhetoric, evidenced in the lengthy conclusion to his discussion of Chronicles' portrayal of David, especially 1 Chronicles 22–29:

> See what Chronicles has made out of David! The founder of the kingdom has become the founder of the temple and the public worship, the king and hero at the head of his companions in arms has become the singer and master of ceremonies at the head of a swarm of priests and Levites; his clear cut figure has become a feeble holy picture, seen through a cloud of incense. It is obviously vain to try to combine the fundamentally different portraits into one stereoscopic image; it is only the tradition of the older source that possesses historical value. In Chronicles this is clericalised in the taste of the post-exilian time, which had no feeling longer for anything but cultus and torah, which accordingly treated as alien the old history...if it did not conform with its ideas and metamorphose itself into church history. Just as the law framed by Ezra as the foundation of Judaism was regarded as having been the work of Moses, so what upon this basis had been developed after Moses—particularly the music of the sanctuary and the ordering of the temple *personnel*—was carried back to King David, the sweet singer of Israel, who had now to place his music at the service of the cultus, and write psalms along with Asaph, Heman, and Jeduthun, the Levitical singing families.[52]

Wellhausen had no need to discuss detailed literary-critical arguments for possible sources; his earlier argument, that the impact of the post-exilic Priestly code altered the perspective of Chronicles, rendered

51. Wellhausen, *Prolegomena*, p. 172.
52. Wellhausen, *Prolegomena*, p. 182.

this superfluous.[53] He thus returned to de Wette in reading 1 Chronicles 23–27 as an integral part of the Chronicler's narrative of the end of David's reign. His avoidance of the literary-critical question, however, rendered his narrative reading of Chronicles ineffective in influencing the next generation of exegetes of Chronicles. As source-critical questions dominated this next generation, most early twentieth-century commentators returned to Graf's analysis, instead of Wellhausen's. Typically, 1 Chronicles 23–27 was isolated literarily from its context in the narrative of 1 Chronicles. The narrative of Chronicles became obscured from the scholar's gaze. Due to the critical appropriation of the apologist's search for sources, Chronicles scholarship became a specialized area for literary-critical analysis on the periphery of the field rather than a key document in constructing the pre- or postexilic history of Israel.

3. *On the Periphery: Büchler and the Literary-Critical Agenda*

Wellhausen's work stilled the field of significant research for over a decade. When A. Büchler's article, 'Zur Geschichte der Tempelmusik und der Tempelpsalmen', appeared,[54] it established the question and the means by which scholars would attempt to understand Chronicles throughout much of the twentieth century. Büchler's concern was to reconstruct the history of the relationship between priests and Levites by isolating and analyzing different compositional layers within Chronicles. No longer concerned with the larger questions of the history of Israelite religion, Chronicles was read for information about the history of the postexilic Temple personnel. Its significant role within earlier nineteenth-century scholarship was soon forgotten.[55]

---

53. In the end, although Wellhausen, like Graf, does admit to the possible employment of sources, it makes no difference because these sources also reflect the postexilic tendency shaped by the Priestly code. Wellhausen writes, 'Thus whether one says Chronicles or *Midrash* of the Book of Kings is on the whole a matter of perfect indifference; they are the children of the same mother, and indistinguishable in spirit and language', *Prolegomena*, p. 227.

54. *ZAW* 19 (1899), pp. 96-133; 329-44.

55. In 1910, A.A. Madsen and E.L. Curtis could write, 'The Books of Chronicles, from their supplementary and, through their genealogical material, their unedifying character, have never been a favourite field of study and investigation, hence their literature has always been relatively meagre', *A Critical and Exegetical Commentary on the Books of Chronicles* (Edinburgh: T. & T. Clark, 1910), p. 44.

Büchler drew upon Graf's earlier conclusions in positing an earlier, though still postexilic, source of Chronicles—a source with a particularly priestly inclination. He, however, narrowed Graf's literary criteria to the relation between priests and Levites and their respective roles in Chronicles. He concluded, for instance, that the Chronicler used sources which neglected the Levites, and so

> [the Chronicler] remedied this deficiency by—whenever possible—adding a mention of Levites to those of priests. Moreover he often named the former thereby pushing the latter. . . into the background. But he [the Chronicler] accomplished this most of all by including the musician- and choir-Levites in the descriptions of the cult.[56]

The Chronicler chiefly contributed to his history by the mechanical conflation of Samuel–Kings with his later 'priestly' source, and by the addition of Levitical figures wherever he might bolster their status.

Büchler incorporated 1 Chronicles 23–27 within his overall framework. Exhibiting a definite Levitical bias, the unit represented one of the few extended compositional units of the Chronicler himself, inserted within the folds of his unknown source, found in 1 Chronicles 22, 28 and 29.[57] Büchler even discovered evidence for his 'priestly' source within the unit itself, in 1 Chron. 24.1-20.[58] Büchler clearly demarcates 1 Chronicles 23–27 from its literary context and posits the existence of literary layers within the unit. The narrative of Chronicles is fragmented in order to detect the presence or absence of emphases on priests or Levites.

Büchler's article had considerable significance in the history of the modern interpretation of Chronicles.[59] First, it preceded the major commentaries of Benzinger and Kittel, and exerted a major influence upon them.[60] Secondly, his literary-critical concern and his criterion—

---

56. Büchler, 'Geschichte der Tempelmusik', p. 123.

57. Büchler, 'Geschichte der Tempelmusik', pp. 130-31.

58. 'Geschichte der Tempelmusik', p. 131, n. 1.

59. Because of this, Graham's failure to include Büchler in his monograph at first seems puzzling. Yet it shows that, by the end of the nineteenth century, Chronicles interpretation became largely a matter of the history of Second Temple Judaean priests and Levites, rather than a central issue in the construction of the history of Israel.

60. I. Benzinger (*Die Bücher Chronik* [Tübingen: Mohr, 1901]), R. Kittel (*Die Bücher der Chronik und Esra, Nehemia und Esther* [Göttingen: Vandenhoeck & Ruprecht, 1902]), and J. W. Rothstein and D. J. Hänel (*Das erste Buch der Chronik*

the relationship between priests and Levites—have provided an important focus of discussion in the interpretation of Chronicles. Finally, his isolation of 1 Chronicles 23–27 and the positing of compositional layers within this unit have emerged as the consensus position regarding the literary origin of these chapters—and the book. With Büchler, the literary-critical agenda initiated by the apologetic response to de Wette entered its final stage as the locus to discover the rivalries between priests and Levites in the Second Temple period. The interpretation of Chronicles became an esoteric adventure for literary critics and historians of the priesthood on the periphery of Hebrew Bible scholarship.

4. *Conclusion*

In the first two-thirds of the nineteenth century, scholarly investigation of Chronicles lay at the center of the historical and theological study of the Hebrew Bible. The project of de Wette that sought to reconstruct the cultic history of Israel over against a traditional reading of the Pentateuch first had to demonstrate the non-historicity of Chronicles. Only as methods of dating the legislative material of the Pentateuch on internal grounds were developed was Chronicles left to serve an illustrative rather than necessary function in the reconstruction of Israel's religious history. After Wellhausen's negative portrayal of the postexilic period, however, Chronicles lost even its illustrative value. Thus, from Büchler on, the study of Chronicles has remained on the margins of the study of the Hebrew Bible, a specialized area of largely literary-critical interest with implications for the history of the Levites.

The twentieth-century source-critical study of Chronicles originated in the apologetic attempt to salvage the historicity of Chronicles. This apologetic use of literary criticism, however, ultimately developed into the isolation of later literary layers as the results were absorbed within the de Wette–Wellhausen perspective. At least in the case of the

[Leipzig: Scholl, 1927]) applied Büchler's method for the entire work. As these scholars investigated the compositional history of Chronicles, the picture became more complex. To Büchler's primary criterion of the relation between priests and Levites these scholars added an ever more stringent criterion of consistency. Hypothetical literary strata proliferated in a manner parallel to the literary-critical investigations of the Pentateuch, ultimately becoming implausible.

nineteenth-century interpretation of Chronicles, the focus on the biblical narrative dissipated in the concerns of the 'defenders of the Scriptures' who sought to protect the sacred writ.

It is an honor to present this essay to my mentor, Joseph Blenkinsopp, 'from whom indeed I gratefully acknowledge myself to have learnt best and most' and whose scholarship has sought to move Second Temple Judaism back to the theological and historical center of Hebrew Bible studies.

DEFENDING THE BOUNDARIES OF ISRAEL
IN THE SECOND TEMPLE PERIOD:
2 CHRONICLES 20 AND THE 'SALVATION ARMY'

Philip R. Davies

The story in 2 Chronicles 20 of a battle in the days of Jehoshaphat has no parallel in 2 Kings. Scholars disagree as to whether it is based on a historical episode otherwise unattested,[1] or is a midrash on 2 Kings 3,[2] or is neither and hence in effect to be regarded as a free composition.[3] I am not participating in that debate, but propose to read the story as a product of the Chronicler without regard to events or sources. However, I do not intend, least of all in an essay dedicated to Joseph Blenkinsopp, a non-historical reading: I shall have clearly in mind the background of the Second Temple period when the Chronicler wrote. Admittedly, little is known in detail of this context, and indeed no generally agreed date for the Chronicler exists; but I shall rely upon a few widely-agreed features which pertain to the whole period in which the Chronicler may have written.[4]

---

1. So M. Noth, 'Eine palästinische Lokalüberlieferung in 2 Chr. 20', *ZDPV* 67 (1945), pp. 47-51; W. Rudolph, *Chronikbücher* (HAT; Tübingen: Mohr, 1955), pp. 258-59. Whereas Noth regards the underlying event as belonging to the fourth or third century BCE, Rudolph proposed the use of a written source relating an event in the time of Jehoshaphat.

2. A view taken largely by earlier commentators: cf. J. Wellhausen, *Prolegomena to the History of Ancient Israel* (New York: Meridian, 1957). 2 Kings 3 is obviously relevant in several respects to our narrative. It describes a battle fought by Jehoshaphat; the enemy is Moab, with the Moabites advancing via Edom (another possible reason for the reading אדום in v. 2?); there is a powerful prophetic figure alongside the king (Elisha), and the battle itself is conducted supernaturally.

3. So P. Welten, *Geschichte und Geschichtsdarstellung in den Chronikbüchern* (WMANT, 42; Neukirchen–Vluyn: Neukirchener Verlag, 1973), pp. 140-53.

4. Dates given for the Chronicler range from 515 BCE (e.g. D.N. Freedman, 'The Chronicler's Purpose', *CBQ* 23 [1961], pp. 436-42; J.D. Newsome, Jr,

Against this historical background, namely that of Yehud (Judaea) in the Persian and/or Ptolemaic period, the surface of the narrative of 2 Chronicles 20 can be read off quite easily. The usual scholarly treatment runs more or less as follows: the Chronicler is writing a history which is relying essentially on a single source (rather like Josephus's *Antiquities*, which for the most part uses the relevant biblical book), namely the books of Samuel and Kings. This source related an epoch in which Judaean and Israelite monarchs went to war, aided and sometimes hindered by prophets and with or without the blessing of their deity. The history of the books of Samuel and Kings is a history of independent kingdoms—for however much in cold fact these kingdoms were subject to other powers, Samuel–Kings treat them as autonomous in theory and nearly always in practice. By contrast, in the period in which the Chronicler writes, the province of Yehud has no king of its own; rather, its inhabitants are subject to the 'king of kings' in Ecbatana, or Susa or Persepolis (or Alexandria). It has, as far as we know, no army of its own but is protected and controlled by Persian (or Ptolemaic—in either case, the troops will have been mostly foreign mercenaries) armies. The Chronicler, in reworking the earlier history—so the accepted reading goes—is concerned not only with drawing his own implications from that history, but also with rearranging the substance of that history, for example by ignoring the deeds of the kings of Israel (unless they impinge on the deeds of the kings of Judah, as in 2 Chronicles 18) and by attributing to David the creation of an elaborate Temple cult. In such ways the history of the Chronicler's 'Israel' is reformed in the direction of contemporary political realities.

From this conventional reading (which, as far as it goes, I do not propose to challenge here), 2 Chronicles 20 can be interpreted as an essay in bridging the gap between the older time of kings and wars

---

'Toward a New Understanding of the Chronicler and His Purposes', *JBL* 94 [1975], pp. 201-17 and favoured by R.L. Braun, *1 Chronicles* [WBC; Waco, TX: Word Books, 1986], p. xxix) to about 200 BCE (M. Noth, *The Chronicler's History* [Sheffield: JSOT Press, 1987]). The possibility of several redactions (e.g. F.M. Cross, 'A Reconstruction of the Judean Restoration', *JBL* 94 [1975], pp. 4-18) or supplementations (e.g. H.G.M. Williamson, *1 and 2 Chronicles* [NCB; London: Marshall, Morgan & Scott, 1982) complicates the dating further, and tends to support the principle of setting a wide historical context to the work (a principle helped by our ignorance of the period!)

and the present time of colonial administration and hierocracy. The opportunity is taken to describe a war as it might be fought now, though obviously somewhat disguised by the presence of institutions from the past. There is, accordingly, a king who summons the people to response, yet no army is mustered. The first act is a public fast, followed by an assembly in Jerusalem at the Temple. After the royal prayer, a Levite delivers the speech of exhortation which, as David Petersen has shown,[5] serves the purpose of presenting Levites as heirs of the prophets.[6] An act of worship follows, then, in the morning, the king appoints singers—maybe we should think of them as 'cheerleaders'—to precede the army. (This is the only mention of an army in the story.) The liturgical performance continues as YHWH sets an ambush against the enemy, with the result that they destroy one another. When the Judaeans arrive on the scene they discover dead bodies only.[7] All that is left to do is plunder, bless YHWH on the battlefield, then return to Jerusalem and the Temple. The moral of such a tale is fairly transparent: if your cause is just and you are faithful to your deity (and if that deity is YHWH), you will not need an army to protect you. Spend your defence budget on hymnbooks and on musical training for your brass band! The only army you need is a Salvation Army. The Chronicler's own circumstances have seen a transformation of values and institutions. The barracks are now the Temple, the warrior is YHWH and his messengers are the Levitical singers.

Again, it is not my wish here to oppose this interpretation. I doubt, however, that it goes far enough in relating the text to its social and historical context. The transformations evident in this story are in fact much more fundamental than is suggested by this interpretation, and I believe that a deeper analysis may expose another layer in which the social world of the text is encoded.[8]

5. D.L. Petersen, *Late Israelite Prophecy* (Missoula, MT: Scholars Press, 1977); on this story see pp. 54-77.

6. We should not forget, however, that according to Deut. 20.1-7 the speech of encouragement to the army was the responsibility of a priest, not a prophet.

7. This idea is perhaps picked up from 2 Kgs 19.35, though in 2 Chron. 32, where that story recurs, this item is not included.

8. By 'social world' I mean not an external social reality, but the world as symbolized by the society as a whole and internalized by society members. This symbolization is expressed in ritual and art. Within a society, each class and each individual has a social world of its/her/his own, which derives from, and contributes to, the social world of the society. In dealing with ancient texts whose authorship is

The key to this deeper analysis lies in the identification of the enemy. There is a textual problem in v. 1, where the MT reading בני מואב ובני עמן ועמהם מהעמונים is emended to either מהמעונים or מהמעינים, following the LXX Μιναίων. Certainly the MT seems corrupt, mentioning Ammonites twice, and 'Meunites' seems a plausible emendation, since they seem to appear in 2 Chron. 26.7. Nevertheless, their identity is extremely uncertain, despite the often confident assertions of commentators.[9] Whatever the explanation of these mysterious Meunim (or Meinim!) I am not at all convinced that the textual corruption in 2 Chron. 20.1 is solved by following the LXX here. Its reading 'Meunites' can hardly be accepted simply because the MT is manifestly at error, since that error itself furnishes a sufficient explanation for the LXX emendation (there is a similar but incorrect amendment in 2 Chron. 26.8). And if the LXX represents the original reading, why are 'Meunites' absent from the rest of 2 Chronicles 20? At the very least, these 'Meunites' are an uncertain element of the enemy forces in this story, and consequently it is precarious to make of them, as Noth has done, the one original historical element! Against

unknown, one is usually dealing with a class (the literate class); the world of society as a whole can only be assumed, and the world of the author differentiated only with very great care; the text and the author must, as a rule, be taken to be identical.

9.   Noth ('Eine palästinische Lokalüberlieferung') is largely responsible for the modern mythology of the Meunites. He suggested that behind the story of 2 Chron. 20 lay an attack of Nabataeans from Meun, which is southeast of Petra. The relevant data concerning 'Meunites' are as follows: 'Meunites' appear twice elsewhere in Chronicles. In 2 Chron. 26.7 MT reads. . .על פלשתים ועל־הערביים היושבים בגור־בעל והמעונים; in v. 8 MT העמונים is read by the LXX again as Μιναῖοι, a reading which is surely wrong, but easily explained as prompted by their presence in the previous verse. Dillard's comment (*2 Chronicles* [WBC; Waco, TX: Word Books, 1987], p. 155) that here these 'Meunites' are 'associated with the Ammonites once again as among those bringing tribute to Hezekiah' is thus questionable on two counts: first, only v. 8 speaks of tribute, and here 'Ammonites' (MT) and 'Meunites' (LXX) are versional alternatives. There is a possible association between the two if one follows the MT at 26.8—but Dillard there favours the LXX! Secondly, the king in question is Uzziah, not Hezekiah.

The other appearance of this mysterious group is in 2 Chronicles 4.41, where the king *is* Hezekiah and the MT has המעינים *kethib*, המעונים *qere*, (LXX again Μιναίους). Finally, outside Chronicles, Ezra 2.50 lists בני מעינים (again *kethib*; *qere* מעונים) among the temple servants of the returning exiles. Taking into account both the *kethib-qere* phenomenon and the LXX/MT variants, one can hardly speak with much confidence about the Meunites at all.

the majority opinion, I suggest that these 'Meunites' have no place either in an event underlying this story nor in the original text of the story itself. Rather, we have either a corruption or a mistake in the MT. If a corruption, we cannot be sure of the original text, and nothing else in the chapter helps identify the original word; while if it is a mistake, the scribe inadvertently mentioned Ammonites twice (in different forms). The safest course is to ignore the peculiarity.

Accordingly, although the identity of the enemy must indeed be discussed further presently, for the moment we can be content with recognizing an attack from at least Ammonites and Moabites. Now what is the significance of Ammonites and Moabites for the Chronicler? In dealing with David's wars with his neighbours (1 Chron. 18–20), the Chronicler keeps the two nations separate, as also does 2 Samuel. In 2 Chronicles 27 we again have Ammonites, but no Moabites. Only in ch. 20 does the Chronicler link the two together. Elsewhere in the Bible, of course, they are quite closely associated. In Genesis 19 Moab and Ammon are portrayed as the two sons of Lot by incest; according to Deut. 23.3 'No Ammonite nor Moabite shall enter into the community of YHWH, not until the tenth generation'. In Neh. 13.1 we are given a concrete setting for this latter ruling, when the 'book of Moses' is read out, in which it is written that 'Ammonites and Moabites should not be admitted to the congregation of God for ever'. Subsequently, Nehemiah discovers that there were Judaeans who had married 'wives of Ashdod, of Ammon, and of Moab' (13.23). Ezra 9.1-2 relates how the 'people of Israel' had not 'separated themselves from the people of the lands (עמי הארצות)', comprising 'the Canaanites, the Hittites, the Perizzites, the Jebusites, the Ammonites, the Moabites, the Egyptians, and the Amorites'; the 'holy seed' has thus been 'mingled' with the 'people of those lands'. The composition of this list of races is instructive. We can easily recognize a Deuteronomic index of nations to be annihilated (Deut. 20.17; cf. 7.1 with slight deviation). But to these nations who inhabit the 'land of Canaan' have been added 'Ammonites', 'Moabites' and 'Egyptians'. Why are these neighbours included with peoples who are presented as indigenous? An answer is forthcoming presently.

The narratives of the 'Former Prophets', in particular Joshua, present the 'land of Canaan' as inhabited by races who were to be expelled or exterminated, and the reason for this is spelt out: lest their religious practices corrupt the Israelites and seduce them from the worship of YHWH. Now, in Ezra the 'people of the lands' also appear as a threat. This time, however, whatever may be implied by way of religious purity, the issue is strictly ethnic purity (though we can probably say that religious purity is already, in the books of Ezra and Nehemiah, inseparable from ethnic integrity anyway: the true 'Israel' is already defined simultaneously in both aspects). In the narratives of Joshua–Kings, however, Israel is defined not so much by its worship (for even when it is said to follow alien religious practices, it is still 'Israel') but by possession of the land given to it and its existence as a political entity (strictly, two entities, Israel and Judah). Thus, Israel's ethnic identity is expressed by geographical and political indices. That is, of course, why removal of indigenous kingship and deportation to Babylonia is represented, in the culmination of those narratives, as invoking a crisis of identity. On the other hand, in the ideology of Ezra–Nehemiah, because the identity is defined in ethnic, not geographical or political terms, the enemies of 'Israel' threaten not by possession of Israel's land, or by aggression against its state, but by ethnic pollution. Israel will not be destroyed by military campaigns but by intermarriage. The presence of Ammonites, Moabites (and Egyptians) in Ezra 9.2 might well be explained by the fact that at the time of composition of the passage the population of Yehud contained significant elements of these people, or perhaps more precisely that such people, always having been living in Yehud, were now being seen as a problem. At all events, we find in Nehemiah a character called Tobiah the Ammonite, one of Nehemiah's opponents. His Yahwistic name is not remarked upon in the text (and perhaps surprisingly, not altered!), and it may indicate that among those adhering to the cult of YHWH in Second Temple Yehud were some not deemed to belong to 'Israel' by the writer (or by Ezra or Nehemiah, or the *Bürger-Tempel-Gemeinde*).[10] The curiosity of the text forbidding Ammonites and Moabites to enter the congregation is the implication that they would want to. But even if we can only guess at the circumstances surrounding this curious ban, it does seem probable that people who could be identified as 'Ammonites and Moabites' (from Transjordan, presumably) were apparently eligible for inclusion in

10. On the *Bürger-Tempel-Gemeinde*, a term coined by J. Weinberg, see the recent exposition and critique by J. Blenkinsopp, 'Temple and Society in Achaemenid Judah', in P.R. Davies (ed.), *Second Temple Studies*. I. *Persian Period* (JSOTSup, 117; Sheffield: JSOT Press, 1991), pp. 22-53.

'Israel'. They were YHWH-worshippers, a problem accounted for by assigning their ancestry to Lot, but illegitimate ones who would not be allowed to belong to Israel—according to one version of the ruling (Deut. 23.3), not for ten generations, according to another version (Neh. 13.1), never.[11]

The profile of Ammonites and Moabites in the Genesis and Deuteronomy texts certainly seems to be a product of the society depicted in the stories of Ezra and Nehemiah. The situation described there seems the most plausible setting for such concern. At all events, we need now to apply the results of the preceding discussion to 2 Chronicles 20. By comparing the geographical-political code of the Joshua narratives with the ethnic-religious code of Ezra–Nehemiah, and by noting that Moabites and Ammonites operate as a category in either code, whether as geographical neighbours or near kin, we gain access to the significance of the enemy in the narrative under discussion. Accordingly, although what is depicted is a military attack by neighbours, using the conventions and the historical context of the 'pre-exilic' situation, the threat from these people in the time of the Chronicler (as in Ezra–Nehemiah) will have been in terms of ethnic identity. Because these Ammonites and Moabites are so like Israelites, even perhaps having Yahwistic names—so runs the Chronicler's argument—they can infiltrate the community of 'Israel'. Indeed, they are physically at its borders. How will Israel defend itself?

The issue, then, cannot in the time of the Chronicler be one of territorial integrity, but one of integrity of the 'congregation of Israel'. The ensuing details of ch. 20 make this clear. Thus the first reaction to the threat is an inward turn, towards the Temple, towards YHWH. A characteristic response of Palestinian Judaism when threatened was to turn inwards, to separate, to isolate itself. Elsewhere and at certain times there was openness, just as sometimes there was a militant counter-offensive. But the inward reflex has persisted, and here it is represented in the initial turning of the king towards his god, not towards his enemy, and in a cultic, not a military, act. The first stage of this inward turning ('seeking YHWH', a common term in

---

11. It is perhaps worth suggesting that the 'Egyptians' here are a cipher for Egyptian Jews, such as those in Elephantine, who also worshipped YHWH, but in a way that might have been disapproved (e.g. in conjunction with other deities, or at an alternative sanctuary).

Chronicles[12]) is the proclaiming of a fast. Although there is ample
evidence of a link between fasting and warfare,[13] in this case the fact
extends to the whole population, not just the soldiers (as, e.g., in Judg.
20.26), and thus should be understood without reference to intended
military action.

The next act of 'seeking YHWH' is a cultic assembly at the Temple.
The importance of this for the Chronicler is that such an assembly
constitutes the קהל יהודה וישראל. It is the קהל יהודה from which,
according to Deut. 23.3, Ammonites and Moabites are barred. Here
too, we find the overlapping of social-ethnic and geographical categories. The identity of the 'new court' is not clear,[14] but the location
symbolizes the wider issue at stake. It seems that in the Second
Temple, and at least by (or perhaps during?) the time of the
Chronicler, the priests and laity were already geographically separated within the Temple buildings through the provision of separate
courts. But such geographical distinctions go further: beyond the
Temple court is the holy city of Jerusalem, whose inhabitants are
distinguished in this text (as of course elsewhere in the OT too) from
the population of Judah which lies further beyond. Even further
beyond are other nations. The pattern of areas of concentric holiness
which we see in the Mishnah (and the Temple Scroll) is visible here
too, and the geographical/geometrical expression of social/ethnic
distinctions is found here as the congregation meets in the Temple
court, while beyond them lie the borders of the land which are being
invaded by those who are 'outsiders' ethnically and geographically.

The speech of Jehoshaphat is, as is well recognized, a lament psalm,
and influenced by Moses' speech in Deuteronomy 4 and by the prayer
of Solomon at the dedication of the Temple (2 Chron. 6.14-42,

12. The root occurs some forty times, thirty of these in 2 Chronicles. Cf.
R. Mosis, *Untersuchungen zur Theologie des chronistischen Geschichtswerkes*
(Freiburg: Herder, 1973), pp. 28-41.

13. Cf. the unpublished paper by D.L. Smith, *Hebrew Satyagraha: The Politics
of Food and Fasting in the Persian Period (6th-2nd century BCE)*.

14. According to 33.5 there were, as also described in Kings, two courts (חצרות);
4.9 terms these the 'priests' court' and the 'great court' (using the term עזרה). But the
references even in 2 Chronicles are very confused. 2 Chron. 7.7 mentions 'the court
before the house of YHWH' where Solomon offers a sacrifice (hence, presumably,
the priests' court); 24.21 has Zechariah stoned in the 'court of the house of YHWH'—
here more probably the outer court; 29.16 may refer to either, and 23.5 speaks of
'the courts of the house of YHWH' (cf. 1 Chron. 23.28; 28.12).

especially vv. 28, 34).[15] More important to us than these matters is
the choice of theme: the dispossessing of the land of Canaan in favour
of the 'descendants of Abraham your friend', but, more importantly
still, the non-dispossession of Ammon, Moab and Mount Seir, which
anticipates the third element of the enemy forces, namely those 'from
the hill-country of Seir' (see vv. 22-23). Now, elsewhere in the biblical literature Seir is the land of Edom (cf., e.g., Gen. 38.8-9; Deut.
2.4-8; Josh. 24.4). According to the majority of scholars, we have
already been introduced to these Edomites in v. 2, where אדם is read
for MT ארם (with 1 m. sing., but no versional support). Certainly this
reading is attractive, and makes proper geographical sense, unlike
'Aram'. Possibly this reading should even be adopted, although even
in that case it might be better considered as a gloss explicating עבר
הים, sc. the Dead Sea, or even harmonizing with the later reference to
'men from Seir'. But for our purposes the reading is something of a
distraction. The point is that the Chronicler refers nowhere to
Edomites by name in this narrative, but only to 'men from Seir'. Why
not? He uses the name 'Edomites' elsewhere, when recording David's
conquest (1 Chron. 18.13) and throughout the next chapter, where he
narrates how they gained independence from Judah. One reason may
be that since in the time of Jehoshaphat they were still subjects, they
could hardly be invaders, and so they had to be disguised. I shall
argue presently that a better explanation is available.

It is not hard to calculate why Edom (in whatever guise) should be
associated with Ammon and Moab. Even more closely than with the
Ammonites and Moabites, the relationship of Edom with Israel is
presented in the Bible as one of kinship; it is brotherly, both in the
Jacob cycle and in Amos 1.11-12.[16] But in Amos, as in Obadiah
(where the term 'mount of Esau' [= Seir?] recurs) the brotherliness is
characterized by anger and violence. The biblical allusions to Edom
thus project both an awareness of close kinship and a strong antipathy,
a not unusual combination of attitudes and one which is entirely consistent with the Hasmonaean Hyrcanus's decision to have them

---

15. For an analysis of the speech, see Petersen, *Late Israelite Prophecy*, pp. 72-
73 and M. Throntveit, *The Significance of the Royal Speeches and Prayers for the
Theology and Structure of the Chronicler* (Atlanta: Scholars Press, 1988).

16. For a detailed treatment of the Amos material, in which Edom is prominent,
see most recently F.L. Andersen and D.N. Freedman, *Amos* (AB; Garden City, NY:
Doubleday, 1989), pp. 264-81.

'Judaized'. On the reason why Esau is depicted as the elder brother in the Genesis cycle, and the possibility of a religious affinity, we are left to speculate.[17]

But why is the term 'men of Seir' used of Edomites in the speech of Jehoshaphat? The answer lies surely in the evident allusion to the story narrated in Deuteronomy 2, where also the name 'Edom' is avoided, and we have references only to 'Mt Seir' (vv. 1, 5), the 'children of Esau' (vv. 4, 5, 8, 22, 29), with the formula 'children of Esau who lived in Seir' at vv. 8, 22, 29. According to Deuteronomy 2 the Moabites (v. 9), Ammonites (v. 19) and children of Esau (v. 22) were all given their lands for a possession by YHWH. In v. 19 we are reminded that the Ammonites are 'children of Lot', an important prompt because it suggests why the three nations have a gift of land similar to Israel's—it is because of their descent from Abraham, via Lot or via Isaac. They are, then, also heirs of the promise of land. In Jehoshaphat's speech, accordingly, we find justified indignation that nations left alone by Israel in the wilderness and given their own land by YHWH are now invading the land given by YHWH to Israel! Of course, Jehoshaphat makes clear that the gift to Israel is superior, and it is Israel who are the true chosen descendants of Abraham—by virtue (v. 8) of their having not only occupied the land of Israel but also having built the sanctuary, on the basis of which they will also be saved by YHWH from their enemies! This royal speech then, whatever its form-critical affiliations, seems to have been very carefully constructed as an ideological key to the entire chapter.

And so it turns out that the battle to follow actually involves four nations all given their territory, as the Bible has it, by the same deity. Let us look at the historical context of the territory in question, which the Chronicler places fairly precisely in an area southeast of Jerusalem. We might commence by noticing that the burial place of Father Abraham was near Mamre—according to Gen. 13.18, 23.19 near the city of Hebron, together with Isaac (Gen. 35.27-28), and that at the time of the Chronicler this lay almost certainly outside Judah, in the territory of Edom, the boundaries of which ran not very far south of Beth-zur. While, for Jehoshaphat, Engedi and Tekoa were well within the boundaries of Judah, in the time of the Chronicler they were both close to the borders of Yehud, with Engedi possibly on the

---

17. See J.R. Bartlett, *Edom and the Edomites* (JSOTSup, 77; Sheffield: JSOT Press, 1989).

other side. Thus, the fundamental question 'who constitutes the real community of Israel' is being complicated, perhaps even compromised, by related considerations—'Who are the heirs of the promise of land? Who are the true descendants of Abraham?' If, as the Bible elsewhere asserts, Israel, Ammon, Moab and Edom are all descended from Abraham and have been given lands to possess by YHWH, what are the boundaries? And who determines them? In the Chronicler's day these boundaries had been drastically changed from what they were thought earlier to have been, and could be expected to remain so. Israel's neighbours, who were also viewed as relatives, were living just beyond where the battlefield of 2 Chronicles 20 lay, in the 'wilderness of Tekoa'. The battle takes place, then, on what are the borders of Israel in the Chronicler's time—and, strictly speaking, in the political geography of the Chronicler's time, those borders are threatened, but not yet transgressed!

How, then, is this kind of conflict to be conducted? After the royal speech we find several substitutions: for speeches of prophets, a Levitical sermon (although with the same words, perhaps); for the speech exhorting the troops (cf. Deut. 20), praise, a call to faith from the king. Instead of the mighty trumpet blast calling to war, the great cry of praise, and in place of captains, the king appoints singers. There is one mention of the 'army' but merely as following the singers. In this story, however, the singing is itself a militarily effective act: v. 22 reads . . . ובעת החלו ברנה ותהלה נתן יהוה מארבים, 'as soon as they began with the singing and praise...'[18] The deliverance apparently happens out of sight of the singers and the army. Fidelity expressed in liturgy is, it seems, an effective military option. A congregation has its weapons after all. After the battle, it remains only to collect the spoil and return, again with singing, to the Temple, and for the Chronicler to record—with or without irony—the formula of Josh. 21.44, 23.1, 2 Sam. 7.1 and so forth.

It is well-known that in 2 Chron. 20 the conventions of warfare have been transposed into the conventions of cult, the army of the king into the worshippers of YHWH. But what sort of situation, what sort of fear, might such transformations serve? Have we here an expression of belief that in the case of a military invasion YHWH will dramatically intervene if appropriately prompted? One should always

---

18. The verb translated 'begin' (החל) has a homonym meaning 'slay'. A possible reading, then, is 'cause to slay, cause to be slain'. Is there a deliberate word-play here?

hesitate before ascribing such radical notions to anyone, and in any case it is unlikely that the threat of military invasion occupied the Chronicler or his[19] contemporaries. Perhaps the narrative is an exercise in imagination, from which no deductions relevant to the social world in which the Chronicler lived should be drawn. However, the preceding exegesis has raised the possibility that a real issue is being addressed here: the integrity of the society of 'Israel' as an ethnically and cultically defined group. The story does indeed originate from an armyless and kingless community. But, for the Chronicler, Temple and people persist without these symbols. Naturally the cult and the people are mutually defined, too: ethnicity and cultic affiliation are gradually being merged as the biblical 'Israel' becomes more closely defined ideologically and practically. Here is a society still anxious about its identity, its ethnic boundaries under real or potential threat, perhaps still seeking to define itself around a cult, an ancestor, an ancient promise, a body of law, a single deity.

The anxieties postulated by this reading of 2 Chronicles are of course speculative. However, if the exegesis is correct, it clarifies just those processes which we know to have taken place during the formation of Jewish society in Palestine during the Second Temple period, processes commonly ascribed to the impact of 'Hellenism' (and the spread of Hellenism was taking place during the entire period within which the Chronicler's work may be dated). More particularly, however, it offers one explanation of the extension of the Hasmonaean kingdom east of the Jordan and south into Idumaea. This expansion is often ascribed to the ambition of recreating the 'Davidic empire'. But such an explanation hardly accounts for the forcible conversion to Judaism of the Idumaeans and others. Is it not more likely that the ambiguous status of these neighbours, particularly the Edomites, resolved narratively by the Chronicler by their repulsion from Israel's borders, is later solved in a more practical way by military means, by which they are brought within the borders of Israel? In the present day, when the issue of 'secure borders' for the state of Israel remains such a major political problem in the Middle East, the not unrelated issue of 'who is a Jew' testifies to the equally vexed problem of defining and maintaining those unseen boundaries which define 'Israel'.

---

19. I use the masculine deliberately here since I believe the author was male and his interests those of males.

EZRA–NEHEMIAH OR EZRA AND NEHEMIAH?*

James C. VanderKam

The thesis that Chronicles–Ezra–Nehemiah form a single literary work, first formulated by L. Zunz in 1832, eventually came to dominate the field and did so until quite recently.[1] Four principal arguments commended the theory to scholars: the three units resemble one another closely in style; they share major themes and interests; 2 Chron. 36.22-23 and Ezra 1.1-3a overlap (thus indicating that the latter resumes the former); and 1 Esdras combines parts of all three (2 Chron. 35.1–36.23; Ezra; Neh. 7.73b–8.13a).[2] Though the conclusion that the three units are one literary work continues to be accepted by some today—including the honoree of this volume[3]—and

* An early draft of this paper was delivered before Professsor Eric Meyers's seminar at Duke University on 13 November 1989. I am grateful for the comments received on that occasion and also for the reactions given more recently by Dr John Wright of the University of Notre Dame. Special thanks are due to Professor Kenneth Hoglund of Wake Forest University for the detailed written critique of another early version.

1. 'Dibre-Hayamim oder die Bücher der Chronik', in his *Die gottesdienstlichen Vorträge der Juden historisch entwickelt* (Berlin: Asher, 1832), pp. 13-36; see also F.C. Movers, *Kritische Untersuchungen über die biblische Chronik* (Bonn: Habicht, 1834).

2. These arguments (not always all of them) have often been repeated; see, e.g., S.R. Driver, *An Introduction to the Literature of the Old Testament* (repr.; New York: Meridian, 1957 [1897]), p. 516; E.L. Curtis and A.A. Madsen, *A Critical and Exegetical Commentary on the Books of Chronicles* (ICC; New York: Charles Scribner's Sons, 1910), pp. 2-5; S. Japhet, 'The Supposed Common Authorship of Chronicles and Ezra–Nehemia Investigated Anew', *VT* 18 (1968), pp. 331-32; and H.G.M. Williamson, *Israel in the Books of Chronicles* (Cambridge: Cambridge University Press, 1977), pp. 5-6.

3. J. Blenkinsopp, *Ezra–Nehemiah* (OTL; Philadelphia: Westminster Press, 1988), pp. 47-54. It may seem churlish to take issue with a distinguished scholar in a volume prepared in his honor, but—perhaps mischievously—I entertain the hope

though there are various theories about different editions of the Chronicler's work which would include varying amounts of Ezra and Nehemiah,[4] it has recently encountered stiff challenges, especially from S. Japhet.[5] She originally centered her case against the unity of Chronicles and Ezra–Nehemiah on what she called 'Linguistic Opposition',[6] 'Specific Technical Terms',[7] and 'Peculiarities of Style'. These varied probes led her to conclude:

> Our investigation of the differences between the two books, which was restricted to one field, has proven that the books could not have been written or compiled by the same author. It seems rather that a certain period of time must separate the two. We are certain that a further study of the literary characteristics, the attitude to the sources and their use and the theological conceptions of the two books will greatly support our conclusions.[8]

Her thesis was later supported and supplemented by H.G.M. Williamson in the first part of his *Israel in the Books of Chronicles*.[9] For his study of the linguistic side of the problem he contented himself with using the lists of the Chronicler's stylistic peculiarities compiled long ago by Driver, and E.L. Curtis and A.A. Madsen.[10] These lists had as their purpose (as Williamson recognizes) to show distinctive traits of the Chronicler's style; their occurrences in Ezra–Nehemiah were also included. After working through the lists item by item, Williamson ended by saying,

that my learned colleague will take some pleasure in reading the case made here and remember that someone almost said: disagreement is the highest form of flattery.

4. D.N. Freedman ('The Chronicler's Purpose', *CBQ* 23 [1961], pp. 436-42) who posits two editions; and F.M. Cross ('A Reconstruction of the Judean Restoration', *JBL* 94 [1975], pp. 4-18 [= *Int* 29 (1975), pp. 187-203]) who argues for three.

5. 'The Supposed Common Authorship', pp. 330-71.

6. For example, formation of the imperfect consecutive for various classes of verbs, the lengthened imperfect consecutive, theophoric names ending with יהו.

7. In these cases Chronicles uses one, and Ezra–Nehemiah another. An example is that 1–2 Chronicles avoids the title כהן גדול, preferring כהן הראש, whereas Ezra–Nehemiah have כהן גדול alone.

8. 'The Supposed Common Authorship', p. 371.

9. *Israel in the Books of Chronicles*, pp. 37-59.

10. Driver's list occupies pp. 535-40 in his *Introduction*; Curtis and Madsen's list can be found in their *Critical and Exegetical Commentary*, pp. 28-36.

. . . for the specific purpose of demonstrating the unity of authorship of Chr. and Ezr.–Neh. on the basis of style, the large majority of the entries are found to be irrelevant or quite inconclusive. Of the remainder, most in fact favour diversity of authorship, and serious questions can be raised about at least four of the six items that might favour unity'.[11]

Around the same time, R. Polzin argued for the distinct but related theses that 'the language of Ezr is almost identical to that of Chr from a linguistic point of view' and that the non-Memoir sections of Nehemiah (7.6–12.26) which differ significantly from the Memoirs, are 'as close linguistically to Chr as Ezr is'.[12] M. Throntveit has provided a convenient summary and critique of Japhet, Williamson and Polzin.[13] According to him, Polzin's evidence shows no more than that Chronicles, Ezra and Nehemiah belong to late biblical Hebrew. He is inclined to accept the Japhet–Williamson position that Chronicles and Ezra–Nehemiah are separate works, although he doubts that *linguistic* arguments can offer definitive proof either way. More recently, D. Talshir has further eroded the linguistic critique of Japhet.[14] He indicated that her data were at times imprecise and are incorrectly assessed by her as pointing to different authors. He also compiled lists of syntactical and idiomatic features and of vocabulary (a total of 62 items) which are shared exclusively by Chronicles and Ezra–Nehemiah; these show the strongest affinities between Chronicles and Ezra (1.1–4.7; 6.19–7.11; 10.1-44, that is, the non-Aramaic, non-Ezra Memoir sections) and the non-Memoir parts of Nehemiah, and the least between Chronicles and Nehemiah's Memoirs. He concludes that

. . . NM [= Nehemiah Memoirs] should not be included within the blocks Ezra–Neh. and that the data examined by my predecessors can be interpreted otherwise: the linguistic oppositions between the books are in fact non-oppositions, and any differences between the books (if such exist) can be interpreted on the level of mere scribal conventions. On the other hand, the language features shared solely by the block Ezra–Neh. . . [less the Nehemiah Memoirs] and Chr. are much more numerous than those

11. *Israel in the Books of Chronicles*, p. 59.
12. *Late Biblical Hebrew: Toward an Historical Typology of Biblical Hebrew Prose* (HSM, 12; Missoula, MT: Scholars Press, 1976), p. 70.
13. 'Linguistic Analysis and the Question of Authorship in Chronicles, Ezra and Nehemiah', *VT* 32 (1982), pp. 201-16.
14. 'A Reinvestigation of the Linguistic Relationship Between Chronicles and Ezra–Nehemiah', *VT* 38 (1988), pp. 165-93.

shared solely by NM and Chr. (or for example by Esther and Chr.); but admittedly lack of linguistic opposition in itself is no proof of identical authorship.[15]

Although there do remain some linguistic points of difference between Chronicles and Ezra–Nehemiah,[16] it is evident that the linguistic data *alone* are insufficient for demonstrating whether the same or different authors penned these works.[17] That is, neither side has been able to prove its case from this angle. A more important and convincing objection to common authorship of the three books centers on thematic differences between Chronicles on the one hand and Ezra–Nehemiah on the other. A number of scholars, including Japhet and Williamson, have also isolated thematic or ideological differences between the two.[18] Japhet, summarizing her views and those of many others, has recently given the following as a partial list:

> We may find illustrations in the role of David, the Davidic monarchy and dynasty in the historiosophical [*sic*] view of Chronicles, and their absence in Ezra–Nehemiah; the hopes for redemption as part of Israelite self-understanding in Chronicles, against the acceptance of the political present of the Restoration community and lack of perspective of change, in Ezra–Nehemiah; the dominant idea of the twelve tribes as a living political reality in Chronicles, the favourable attitude to non-Israelites and the concept of 'pan Israel', against the extreme separatism of Ezra–Nehemiah, the decline of the concept of the twelve tribes, and the major function of 'the Exile' (Golah) as the embodiment of Israel's identity; the central role of divine justice as a formulating factor of the whole history of Israel with a specific theory of retribution, in Chronicles, and its complete absence as a formulating force in Ezra–Nehemiah; the function in Ezra–Nehemiah of foreign rulers as a vehicle of God's benevolence in the restoration of Israel, and the absence of this idea in Chronicles; the strict stand on the matter of mixed marriages in Ezra–Nehemiah, versus the different attitude of Chronicles.[19]

15. Talshir, 'A Reinvestigation', pp. 192-93.
16. Cf., e.g., Talshir, 'A Reinvestigation', pp. 174-75 (lengthened imperfect consecutive, theophoric names ending in יה or יהו).
17. This is now the view of Japhet, 'The Relationship Between Chronicles and Ezra–Nehemiah', in J.A. Emerton (ed.), *Congress Volume Leuven 1989* (VTSup, 43; Leiden: Brill, 1991), pp. 301-304.
18. In *Israel in the Book of Chronicles*, pp. 60-70, Williamson deals with the themes of mixed marriages, the early history of Israel, the fall of the northern kingdom, immediate retribution, and historiography.
19. 'The Relationship Between Chronicles and Ezra–Nehemiah', pp. 305-306.

Some of these are more convincing than others. For example, the treatment of the Davidic line in the two stands in stark contrast— powerfully stressed in Chronicles and never mentioned in a dynastic sense in Ezra–Nehemiah. But others, such as the benevolent role of foreign rulers, may have more to do with the different situations which the works purport to describe than with any ideological distinction.[20]

The argument that the end of 2 Chronicles and the beginning of Ezra 1 overlap (both cite Cyrus's decree) and that this indicates that Chronicles continues in Ezra is hardly convincing. The repetition could also be interpreted as an indication by another writer that his book resumes the story from the point where Chronicles breaks off, or possibly the repetition is the result of two writers quite independently having the same source at their disposal (the two do not cite it in exactly the same way).[21] In the Hebrew manuscript tradition the

B. Uffenheimer (*The Visions of Zechariah: From Prophecy to Apocalyptic* [Jerusalem: Kiryat Sepher, 1961 (Hebrew)], Appendix) points to the prevalence of the miraculous and exaggerated in Chronicles and the more straightforward approach in Ezra–Nehemiah.

20. For objections to some of these proposed differences of theme, see Blenkinsopp, *Ezra–Nehemiah*, pp. 51-53; K.F. Pohlmann, 'Zur Frage von Korrespondenzen und Divergenzen zwischen der Chronikbücher und dem Esra/Nehemia-Buch', in Emerton (ed.), *Congress Volume*, pp. 314-30. Pohlmann's argument about the treatment of the Davidic line in the two works is unconvincing: Zerubbabel's Davidic origin is not mentioned in Ezra because the name spoke for itself; there was the unfortunate end of Zerubbabel's messianic ambitions which need not have been dredged up for the writer's picture of new beginnings (pp. 320-21). The fact is that neither in Ezra nor in Nehemiah is the connection of anyone with the house of David noted other than Hattush (Ezra 8.2) who plays no noteworthy role in Ezra.

21. See the discussion in Williamson, *Israel in the Books of Chronicles*, pp. 7-11. M. Haran ('Book-Size and the Device of Catch-Lines in the Biblical Canon', *JJS* 37 [1986], pp. 5-11) has argued that the repetition is an example of the practice of indicating at the end of one scroll what followed in the sequel. As the scroll containing Chronicles had reached the maximum length possible, it was necessary to resume the narrative on a new one and to assist the reader in finding the continuation by suggesting at the end of the now completed scroll the subject taken up at the beginning of the new one. It is not clear, however, why one should think all of Chronicles filled one scroll to the maximum, thus necessitating a break at that point; also, would a catch-line be likely to run to the length it has at the end of Chronicles and the beginning of Ezra?

books never appear in the order Chronicles–Ezra–Nehemiah: their arrangement is always Ezra–Nehemiah–Chronicles or, if Chronicles precedes, it is separated from Ezra–Nehemiah by others of the Writings.[22] The argument from 1 Esdras is also a fragile one. The apocryphal book does indeed contain sections from all three works, but this is an argument for their original unity only if one accepts the fragment hypothesis, that is, that 1 Esdras is merely part of a once complete translation which would have included at least all of Chronicles. However, as it has survived, it combines only the last two chapters of 2 Chronicles with Ezra and a couple of verses from Nehemiah 7 and 8. It has the appearance of a composite which an editor has drawn from the three canonical works and is quite irrelevant to the issue of unified authorship for Chronicles–Ezra–Nehemiah.[23]

From a thematic point of view, there are good reasons for doubting that Chronicles–Ezra–Nehemiah constitute a single work; and the other standard arguments for their unity are susceptible to other interpretations. The concern in this paper is not, however, primarily with the separation of Chronicles and Ezra–Nehemiah. All writers who deal with the issue frame it as though the only problem were whether there are two or one compositions: Chronicles and Ezra–Nehemiah or Chronicles–Ezra–Nehemiah. Another possibility is that there were three: Chronicles, Ezra and Nehemiah. The hypothesis proposed and defended here is that all three may originally have been independent of one another. Thematic arguments of the kind listed above go far toward demonstrating that Chronicles should be separated from the other two; the remainder of this essay sets forth three lines of evidence which suggest that Ezra and Nehemiah as well may not come from one author/editor but are discrete literary works.

The arguments for taking Ezra–Nehemiah as a single editorial product include most of those which are thought to support the unity of Chronicles–Ezra–Nehemiah: language, themes and the arrangement of 1 Esdras. In addition, one finds statements such as the following from L.W. Batten:

---

22. For the evidence, see R. Beckwith, *The Old Testament Canon of the New Testament Church* (Grand Rapids: Eerdmans, 1985), pp. 452-64.

23. W. Rudolph, *Esra und Nehemia samt 3. Esra* (HAT; Tübingen: Mohr [Paul Siebeck], 1949), p. xiv.

The books of Ezr. and Ne. were originally one, and ought really to be so combined now. The evidence of this is overwhelming. Two points suffice for a demonstration: (1) The story of Ezr. is partly in one book, Ezr. 7–10, and partly in the other, Ne. 7.70–8.12. In 1 Esd. these two parts are united in a single book. (2) At the end of each book of the OT there are certain Massoretic notes, giving the number of verses, the middle point in the volume or roll, etc. There are no such notes at the end of Ezr., and those at the end of Ne. cover both books, showing that the two constituted a single work when those notes were made.[24]

One may add to the latter point that the Greek translation (Esdras β) also combines the two books in its 23 chapters.

Batten's first argument is weak indeed: if mention of one character in two works implied that the same author wrote them, we would have some wonderful combinations—2 Kings and Jonah should on these grounds be from the same writer. It is surely quite possible that two authors wrote about different points in Ezra's career, as was to happen later with the NT Gospels. Also, 1 Esdras does not combine the *books* of Ezra and Nehemiah. It merely attaches most of the remaining parts of the Ezra story to the book of Ezra (and prefixes a small part of 2 Chronicles to these elements). The second point is interesting but hardly compelling. It is true that at the later time for which they provide evidence the notes of the Massoretes show that they combined Ezra and Nehemiah. The total of 685 verses, mentioned at the end of Nehemiah, and the specification of Neh. 3.32 as the midpoint (in verses) fit the combined Ezra–Nehemiah. But even the data from these relatively late Hebrew copies are not unambiguous, since some MSS supply at Neh. 1.1 the marginal notation ספר נחמיה.[25] Such information, however, seems to be more significant for the history of transmission or for canonical history than for the question of original unity. It may be, too, that Ezra and Nehemiah were combined into one to help make the number of biblical books total 22 or 24, the same as the number of letters in the alphabet (Hebrew and

24. *A Critical and Exegetical Commentary on the Books of Ezra and Nehemiah* (ICC; Edinburgh: T. & T. Clark, 1913), p. 1. For a fuller listing of the ancient evidence for their unity, see H.G.M. Williamson, *Ezra, Nehemiah* (WBC, 16; Waco, TX: Word Books, 1985), pp. xxi-xxii.

25. See *BHK* or *BHS*, and S. Talmon, 'Ezra and Nehemiah [Books and Men]', *IDBSup*, p. 318. Actually, Josephus (*Apion* 40) may be the first writer to offer at least indirect evidence for considering the two as one because his count of biblical books works if one assumes that he treated Ezra–Nehemiah as a single book.

Greek respectively).[26] Qumran provides no information which favors either view. Three fragments of Ezra were found in cave 4, but thus far no scrap of Nehemiah has been identified.[27] What does this mean? It may imply that Nehemiah joins Esther as the only books of the Hebrew Bible not attested at Qumran; or it may not signify this at all if the books of Ezra and Nehemiah were already regarded as one composition.

While the special arguments for the unity of Ezra and Nehemiah lack convincing force, there are on the other side of the ledger three kinds of evidence which point to the conclusion that Ezra and Nehemiah were originally separate works.

The first category is that of language. Anyone consulting Driver's and Curtis and Madsen's lists of the stylistic peculiarities of the Chronicler soon becomes impressed, not so much by the force of the conclusion which the lists were supposed to document, but by how they illustrate numerous minor differences between Ezra and Nehemiah.[28] If one uses only these lists, the following gross figures result. (a) Driver gives 46 entries; of these, 11 show no examples from either Ezra or Nehemiah and are thus irrelevant to the present context. Of the remaining 35 entries, 18 (in whole, or in part where the entry has sub-categories) reveal differences between Ezra and Nehemiah in the sense that one book has the item in question while the other does not. Consequently, about one half of Driver's entries show linguistic distinctions between Ezra and Nehemiah. (b) Curtis and Madsen compiled a list of 136 items. Of these, 58 include no examples from

---

26. For the historical data on these enumerations, see Beckwith, *The Old Testament Canon*, pp. 235-41 (where the treatment of *Jub.* 2 is misguided), pp. 250-56.

27. The first contains Ezra 4.2-6, the second 4.9-11 and the third 5.17–6.5. Cf. Blenkinsopp, *Ezra–Nehemiah*, pp. 70-72; and now Ulrich's article in this volume.

28. That these lists do not go very far toward showing the presence of characteristic traits of the Chronicler's diction in Ezra and Nehemiah is evident from the following: in the Curtis-Madsen list of 136 entries, they mark 50 with an asterisk as being unique to the Chronicler (that is, the writer of Chronicles–Ezra–Nehemiah). Of these 50, 30 examples are found only in 1–2 Chronicles (no. 78 could be added here because the phrase in question is worded differently in Chronicles and Ezra). For the remaining 20, one (no. 77) occurs only in Nehemiah, three in Chronicles and Nehemiah alone, four in Chronicles and Ezra alone, and 12 in Chronicles–Ezra–Nehemiah. Some items in this last category are of dubious value as indicators of a writer's style: דרכמונים (no. 22), for example, says less about style than about the period when the writer was active.

either Ezra or Nehemiah. Of the remaining 78, 40 show disagreement between the two books. No great importance should be attached to such numbers, since the compilers did not distinguish editorial layers from sources in the various compositions. Moreover, the lists were drawn up to illustrate the stylistic traits of the writer of Chronicles. The true nature of the situation would emerge only if each item were examined and if due weight were given to all the other potential flaws in such comparisons (see above in connection with the unity of Chronicles–Ezra–Nehemiah). But even the raw numbers do allow one to conclude that the Driver and Curtis and Madsen lists highlight a number of minor differences in language between Ezra and Nehemiah.

There are, however, more weighty pieces of evidence. In studying whether the styles of two works are so similar that one should posit a common author/editor—and precisely how similar they should be to establish such a point is not easy to define—one should limit the comparison to those sections which are supposed to come from the author/editor. Including his sources is likely to skew the comparison by introducing irrelevant information, even if he may have touched them up to some extent. If one limits the comparison between Ezra and Nehemiah to recognized editorial material, a curious fact emerges, viz., there is little to compare, since so much of their texts comes from sources. That this is the case can be seen from any study of the two books. Consider, for example, Williamson's analysis in his recent commentary. He confines the editor's contribution to these passages: Ezra 1.1, 5-8; ch. 3; 4.1-5; 4.23–5.5; 6.1-2, 13-22; 7.11, 27-28; Neh. 9.1-5 (?); 10.1, 29-40; 12.44-47.[29] If his conclusions are mainly on the mark, it would mean that the editor contributed some

---

29. *Ezra, Nehemiah*, pp. xxiv-xxxiii. This is a minimal list, as Williamson does think that the editor revised a passage such as Ezra 7.1-10 from a first- to a third-person account. An older survey (O. Eissfeldt, *The Old Testament: An Introduction* [New York and Evanston: Harper & Row, 1965], pp. 542-48) arrives at similarly slim results. For Eissfeldt, the editor (he identifies him as the Chronicler) added, Ezra 3, 6.19-22, 7.1-11 and possibly Ezra's prayer in 9.6-15, Neh. 12.27-43 and perhaps the prayer in 9.6-37. For the book of Nehemiah, U. Kellermann (*Nehemia: Quellen Überlieferung und Geschichte* [Berlin: Töpelmann, 1967], pp. 4-56) spots the editor's hand in (apart from a few glosses elsewhere), 8.1–9.2, 9.4–10.1, 10.29-40, 11.1-2, 20, 25, 36, 12.30, 33-36, 41-45, 13.1-3—85 verses. Most of his extra verses vis-à-vis Williamson are found in chs. 8–9. Rudolph (*Esra und Nehemia*, pp. xxiii-xxiv) found the Chronicler's hand in Ezra 1.1-7, 11b, 3.1–4.5; 4.24; 6.19-22; 7.1-11; Neh. 9.3-5a; 10.1; 10.29–11.2; 11.20-25a;12.44–13.3.

45 verses in Ezra and just 22 in Nehemiah, for a grand total of 67. The small size of his contribution makes it difficult to establish whether one or more redactors contributed to the compilation of Ezra and Nehemiah.

Though there is not much to go on, the verses in Ezra and Nehemiah that are attributed to one or more editors exhibit both points of agreement and disagreement. Agreements in style and vocabulary can be gleaned to some extent from lists such as those of Driver and Curtis and Madsen as well as from the ones compiled by Talshir. A familiar stylistic trait which the two works share is the phrase 'the hand of the Lord upon me' (with variations it figures in Ezra 7.6, 9, 28; 8.18, 22, 31; Neh 2.8, 18), although it does not occur in the editorial sections of Nehemiah (or in Chronicles). Although there are resemblances of these kinds and the later Hebrew tradition does consider them one literary unit, there are also some rather startling differences which have not always been properly appreciated by scholars. First, some minor points should be listed.

1. Both Ezra and Nehemiah refer to the temple by its common name בית האלהים (Ezra 3.8, 9; Neh. 12.40), but Ezra alone calls it בית יהוה (3.8, 11; cf. 7.27 [8.29]).

2. Persian monarchs: (a) Although Ezra and Nehemiah mention Persian kings often, Ezra alone refers to one as מלך אשור (6.22). Neh. 9.32, which Kellermann attributes to the editor, does have the phrase מלכי אשור, but the ones intended are the actual Assyrian monarchs who had played parts in Israel's past. (b) In editorial and source passages Ezra calls the monarch מלך פרס (3.7; 7.1; cf. 1.1, 2, 8; 4.3, 5, 7, 24; 6.14; 9.9 [plural]). In Nehemiah, however, although one finds the phrase מלכות דריוש הפרסי in 12.22 [non-editorial], the noun פרס is never used with מלך.[30] (Note, too, the titles מלך בבל in Neh. 13.6 for Artaxerxes and מלך בבל for Cyrus in Ezra 5.13 [both are in sources].)

3. Ezra, both in source and redactional passages, employs the divine title אלהי ישראל (1.3; 3.2; 4.1, 3, 6, 21; 5.1; 6.14, 22; 7.6, 15; 8.25; 9.4, 15). It is not attested in Nehemiah.

4. Both books offer a phrase that seems to have the same meaning in a similar context but is worded slightly differently in them:

30. A.S. Kapelrud, *The Question of Authorship in the Ezra-Narrative* (Skrifter Utgitt av det Norske Videnskaps-Akademi i Oslo, 1944; II. Historisk-Filosofisk Klasse; Oslo: Dybwad, 1945), p. 19.

Ezra 3.13   הקול נשמע עד למרחוק

Neh. 12.43   ותשמע שמחת ירושלם מרחוק (editorial for Kellermann, not Williamson).

5. If Ezra's prayer in 9.6-15 and the historical survey with confession in Neh. 9.6-37 are included among the editorial contributions,[31] other differences emerge:

    a.   Although both texts make regular reference to sins of sundry kinds, Ezra uses forms of אשמה four times (9.6, 7, 13, 15; cf. 10.10, 19); in Nehemiah this word never appears, here or elsewhere in the book.[32]

    b.   Ezra employs נכלם (9.6) and בוש (9.6; the noun בשת appears in v. 7); these words do not figure in the Nehemiah passage (or elsewhere in the book).

    c.   In his prayer Ezra uses עון in 9.6, 7, 13; it is not found in Neh. 9.6-37, although it is in Neh. 3.37, 9.2 (Williamson and Kellermann consider this verse redactional). Conversely, Neh. 9.35 calls certain misdeeds מעלליהם, but one searches in vain for this word in Ezra.

    d.   Ezra refers to himself and the other returnees as פליטה (9.8, 13, 14, 15); the word does not occur in Nehemiah 9, although it is used in 1.2 (source).

    e.   The word יתד in Ezra 9.8 is not found in Nehemiah.

    f.   Terms for the deity: Nehemiah uses the two less frequent designations אלה (9.17) and אל (9.31, 32 [cf. 1.5]); neither term appears in Ezra.

    g.   Lists of groups: in Ezra 9.7 the writer details several categories of those who have sinned: אנחנו מלכינו כהנינו. In Nehemiah 9 the same sorts of lists occur but they are longer: למלכינו לשרינו ולכהנינו ולנביאנו ולאבתינו (9.32) and מלכינו שרינו כהנינו ואבתינו (9.34).

---

31. Kellermann (for Ezra 7–10, see *Nehemia*, pp. 56-69; for Nehemiah 9, see n. 29 above) considers these two pericopes to be the work of the Chronicler.

32. Williamson (*Israel in the Books of Chronicles*, p. 58) includes this word as one of the six cases which alone remain as positive evidence that one editor combined Chronicles–Ezra–Nehemiah; but he operates with the conclusion that Ezra–Nehemiah are the work of one editor. Hence the appearance of the word in just one of these books would be sufficient.

Admittedly, these are small details (and there are probably others like them), but when coupled with the statistics regarding linguistic differences and when one remembers the small basis for comparison, they should perhaps be accorded some value. On the level of language, one cannot make a very strong case for the editorial unity of Ezra and Nehemiah.

A second category of evidence involves a larger issue that moves beyond the linguistic surface and touches on a more significant characteristic of these two books, viz., the ways in which they employ sources. Clearly there are some fundamental similarities between the stories the books tell. Thematically, they are joined by their principal subjects: restoration (of people, temple and city); their two protagonists are parallel to some extent; and both are concerned with similar problems (e.g. intermarriage). Nevertheless, with regard to the sources there are major differences which offset the shared features.

1. As noted above, both books rely heavily on sources; once these are subtracted surprisingly little remains. Nevertheless, there is a marked, if transparent, difference here: Ezra quotes extensively from official, apparently largely authentic Aramaic documents (and one Hebrew proclamation in 1.2-4) which provide imperial sanction for the restoration project.[33] The Aramaic documents come from the reigns of each of the three kings who are important in the book of Ezra: Cyrus (6.3-5), Darius (6.3-12) and Artaxerxes (4.17-22; 7.12-26). Nehemiah makes a few allusions to official royal documents: 1.7 (royal letters for the governors of Beyond the River; cf. 1.9); 1.8 (a royal letter to Asaph, keeper of the king's forest). However, the writer never quotes one in support of his hero's efforts at restoring the wall of Jerusalem, even though he encounters the same sort of local opposition as befell the builders and restorers in Ezra (e.g. Neh. 6.1-9). The author/editor of Nehemiah does quote from documents, of course, such as the list of returnees in ch. 7 and the Nehemiah Memoirs; moreover, in the Memoirs a letter of Sanballat is cited (6.6-7). But, while royal approval undergirds Nehemiah's

33. For a recent and detailed comparison of the documents in Ezra with the pertinent extra-biblical material, see B. Porten, 'The Documents in the Book of Ezra and Ezra's Mission', *Shenaton* 3 (1978–79), pp. 174-96 (Hebrew). The remarkable authority granted to Ezra in 7.12-26 gives one pause, but this document, too, shares many of the traits of Aramaic letters from roughly the time in which it is set (see especially pp. 186-89).

efforts (2.4-10, 18), no letter or decree is quoted to support the point. The contrast, especially with Ezra 7, is stark indeed. One wonders why the same editor would parade a full and extraordinary document before his readers in one case (note that it includes a message for the treasurers in Beyond the River [vv. 21-24]), but under strikingly similar circumstances merely allude to such texts in the other instance? There may be a reason for this—even one that is compatible with the unified hypothesis (e.g. he had no access to such documents for Nehemiah); yet, whatever the cause(s), the contrast remains.

2. The list of returnees who accompanied Zerubbabel and Joshua when they came up from Babylon to Jerusalem at some point in Cyrus's reign appears in largely the same form in Ezra 2 and Nehemiah 7. In Ezra it is adduced to identify the groups and individuals who are supposed to have returned in the time of Cyrus; in Nehemiah it is cited as a document which belongs to a time long past ('I found the book of the genealogy of those who came up at the first' [7.5])[34] and which Nehemiah used as the basis for his effort to repopulate Jerusalem (7.4-5). Thus, the same list serves different purposes in the two books, yet there is no reason to think it strange that it should figure in both places. A problem arises, however, with the way in which the list is attached to the sequel in the two books. The material that is common to Ezra and Nehemiah includes more than just the list itself. The heading of the document is quoted in both books (Ezra 2.1-2 = Neh. 7.6-7; Ezra has 11 leaders, Nehemiah 12), and the end is cited as well. The final parallel words are in Ezra 3.1 and Neh. 7.73b–8.1a. In Ezra one reads, 'When the seventh month came and the sons of Israel were in the towns, the people gathered as one man to Jerusalem'. It then continues with events of the seventh month—the episode of Joshua, Zerubbabel and construction of the altar during Cyrus's reign (therefore between 538 and 530). The parallel in Nehemiah reads, 'And when the seventh month had come, the children of Israel were in their towns. And all the people gathered as one man into[35] the square before the Water Gate...' The book then continues with what happened in the seventh month mentioned in it: the reading of the law by Ezra which occurred no earlier than the

---

34. All biblical quotations are from the RSV.

35. To this point, although the English renderings differ somewhat, the Hebrew texts of Ezra and Nehemiah are identical except for the suffix on עריהם and the use of כל before העם, both in Nehemiah.

twentieth year of Artaxerxes (445 or perhaps somewhat later). There is, therefore, a gap of about 90 years between the events of the seventh month in the two books, although the reference to the seventh month is quoted from the same document in each. If the same editor inserted the list into both Ezra 2 and Nehemiah 7, then he would be interpreting the seventh month of the text in one case to refer to a year in Cyrus's reign and in the other to a year in Artaxerxes' reign—a sizable historical blunder. However, if one posits one editor for the book of Ezra and another for the book of Nehemiah, then the phenomenon is more readily explicable and no historical problem arises. That is, the author of Nehemiah, when he quotes this document, continued the quotation through the reference to the seventh month, not because he put Ezra's reading of the law in Cyrus's reign, but because the next event that he narrated happened also to have occurred in the seventh month. Since he was not responsible for how the list was used in Ezra, no conflict within his book resulted.

In this connection it is worthwhile to examine T. Eskenazi's explanation of the twofold citation of the list. Eskenazi explains its double appearance as a hefty case of *inclusio*.[36] She accepts the unity of Ezra–Nehemiah (pp. 11-14) and regards the repetition of the list as evidence for that oneness. She introduces her section on Neh. 7.6-72 with words that express what she considers the artistic results of the repetition:

> The resumptive repetition of Ezra 2 in Nehemiah 7 clamps together everything and everyone in between, i.e., the earlier movements and characters from Ezra 2 to Nehemiah 7. The repetition welds diverse groups into a unity, into עם, a 'people'. This document also effects the unity of past events with the present via the written mode. Previous generations become partners in present events through this document' (p. 88).

This would be an impressive accomplishment indeed for a quite ordinary list which is repeated in two rather prosaic books. Eskenazi's conclusion arises, as nearly as one can tell, from no clear indication in the text, but more from what contemporary literary criticism leads one to believe that *inclusios* achieve. She asserts that the repetition of the list is the 'major structuring device of Ezra–Nehemiah' and that

---

36. *In an Age of Prose: A Literary Approach to Ezra–Nehemiah* (SBLMS, 36; Atlanta: Scholars Press, 1988), pp. 88-95. The page references in the text are to this book.

'the list reiterates, both formally and thematically, the major concerns of the book'. Formally, it unifies the movements of return and reconstruction; thematically, its contents express the emphasis of the book on the reconstituted people (p. 88).

Eskenazi lists six results that come about from the double quotation: (1) it unifies what comes between these two extremes; (2) it emphasizes the people listed and the role they play; (3) it articulates the 'wholeness of the people'; (4) it 'bridges past and present' (p. 91); (5) it 'suggests broadening of communal participation' (note 'rest of the people' in Neh 7.71 which is lacking from Ezra); and (6) (with hesitation) 'interpretation of the repetition implies that the list sets equivalencies between Torah reading and sacrifices', that is, these are what follow the list in its two locations (p. 92). She ends her creative analysis in poetic fashion: 'Like a funnel through which sand flows, so does Nehemiah 7 channel persons and events from Ezra 2 through Nehemiah 7 into the final celebration which comes next to conclude the book' (p. 95).

It would be satisfying in a way if all this were the case, but the essential assumption behind interpreting the two appearances of the list as an *inclusio* is that Ezra and Nehemiah are one work. If Ezra and Nehemiah were originally separate books, then one would be left with the quotation of one document in two compositions, as with the Decalogue in Exodus 20 and Deuteronomy 5 or the Lord's Prayer in Matthew 6 and Luke 11. Surely those are not instances of *inclusio*. The larger question can be settled only after examining a third kind of evidence that the two books are separate compositions.[37]

The third category of evidence that Ezra and Nehemiah were originally independent is probably the most important one: the themes of the book of Ezra. If one pays close attention to the central thematic statement in Ezra, it becomes evident that it embraces all of the material in Ezra and leaves no room for the contents of the book of Nehemiah which has other fundamental concerns.[38] Ezra in its

37. Williamson ('The Composition of Ezra i-vi', *JTS* 34 [1983], pp. 1-30) maintains that the list and accompanying material in Ezra 2 are derived from Nehemiah 7 and that Ezra 1–6 was composed after the Ezra and Nehemiah materials were combined. His arguments from the two lists and their contexts have been refuted by Blenkinsopp, *Ezra–Nehemiah*, pp. 43-44.

38. Blenkinsopp (*Ezra–Nehemiah*, p. 54), who, as noted earlier, considers Chronicles–Ezra–Nehemiah to be an editorial unity, points to a structural feature

entirety focuses on the restoration of temple and people, while
Nehemiah centers more on rewalling and repopulating Jerusalem. For
this point it will again be helpful to use the analysis in Eskenazi's
monograph.

She has correctly perceived that the thematic verse of Ezra is
6.14.[39] Although this verse occurs in the Aramaic section of the
chapter, it is found in the narrative part of it that is often thought to
have been contributed by the compiler of the book.[40] It would not be
the only case in which he continued a narrative that had to do with an
Aramaic document in the same language (see 4.23–5.5). In ch. 6,
after recording that Darius confirmed Cyrus's decree and ordered that
the Jerusalem temple be completed, the author/editor writes: 'And the
elders of the Jews built and prospered, through the prophesying of
Haggai the prophet and Zechariah the son of Iddo.[41] They finished
their building by command of the God of Israel and by decree of
Cyrus and Darius and Artaxerxes king of Persia...'[42] In Ezra 6.14
the full message of the book of Ezra is served up to the reader in
succinct but comprehensive form: the people, represented by their
elders, are at the head of the building project, but they proceed, not
by their own authority or power, but through the prompting of God's

which unites Chronicles with Ezra–Nehemiah: 'the retrospective comment accompanying the epoch-marking festivals throughout the work'. He mentions Hezekiah's
passover (2 Chron. 30.26), Josiah's passover (2 Chron. 35.18), and the festival of
tabernacles in the time of Ezra and Nehemiah (Neh. 8.17). While these passages
constitute an interesting progression and in this way tie Chronicles and Nehemiah
together, the book of Ezra falls outside the pattern. It is curious, too, that Neh. 8.17
says no festival of tabernacles like this one had been celebrated since the days of
Joshua son of Nun, whereas Ezra 3.4 says that Zerubbabel, Joshua and the others
observed it as prescribed in the law. Would one editor claim both?

39. *In an Age of Prose*, pp. 37, 41-42.

40. Williamson regards it as redactional (*Ezra, Nehemiah*, p. xxiv). It may say
something about the degree of certainty which may be accorded to the scholarly
identification of editorial additions that C.C. Torrey wrote regarding the contribution
of the Chronicler here: 'From Ezr. 4.8 to 6.8, and again through 6.11-14, there is no
sign of his presence'. (*Ezra Studies* [The Library of Biblical Studies; New York:
Ktav, 1970], p. 224 [the chapter in which these words appear is a revision of one
that had been published in 1909]).

41. The reference here to the two prophets does in fact form an *inclusio* with 5.1.

42. One may safely dismiss Eskenazi's suggestion that the singular 'king of
Persia' expresses the thought that all three are somehow one, 'as if they spoke with
one voice' (*In an Age of Prose*, p. 60). Esdras β reads a plural.

prophets and under the aegis of the Persian sovereigns Cyrus, Darius and Artaxerxes—that is, the three kings whose decrees about the temple play a role in Ezra. Yet, although these three great kings are named, God is listed as the first authority. His people, with divine and royal authorization, build God's house—the only building mentioned in the context.

So much is transparent, but Eskenazi moves beyond her recognition that Ezra 6.14 is the thematic verse of the book to an ill-fated attempt to include the book of Nehemiah within its purview. These are her words:

> The major repetition of the list of returnees (Ezra 2 and Nehemiah 7) is the clue to the structure. The opening verses of the book, i.e., the edict of Cyrus and the response to it (Ezra 1.1-6), encapsulate the major themes. Ezra 6.14 is a key verse, summarizing the book by stating that the house of God was finished in accordance with the decree of God and the decree of the three Persian kings.[43]

On her analysis the editor handles these central themes of the combined Ezra–Nehemiah by describing their potentiality (Ezra 1.1-4), their actualization (Ezra 1.5–Neh 7.72; this central section is framed by the repeated list) and success (Neh. 8.1–13.31) (pp. 38-39). Her 'actualization' section traces the three movements that effected the potential of Cyrus's decree: Ezra 1.5–6.22, 7.1–10.44 and Neh. 1.1–7.5.

> I label these three stories 'movements' because they represent three actual, spatially determined movements from diaspora to Jerusalem. They are also distinct movements in the sense of pertaining to different streams of populations. Each of these movements actualizes a specific aspect of building the house of God by a group of people; it is thus embedded as a detail of the overall 'process of actualization' (p. 39).

She is surely correct in highlighting the twin themes of temple and people that are introduced immediately in Cyrus's proclamation: '...he has charged me to build him a house at Jerusalem... Whoever is among you of all his people...let him go up...and rebuild the house of the Lord...let each survivor...be assisted by the men of his place...' (1.2-4). Also, there is no doubt that both Ezra and Nehemiah detail movements of Jewish groups from the east to

---

43. Eskenazi, *In an Age of Prose*, p. 37. In the following paragraphs the page references are again to this work.

Jerusalem, although Nehemiah's contingent appears to have been small
and his acceptance of a military escort casts him in an unfavorable
light vis-à-vis Ezra. What is surprising about Eskenazi's analysis is
her contention that the book of Nehemiah actualizes the building of
the house of God and that the last chapters of the book chronicle
success in this area. In order to fit the book of Nehemiah into this
theme which is articulated in Ezra she is forced to expand the meaning
of the phrase 'house of God' in Cyrus's decree and in Ezra 6.14 to
encompass not only the temple but also the entire city of Jerusalem.
Thus one meets in her book the odd-sounding claim that the third
movement 'finished the house of God by restoring the wall (under
Artaxerxes)' (pp. 40, 77-78).

Among the pieces of data which she marshals for her thesis are
some hints in the book of Ezra that the 'house of God' involved more
than the new building on the temple mount. The ceremony at the
completion of the second temple is briefly described in ch. 6
'...because only a certain stage has concluded. The house of God is
not yet finished.' (p. 56). The curious temple dimensions that are
specified in Cyrus's decree (6.3: 60 cubits high and 60 cubits wide;
Solomon's temple was only 30 cubits high and 20 cubits wide [1 Kgs
6.2]) also suggest that the emperor had provided for a larger house of
God than just the temple itself. 'This expansion of the house of
God... culminates in Ezra's and Nehemiah's activities, during the
reign of Artaxerxes, thus reflecting the notion of temple and city
composing together the house of God' (p. 57). She quite properly sees
Ezra 7.1–10.44 as filling out the themes of Ezra 1 and 6 (although her
interpretation of השלם in 7.19 as 'complete' is unacceptable).[44] She
adds that the term יתד in 9.8 also implies that more is coming—the
tent itself (p. 73).

While in Eskenazi's view such hints are present already in Ezra,
clearer indications surface in the account of the third movement—
Neh. 1.1–7.5.[45] She believes that Ezra 4.7-24, the famous section
which is out of chronological order and deals with the city of
Jerusalem, not the temple, connects in an implicit way the temple and
the city walls. Or, as she writes, in this section 'it has been established
that the house of God and the city walls are coextensive' (p. 84). In

44. Eskenazi, *In an Age of Prose*, pp. 60-77. She deals with השלם on p. 71.
45. For the material in this paragraph, see Eskenazi, *In an Age of Prose*, pp. 77-88, especially pp. 83-87.

some way parallels between the building reports in Ezra 1–6 and Nehemiah 1–7 are supposed to demonstrate this point. More plausible arguments emerge from a few statements in Nehemiah. Neh. 2.8 has the hero requesting from the king wood for the 'gates of the fortress of the temple' as well as for the walls and for his own house. Because the house of God is being constructed in the building of the city wall, sanctification of that wall is necessary. Thus, Neh. 3.1 uses the word קדש, and participation by the high priest (absent in Ezra, and here given the title for the first time in Nehemiah) evidences the religious nature of the enterprise (he is not, however, mentioned in connection with the dedication of the wall in 12.27-43). One more clue that the whole city is the house of God is found in the appointing of gatekeepers, singers and Levites as guards (7.1; 13.22). Previously, singers and Levites guarded only the temple gates, but now the entire holy city (11.1) is the house of God. Hence the area which they must watch is enlarged. Finally, the seemingly innocuous references to the tower of Hananel (3.1; 12.39) may have more than architectural or geographic significance. This tower appears in prophetic passages that talk of 'completed restoration' (Jer. 31.38-39; Zech. 14.10-11). For Eskenazi the repair of the tower of Hananel becomes '...the enactment of a larger theological-salvific vision' (p. 86). With the completion of the sanctified city walls, which themselves render holy all that is within them, the house of God, whose reconstruction had been commanded by Cyrus, Darius and Artaxerxes, is finished.

There are many objections that could be lodged against Eskenazi's forced attempt to include Nehemiah within the scope of Ezra's themes. One of the more telling ones is that the writer of Nehemiah seems not to have been privy to this feature of his book because he continues to distinguish clearly between the house of God and the city of Jerusalem (e.g., 6.10; 8.16; 10.32-39 [8×]; 11.11 [cf. v. 12], 16, 22; 13.4, 7, 9, 11, 14). There is every reason to believe that throughout both Ezra and Nehemiah the house of God is the temple; furthermore, Jerusalem is never called 'the house of God'. Alas, Jerusalem is not Bethel. Furthermore, sanctifying something like a part of a city wall does not transform it into a temple; and the tower of Hananel is mentioned only to mark a fixed geographical point on the north side of the city. As for the members of the clergy who guard the city gates, it should be noted that 7.1 does not say that the Levites and singers actually guard gates of the city. It is often taken in this sense (cf. 13.22), but it may be that, if in fact the text means that they served as sentries, they were responsible for gates in the temple area at the east end of the city. The reference in 13.22 to Levites guarding gates on the Sabbath is often regarded as a special case because Sabbath observance at that particular time was being strictly enforced.

Eskenazi's intriguing attempt to inflate the meaning of 'the house of God' should therefore be rejected. The themes of the book of Ezra will not accommodate the contents of the book of Nehemiah. She is correct in seeing that the themes of Ezra are executed in three movements, but all of them are within that one book. Its two principal entities—temple and people—are restored within the confines of Ezra's 10 chapters. The first movement was that of Sheshbazzar, who, despite all the modern uncertainty about his identity and accomplishments, is said to have brought the temple vessels back to Jerusalem (1.8-11) and to have laid the אשׁיא, the lowest parts of the temple foundation (5.14-16). The second movement centers on Zerubbabel and Joshua, who returned at the head of a large company of exiles, built the altar during Cyrus's reign, and started work on the temple itself (chs. 2–4). Later, in Darius's second year they with the two prophets led the successful effort to finish the temple building (chs. 5–6).

Chapter 6 may appear to bring the themes of the book to a conclusion because at this juncture in the story there is a substantial community of Jews in Yehud and the temple has been rebuilt. But the author of Ezra ties the contributions of Artaxerxes into his themes by stressing how he restored the sanctuary in splendid fashion through his contributions and how Ezra refined the new Israel by implementing provisions of the royally supported lawbook that he brought in his hand.[46] Ezra 7–8 is replete with indications of Artaxerxes' contributions to the adornment and service of the temple in Jerusalem. Among others, he permits Levites to return with Ezra (7.13; cf. v. 7). Also, Ezra is

> to convey the silver and gold which the king and his counselors have freely offered to the God of Israel, whose dwelling is in Jerusalem, with all the silver and gold which you shall find in the whole province of Babylonia, and with the freewill offerings of the people and the priests, vowed willingly for the house of their God which is in Jerusalem. With

46. Porten ('The Documents in the Book of Ezra', pp. 191-93) stresses the continuity between Ezra and Zerubbabel as evidenced in the text.

this money, then, you shall with all diligence buy bulls, rams, and lambs, with their cereal offerings and their drink offerings, and you shall offer them upon the altar of the house of your God which is in Jerusalem. Whatever seems good to you and your brethren to do with the rest of the silver and gold, you may do, according to the will of your God. The vessels that have been given to you for the service of the house of your God, you shall deliver before the God of Jerusalem. And whatever else is required for the house of your God, which you have occasion to provide, you may provide it out of the king's treasury (7.15-20; see also vv. 23-24).

As one reads on, there are references to Ezra's efforts at getting temple personnel to accompany him (8.15-20), valuables placed in priestly hands for the temple (8.24-30), goods for priests and temple (8.33-34), sacrifices at the temple by those who returned (8.35), and notes on how the returnees 'aided the people and the house of God' (8.36). There will be no more unfavorable comparisons between the first and second temples after Artaxerxes had finished adorning the latter. It causes little wonder then that Ezra exclaimed, 'Blessed be the Lord, the God of our fathers, who put such a thing as this into the heart of the king, to beautify the house of the Lord which is in Jerusalem...' (7.27). The final chapters of the book round out the themes by identifying those who returned with Ezra (8.1-20) and by relating how Ezra purified the restored nation according to the dictates of the lawbook by enforcing the end of mixed marriages. The chronology of the book implies that Ezra executed his mission in 458; what he may have done at later points in his career is not recorded here—for whatever reason.

These three kinds of evidence that have been presented support the thesis that the book of Ezra was composed as an independent work. Its author or editor wrote in a style and with a vocabulary that are not the same as those of the Chronicler or the editor of Nehemiah, made heavy use of official Aramaic sources, and enunciated, pursued and carried to completion his own two themes of a restored people and temple which came into being by the mercy of God exercised through Cyrus, Darius and Artaxerxes.

EZRA AND NEHEMIAH: ON THE THEOLOGICAL
SIGNIFICANCE OF MAKING THEM CONTEMPORARIES

Judson R. Shaver

Despite significant scholarly interest in the book of Ezra–Nehemiah, a number of critical issues remain unresolved. Among these are questions regarding the genre and historical reliability of the book's sources, its date and editorial history, the nature and extent of literary dislocations in the text, and the relationship of Ezra–Nehemiah to Chronicles. One of the most intractable and well known issues, however, is the question of the relative chronology of Ezra and Nehemiah. I do not intend to contribute to the literature on this problem; it is already extensive, and has been reviewed elsewhere.[1] But despite the fact that a great deal has been written on the question of Ezra and Nehemiah's relative chronology, much of it arguing or assuming that their missions did not overlap, little attention has been paid to the theological significance of making them contemporaries.

According to the book of Ezra–Nehemiah, however, there is nothing obscure about their relationship; the two men were contemporaries. Ezra preceded Nehemiah to Jerusalem in the seventh year of Artaxerxes (Ezra 7.8), Nehemiah arrived some fourteen years later (Neh. 2.1), and thereafter they cooperated in the restoration of the political and religious life of the Jews in Beyond the River (Neh. 8–12). If in fact they were contemporaries, it follows, of course, that no treatment is required of the theological significance of making them so. It is also true, however, that for the most part the book describes the activities of each without reference to the other; in only two places does the text explicitly place them side by side (Neh. 8.9; 12.36; cf also 12.26). An attentive reader, therefore, might wonder why, if they

---

1.   See the comments and bibliography in J. Blenkinsopp, *Ezra–Nehemiah* (Philadelphia: Westminster Press, 1988), pp. 139-44.

were indeed cooperating in the restoration, there are so few references to that fact. The question of whether they were contemporaries thus seems unavoidable. Likewise, if they were not contemporaries, can one explain the text without dealing with the editorial shaping which, although it created a flawed history, produced the canonical text?

Predictably, the exegetical literature represents a variety of ways of dealing with this set of issues. Without any effort to provide an exhaustive survey, I would suggest that this literature represents three basic approaches, which are themselves a reflection of the authors' theological assessments of the nature of biblical texts.

Those who take the more conservative approach, who understand the Bible primarily as divine revelation, begin with a radical commitment to the text that we have. The exegete's questions are: what does the text say and what does that mean? But since the Bible is an intentional divine disclosure, one need not doubt that it is true. Thus, Fensham, in his commentary on Ezra and Nehemiah, states that Neh. 8.9 is a very important text because from it we learn that Ezra and Nehemiah were contemporaries.[2] Although Fensham demonstrates thorough familiarity with the critical literature, almost all of which regards the inclusion of Nehemiah in this text as a secondary (and historically inaccurate) interpolation, he finds no *text-critical* basis to emend the verse and thus no reason to treat it as other than a straightforward statement of historical fact.[3] Surprisingly, he is little inclined to comment on the theological significance of this important historical detail. This lack is filled by J.G. McConville's volume in the Daily Study Bible series.[4]

According to McConville, the two leaders were contemporaries, but responsible for different spheres. Ezra the priest takes precedence in religious matters, but defers to Nehemiah the governor when it comes to politics.[5] That, of course, explains the paucity of texts which actually associate the two. But it also explains the two occasions when the

2. F.C. Fensham, *The Books of Ezra and Nehemiah* (Grand Rapids: Eerdmans, 1982), p. 218.
3. Fensham, *Ezra*, p. 218.
4. J.G. McConville, *Ezra, Nehemiah, and Esther* (Philadelphia: Westminster Press, 1985).
5. McConville, *Ezra*, p. 115.

men did act together. The sequence of their activities was: Ezra's initial religious reforms, then Nehemiah's political efforts to restore the city, especially the wall, followed by an interim religious celebration of the wall's completion. This, the law-reading ceremony of Nehemiah 8, occurred some four or five days after the wall was finished and would understandably have been led by Ezra, but must also surely have included Nehemiah as, indeed, Neh. 8.9 states. The formal dedication of the wall was necessarily postponed until the people as a whole had made a great confession and had dedicated themselves to the Torah and the upkeep of the Temple. Only then did Nehemiah and Ezra join the people in a procession which circled the new wall and converged at the Temple. According to McConville, the theological significance of this historical order of events is that it relativizes the importance of the human accomplishment of rebuilding the walls, and the importance of the walls themselves. What is important and what is celebrated by the restored community is the gift of God's presence and protection represented by the restored Temple and wall.[6]

The major virtue of this first approach is its attempt to explain the text that we have; its primary flaw is that its explanation depends on the historical accuracy of the text. As a result it constitutes an explanation not so much of the text as of the historical events which it assumes are reliably narrated by the text. But with regard to the relationship of Ezra and Nehemiah, it is doubtful that the present text is historically accurate.

This brings us to the second basic way of reading the text. If the historical-critical investigation of the Bible has taught us anything it is that biblical texts have complex editorial histories in which one finds reflected all the evidence of any human endeavor. We are thus accustomed to a great deal of diversity within the unity of, for example, the Pentateuch. With regard to Neh. 8.9, a majority of scholars concur with Rudolph that since the verb is singular, the reference to Nehemiah and the Levites is secondary, an interpolation made by the same hand that destroyed the symmetry of the procession around the walls in Nehemiah 12 by including Ezra.[7] For these scholars it appears that the Ezra and Nehemiah traditions developed independently of each other

---

6. McConville, *Ezra*, p. 141.
7. W. Rudolph, *Esra und Nehemia* (Tübingen: Mohr, 1949), p. 148. Cf. R.A. Bowman, 'Ezra and Nehemiah', *IB*, III, pp. 796-97.

until a very late stage in the formation of our book. Believing that independence to reflect the historical reality, these authors attempt to restore or reconstruct the present text so that it will more accurately reflect the actual events. In reference to Neh. 8.9 we find statements such as 'this section deals with Ezra; Nehemiah has no part in it',[8] or, 'As Ezra and Nehemiah were not contemporaries...the name of Nehemiah must be an addition'.[9] The assumption here is not only that the book of Ezra–Nehemiah was written and preserved as history in a fairly modern sense, but that in its original form it was completely accurate as well. We find this logic again in Bowman's treatment of Neh. 12.36, which includes Ezra in the dedication of the walls in the time of Nehemiah. He writes, 'Ezra...intrudes into the narrative, since he and Nehemiah were not contemporary'.[10] Assuming that the author's intentions are historical, can we expect the work to conform to the standards of modern historiography? Could the author have erred? The question is more acute if we reckon with the likelihood that Ezra–Nehemiah, for all its apparent interest in historical narrative, actually was produced and preserved in the service of a theological rather than a merely historical agenda. If, indeed, our text has been shaped by theological concerns, are we justified in dismissing it in favor of a reconstructed text which we suppose to be historically more accurate?

Given historical criticism's emphasis on the so-called original text, it is not surprising that the majority of scholars, in fact, do just that. Having argued or asserted that the two leaders were not contemporaries, they emend or rearrange the text accordingly, and then provide commentary on their restored text, a text which is hypothetical at best, and which, of course, never enjoyed canonical status in either the Jewish or Christian community. In the meantime the overall shape and structure of the canonical text is ignored, the question of its theological meaning not even raised because it is historically incorrect. The book of Ezra–Nehemiah, however, is not a piece of modern historiography, neither does it appear to function in the canon, nor to have been preserved, simply to provide historical information. It is one

---

8. R.J. Coggins, *The Books of Ezra and Nehemiah* (Cambridge: Cambridge University Press, 1976), p. 107.
9. Bowman, 'Ezra', p. 738.
10. Bowman, 'Ezra', pp. 796-97.

thing, a legitimate thing, to use Ezra–Nehemiah as a source for the history of the restoration, and thus on literary and historical grounds to suggest how a reorganized text or the text at some earlier stage of its development could be historically more accurate. That enterprise, however, should not be confused with exegesis which seeks to understand the canonical text itself and which is, therefore, reluctant to emend the text.

The third, less common, approach to our issues is distinguished by its attempt to take seriously both the apparent fact that a prior stage of the tradition was more historically accurate and the fact that our present text makes the two men contemporary. The representatives of this position agree with the scholars cited above that Ezra and Nehemiah were not contemporaries, and that the indications otherwise are both secondary and inaccurate. Unlike the representatives of the second position, however, they do not limit their attention to a hypothetical, reconstructed text.

Clines, for example, explains Neh. 8.9 as follows.[11] Ezra came to Jerusalem in 458, and the law-reading ceremony took place shortly thereafter in the same year. Nehemiah was not yet in Beyond the River, and so of course did not play the role assigned to him by Neh. 8.9. The Chronicler has reorganized his sources (Neh. 8, a part of the Ezra story, was originally much closer to Ezra 7) and included Nehemiah in the ceremony perhaps to make the point that Nehemiah repopulated Jerusalem with a community that was faithful to the Torah. That is, the sequence the Chronicler created (ch. 7, a list of those entitled by genealogy to live in Jerusalem; ch. 8, the reading of the law; chs. 9–10, repentance and re-dedication; and ch. 11 the repopulation of the city) is not historically accurate, but is theologically meaningful.[12] Clines is less certain about the historicity of Ezra's involvement in the dedication of the wall (Neh. 12.36). He doubts Ezra was there, but allows that he might have been. Putting him there, or (less likely) his actual presence there, makes the point that the foundation of the postexilic community was the joint work of Ezra and Nehemiah.[13] Unfortunately, Clines does not discuss the theological significance of making this point.

11. D.J.A. Clines, *Ezra, Nehemiah, Esther* (Grand Rapids: Eerdmans, 1984).
12. Clines, *Ezra*, p. 181.
13. Clines, *Ezra*, p. 232.

A theologically more sophisticated example of this third category is the canonical approach Childs takes in his *Introduction to the Old Testament as Scripture*.[14] While Childs does not explicitly embrace the consensus that Ezra and Nehemiah acted independently, he does acknowledge that it is very widely held and likely to be correct. This relative lack of interest in historical detail is consistent with one of the guiding convictions of his enterprise. As he put it in his Preface, 'To determine the degree of a narrative's historicity, whether slightly more or less...makes little difference in one's total understanding of the literature'.[15]

In his treatment of the book of Ezra–Nehemiah, Childs discusses numerous historical-critical issues which have led to a variety of proposed solutions. These proposals are all, in his view, inadequate, as the closing statement of his section on 'Historical Critical Problems' makes clear:

> To summarize, the great majority of scholars. . . approach the interpretation of Ezra–Nehemiah with the assumption that its proper interpretation depends on establishing an accurate historical sequence of events to which these writings must obviously be correlated. Because of the difficulty of accomplishing this task and the radical reconstructions of the literature involved, the interpretation remains unusually tentative and vulnerable to excessive speculation. In addition, an implicit judgment is rendered on the canonical text that it is fragmentary, tendentious, and in much need of improvement.[16]

This judgment is all the more regrettable since the canonical text is in fact not fragmentary. Rather, Childs argues, 'The present structure of the books of Ezra–Nehemiah shows a clear mark of intentionality which an author or editor established by means of a chronological sequence. . .'[17]

Of special historical and theological importance, given this purposeful chronology, is the question of the chronological relationship of Ezra and Nehemiah. Childs notes that this problem has provoked 'the

14. B.S. Childs, *Introduction to the Old Testament as Scripture* (Philadelphia: Fortress Press, 1979).

15. Childs, *Introduction*, p. 16.

16. Childs, *Introduction*, p. 630.

17. Childs, *Introduction*, p. 631. Childs notes that Neh. 8 could be relocated following Ezra 8 without disturbing this chronology, but argues against such a move (*Introduction*, p. 632).

major historical reconstructions from critical scholarship', but maintains that, 'it is also the area in which the special shaping of the tradition by the biblical authors can be most clearly discerned'.[18] It is his view, then, that the standard approach (the second approach described above), with its emphasis on historical and literary issues at the expense of attention to the present text, will likely fail to appreciate the theology of the canonical book. A book which, Childs argues, was clearly not intended to be a historical account of the Persian period 'according to the canons of modern historical writing. . .but [which] has been shaped and transmitted toward another end'.[19] And that end is theological.

An essential feature of this theological shaping of the tradition is that Ezra's initial reforms (Ezra 7–9) and Nehemiah's repairs on the wall (Neh. 1–6) are preliminary to—and find their meaning only in light of—their joint work of restoration which follows in Nehemiah 8–12. Thus when Ezra, in Ezra 9, wants to bring the people to repentance for their exogamy he reminds them of the Mosaic prohibition of intermarriage. But Ezra's paraphrased reference to the Torah on mixed marriages in his public prayer is unlike the later event recorded in Nehemiah 8. The great, open-air, public reading of the law, as we find it in the canonical book, is not an attempt by Ezra to impose a new law code brought from Babylon, nor should it be relocated, literarily or historically, in order to bring it into closer proximity to the account of Ezra's commission and early reforms. According to the book's theological interpretation of the restoration, 'Ezra does not read the law in order to reform Israel into becoming the people of God'.[20] Rather, it is the reformed people of God who, to quote the biblical text, 'told Ezra the scribe to bring the book of the law of Moses which the Lord has given to Israel' (Neh. 8.1). Ezra's subsequent reading of the law is not intended to convict or reform, as is clear from the fact that when the people do weep, they are admonished by the Levites to rejoice. 'The observation to be made', according to Childs, 'is that the reading of the law in Neh. 8 is a part of the liturgical celebration by the people of God'.[21] The theological point,

18. Childs, *Introduction*, p. 635.
19. Childs, *Introduction*, p. 635.
20. Childs, *Introduction*, p. 636.
21. Childs, *Introduction*, p. 636. This view has been given additional support by

in his view, of this narrative chronology is that it was only after the wall had been rebuilt and the city repopulated by the re-formed people of God 'that the conditions for the full restoration of the community were met'.[22] What follows in the rest of Nehemiah is a description of the formation of the community in terms of the author's theocratic ideal. As in the case of the earlier period of Zerubbabel and Jeshua, this required the combined efforts of the sacred and secular leadership represented here by Ezra and Nehemiah. Thus the account of the dedication of the wall concludes with two 'on that day' passages, which, whatever their provenance, provide the book's concluding statement about the restoration begun under Cyrus and now, finally, in the reign of Artaxerxes, completed by Ezra and Nehemiah. The Temple is rebuilt, the people are reformed, the wall rededicated, and '"On that day" (12.44; 13.1) both the service of worship and the purity of the people were established'.[23]

In my opinion, Childs's work represents a major advance over the mainstream exegetical tradition represented by the second approach to the text described above. By refusing to edit the canonical text, Childs has restored the Bible as the object of biblical exegesis. At the same time, by acknowledging the multiple historical-critical problems presented by the text in its canonical shape, Childs has distanced himself from the representatives of the more conservative approach who, I have argued, interpret a dubious history rather than the biblical text. On the other hand, Childs's interest in the final, canonical shape of the tradition leaves him little room for a treatment of the theological motives or significance of Ezra–Nehemiah's editorial history.

Blenkinsopp, who in his *Ezra–Nehemiah* treats both the editorial history and the final form of the text, raises a more substantive challenge to Childs's approach. Blenkinsopp notes, very much as Childs does, that 'The serious disturbances of an original order... also draw attention, more acutely than in most other biblical books, to the theological significance of the final form in which the material has come

R. Rendtorff, who has argued that the דת of Ezra 7 is not the תורה of Neh. 8, which refers to a liturgical event and not to the promulgation of the Torah ('Esra und das "Gesetz"', *ZAW* 96 [1984], pp. 165-84).

22. Childs, *Introduction*, pp. 636-37.

23. Childs, *Introduction*, p. 637.

down to us'.[24] Blenkinsopp, refuses, however, to wash his hands of the historical-critical task because, as he points out:

> One of the problems of 'canonical criticism'. . . is a tendency to circumvent the tension between confessional and critically reconstructed history. This tension seems to be inescapable, and it is difficult to see how theology can maintain its integrity, or avoid degenerating into ideology in the pejorative sense, if it is avoided. Hence the necessity of juxtaposing a critical reconstruction of a text like Ezra–Nehemiah with the form imposed on it by its successive authors or editors.[25]

With regard to the contemporaneity of Ezra and Nehemiah, Blenkinsopp's analysis yields the following conclusions. The two were not contemporaries, Ezra having arrived in Jerusalem in 458 and Nehemiah in 445.[26] The texts which indicate otherwise may be explained as follows. Nehemiah 8 is clearly about Ezra; the reference to Nehemiah in v. 9 is a late addition as the singular verb indicates.[27] Likewise, the inclusion of Ezra in Neh. 12.36 comes from 'the time when the activity of the two men had been amalgamated into one movement of reform'.[28] Neh. 12.26, which associates Ezra and Nehemiah during the period of Joiakim, is the product of a compiler for whom the synchronicity of the two men had long been accepted.[29]

In Blenkinsopp's view, the association of the two men was motivated by the desire to give the priest Ezra, whose mission was only partially successful, co-equal status with the more effective governor.[30] The result is a canonical text in which the two men, with the support of the Persian kings and despite the opposition of their neighbors, 'bring to a successful conclusion the task of unifying and purifying the community' by teaching the law, rebuilding the wall and restoring the city.[31] 'The religious and civic foundations of the Jewish commonwealth', Blenkinsopp concludes, 'are thus securely laid'.[32]

Very clearly, then, as both Childs and Blenkinsopp have shown, the

---

24. Blenkinsopp, *Ezra–Nehemiah*, p. 39.
25. Blenkinsopp, *Ezra–Nehemiah*, p. 42.
26. Blenkinsopp, *Ezra–Nehemiah*, pp. 65, 205.
27. Blenkinsopp, *Ezra–Nehemiah*, p. 284.
28. Blenkinsopp, *Ezra–Nehemiah*, p. 346.
29. Blenkinsopp, *Ezra–Nehemiah*, p. 341.
30. Blenkinsopp, *Ezra–Nehemiah*, p. 54.
31. Blenkinsopp, *Ezra–Nehemiah*, p. 41.
32. Blenkinsopp, *Ezra–Nehemiah*, p. 41.

author or editor of Ezra–Nehemiah has imposed his own chronology on his sources. In addition, however, to creating a structure which, as we have seen, climaxes, both sequentially and theologically, in the shared accomplishments of Ezra and Nehemiah, Childs argues that the author has also emphasized three themes 'to explicate his theological intent'.[33] These are: God's use of foreign rulers for Israel's sake, the contrasting theme of bitter opposition from the people of the land, and especially, the separation of Israel from foreigners of the land in order to reflect the purity of the people of God.[34]

One way that the book stresses these three themes is to divide the history of the restoration from Cyrus to Nehemiah into two periods (that of Zerubbabel and Jeshua, and that of Ezra and Nehemiah) and then to detail how both sets of leaders were armed with Persian mandates and support, faced intense local opposition, and insisted that the members of the *golah* group separate themselves from the people of the land.

In the case of the period of Zerubbabel and Jeshua, Japhet has persuasively argued an even stronger case.[35] In her view, it is not just that the Persians supported the return. The author of Ezra 1–6 celebrates their help, gives the credit to God, and goes to extraordinary lengths to suppress the Davidic origins of the governor Zerubbabel. She writes,

> In the framework of this sort of political thought there is no room for change, and even less room for hopes of redemption. The House of David, as the vehicle of aspirations to national unity and as the symbol 'par excellence' of salvific hopes, has no place in this world view and therefore is conspicuously absent from the book.[36]

While it is clear that Zerubbabel played an important part, the author stresses instead the role of the people as a whole. Japhet concludes from this that the author of Ezra 1–6 both reflects and endorses a process of 'democratization'.[37] But this is in stark contrast, she notes, to what we find in Nehemiah's memoirs and the story of Ezra, the two other important components of the book. There,

33. Childs, *Introduction*, p. 633.
34. Childs, *Introduction*, p. 633.
35. S. Japhet, 'Sheshbazzar and Zerubbabel', *ZAW* 94 (1982), pp. 66-98.
36. Japhet, 'Sheshbazzar', pp. 75-76.
37. Japhet, 'Sheshbazzar', p. 87.

the personalities of the leaders are placed in [the] center. Even the struggle between the people of Judah and their adversaries becomes in the story of Nehemiah a struggle between Nehemiah himself and his enemies—Sanballat. . . Tobiah. . . and Geshem.[38]

In my view, Japhet has provided a valuable analysis of Ezra 1–6. Her treatment of the remainder of Ezra–Nehemiah, however, is unconvincing for two reasons. In the first place, while in very much of the Ezra tradition and the Nehemiah memoir the leader rather than the people occupies center stage, this is clearly not the case in the account of the law-reading liturgy of Nehemiah 8, one of the most important events included in the Ezra tradition. It seems to me that by gathering together and telling Ezra to bring the law book, the people in Nehemiah 8 play just the sort of role Japhet finds only in Ezra 1–6. But while, then, for the most part it is true that Ezra 1–6 is distinct from the Ezra story and the Nehemiah memoir in terms of the roles assigned to the people and their leadership, we must go on to observe that this distinction, which is based on a comparison of the final form of Ezra 1–6 with a preliminary or hypothetical form of the rest of the book, has been virtually eliminated in the book's canonical form as a consequence of making Ezra and Nehemiah contemporaries.

Had the canonical account of the period(s) of Ezra and Nehemiah attained its final form without undergoing the editorial shaping which linked their memoirs and made them contemporaries, we would indeed have an account in which the role of the laity would contrast sharply with that narrated for the early period of the restoration. In addition, Ezra the priest and authoritative interpreter of the Torah of Moses might well appear to have been outclassed by his secular counterpart, the governor Nehemiah, and the restoration of the sacred and the secular spheres would appear to have been sequential, perhaps with the latter appearing to be the more important.

In the present form of the narrative, however, the activities of Ezra and Nehemiah parallel the earlier work of Jeshua and Zerubbabel, and in so doing they balance the book structurally, and give full expression to the author's conception of the ideal community of God as a union of the sacred and secular life of the people in a democratic theocracy established by God through the agency of the Persian kings.

---

38. Japhet, 'Sheshbazzar', p. 86.

COOPTING THE PROPHETS: NEHEMIAH AND NOADIAH

Robert P. Carroll

> The potential data of history are limitless, and by selecting for attention only those bits and pieces that fit in with one's notions, a convincing 'empirical' validation of the preconception with which one started out may often, if not always, be achieved.[1]

> It is not a passive surrender to the spell of another's mind; it is a labour of active and therefore critical thinking. The historian not only re-enacts past thought, he re-enacts it in the context of his own knowledge and therefore, in re-enacting it criticizes it, forms his own judgement of its value, corrects whatever errors he can discern in it. This criticism of the thought whose history he traces is not something secondary to tracing the history of it. It is an indispensable condition of the historical knowledge itself. Nothing could be a completer error concerning the history of thought than to suppose that the historian as such merely ascertains 'what so-and-so thought', leaving it to someone else to decide 'whether it was true'. *All thinking is critical thinking*; the thought which re-enacts past thoughts, therefore, criticizes them in re-enacting them.[2]

Joe Blenkinsopp belongs to the great and the good of the Guild of Biblical Studies (Hebrew Bible section) and therefore poses some real problems for the would-be Festschrift article writer. How can the aspiring writer hope to match the range and depth of his erudition or illuminate in a short space any of the many topics covered by his work? In this celebration of his many talents I shall confine my attention to just two areas of biblical studies graced by significant works of his: prophecy and the Ezra–Nehemiah literature.[3] In

---

1. W. McNeill, *Mythistory and Other Essays* (Chicago: University of Chicago Press, 1986), p. 138. The subject of McNeill's discussion at this point is that of Arnold J. Toynbee's work.

2. R.G. Collingwood, *The Idea of History* (London: Oxford University Press, 1961), pp. 215-16; emphasis added.

3. J. Blenkinsopp, *A History of Prophecy in Israel: From the Settlement in the*

combining these two quite different topics I wish to work a small corner of Second Temple studies which is an area of mutual interest for both of us.[4]

Prophets are alluded to a number of times in the Ezra–Nehemiah literature. Most notably in Ezra 5.1-2, 6.14 and in Neh. 6.7, 10-14 various prophets are referred to, especially by name. These references will constitute the heart of my paper. Other allusions to prophets in Ezra–Nehemiah may be noted, but only in the passing. The great stereotypical prayers of Ezra set out in Ezra 9 and Nehemiah 9 refer to 'the prophets' (Ezra 9.11; Neh. 9.26, 30, 32), but in very uninformative ways. The essential point of these allusions is a Deuteronomistic one: the past is the time of prophets preaching against the sins of the people and being killed for their pains. It is a far cry from the more usual denunciation of prophets to be found in the so-called 'prophetic' texts which blame the prophets for the corruption of the people (e.g. Isa. 9.15; 28.7; 29.10; Jer. 23.9-32; Ezek. 13; Lam. 2.14). Yet the deeply ambivalent attitude of the Bible to prophets can also be found in Ezra–Nehemiah, so I shall concentrate on those references which contribute to an exploration of this attitude.

The positive assessment of prophets is to be found in Ezra 5.1-2 and 6.14 where the prophets Haggai and Zechariah are represented as supporting the rebuilding of the Temple in Jerusalem. As the Temple rebuilding project is described as an enterprise having the official backing of the God of Israel *and* three notable Persian emperors (Cyrus, Darius, Artaxerxes), Haggai and Zechariah must be seen as positive prophets and ideologically sound. They stand for what the writer(s) of Ezra–Nehemiah stood for and the shared ideology of text and task indicates the truth of the claim that they were 'the prophets of

Land to the Hellenistic Period (Philadelphia: Westminster Press, 1983); *Ezra–Nehemiah: A Commentary* (OTL; London: SCM Press, 1988).

4. Blenkinsopp's contributions to Second Temple studies are too numerous to list here, but see by way of example his 'Interpretation and the Tendency to Sectarianism: An Aspect of Second Temple History', in E.P. Sanders, A.I. Baumgarten and A. Mendelson (eds.), *In Jewish and Christian Self-Definition*. II. *Aspects of Judaism in the Graeco-Roman Period* (London: SCM Press, 1981), pp. 1-26; 'The Mission of Udjahorresnet and those of Ezra and Nehemiah', *JBL* 106 (1987), pp. 409-21; 'A Jewish Sect of the Persian Period', *CBQ* 52 (1990), pp. 5-20; 'Temple and Society in Achaemenid Judah', in P.R. Davies (ed.), *Second Temple Studies*. I. *Persian Period* (JSOTSup, 117; Sheffield: JSOT Press, 1991), pp. 22-53.

God' (Ezra 5.2). The presence in the canon of the Hebrew Bible of the books of Haggai and Zechariah is further evidence of these prophets' political (i.e. ideological) correctness. In the canonic literature of the Second Temple cult community (what Joel Weinberg calls *Bürger-Tempel-Gemeinde*) only the ideologically sound material can hope to appear. To have opposed the Temple would be to have silenced oneself. Prophets who support the right causes will become canonical prophets, all others will be spoken against and marginalized. In this paper Noadiah the prophetess will stand for negative prophets. That is, she will be the representative of prophetic groups who failed to side with Temple or city building or who opposed Ezra or Nehemiah.

The negative assessment of prophets will be found in Neh. 6.1-14. Different aspects of prophets and prophesying are contained in this complex piece of narrative. In the first instance Sanballat writes an open letter to Nehemiah accusing him of having established prophets in Jerusalem to proclaim himself as king. Whether this is an allusion to the activities of Haggai and Zechariah or an interpretation of what they were doing is beyond the wit of any reader to discover. Nehemiah is such an unreliable narrator, with a Maileresque ego to boot, that modern readers must despair of believing anything they may read in the 'I' sections of the Ezra–Nehemiah literature.[5] In the second instance Shemaiah ben Delaiah is represented as speaking a prophecy (the rarely used word $n^e b\hat{u}'\hat{a}$ appears here) against Nehemiah. Nehemiah claims to have been able to recognize that this prophecy was not from God because Shemaiah had been hired by Sanballat and Tobiah. There are some real linguistic and interpretative difficulties in this section (Neh. 6.10-14), but the enquiring reader may consult all the best commentaries for the textual and exegetical technicalities. The third instance appears as a throwaway phrase in a generalization: '*and also Noadiah the prophetess* and the rest of the prophets who were making me afraid' (6.14). This is the first time in the narrative that we have heard of any prophets—in v. 7 the reference to prophets was in a charge made about Nehemiah's activities—so we do not know who or what they may have been. Had Tobiah and Sanballat hired prophets to frighten Nehemiah? Were there other

5. On this very important point, see the illuminating study by D.J.A. Clines, 'The Nehemiah Memoir: The Perils of Autobiography', in his collection *What Does Eve Do to Help? and Other Readerly Questions to the Old Testament* (JSOTSup, 94; Sheffield: JSOT Press, 1990), pp. 124-64.

prophets in Jerusalem who disapproved of Temple building or of urban renewal in the old city? Were there warring factions of prophets roaming the streets of Jerusalem, some siding with Nehemiah and others opposing him? Was Jerusalem ever free of opposing factions of prophets? Who can tell? I shall not rehearse all the different opinions expressed in the numerous commentaries on Ezra–Nehemiah on this point because the truth of the matter is that we do not know. The text tells us absolutely nothing about these prophets except for the 'fact' that Nehemiah says that Noadiah and these prophets were scaring him.

These then are the prophets formally opposed to the prophets Haggai and Zechariah in the Ezra–Nehemiah literature. Whether they ever existed historically or had any real existence outside the imagination of the textual Nehemiah cannot be ascertained. They exist in the text and must therefore be considered as having a real textual existence by the reader. They formally balance the role of Haggai and Zechariah and may be grouped with the prophets in the prayers of Ezra as figures rejected by Nehemiah and/or the community. The only prophets supported actively in Ezra–Nehemiah are Haggai and Zechariah, all other prophets are rejected. While the prophets in Ezra's prayers will not concern me in this paper, I wish to focus attention on the polarities represented by Haggai and Zechariah on the one hand and Noadiah and the other prophets on the other hand. In terms of the dynamics of the Ezra–Nehemiah literature these different sets of prophets may be characterized as pro-building and anti-building figures in the text. What seems to differentiate them is whether the writer of the text regards them as supporting the ideological projects defended in the text or as opposing such projects. In other words, there is a cooption of prophets and a refusal of prophets.

The model of prophecy often developed by readers of the Bible, including especially biblical scholars and theologians, is that of speakers of the divine word who must be listened to and obeyed. It is very much a Deuteronomistic one (cf. Deut. 18.15) which is succinctly expressed by the Chronicler's command 'Believe in YHWH your God, and you will be established; *believe his prophets*, and you will succeed' (2 Chron. 20.20). Yet everything in the so-called 'prophetic' books speaks out against this facile univocal definition of prophets. The books of Isaiah, Jeremiah, Ezekiel and Micah in particular speak out very strongly *against* the prophets.[6] There is certainly no sense in these writings of prophets as speakers of the divine word *tout court*. On the contrary, they are liars and deceivers, charlatans and con artists. The Chronicler may advocate believing the prophets and may explain the destruction of city and nation as the result of persistent scoffing at the prophets (2 Chron. 36.15-16), but the other traditions contained in the Hebrew Bible would take a quite contrary view of prophets. Ezra–Nehemiah reflects elements of both attitudes. That is, there is the rather conventional expression of the rejection of the prophets in the prayers of Ezra as well as Nehemiah's dismissal of prophecy and prophets in Neh. 6.10-14. In the treatment of Haggai and Zechariah in Ezra 5.1-2, 6.14 there is an acceptance of prophets. So both attitudes towards prophets can be found in the same collection of texts.

In order to clarify the distinctions between prophets in the Hebrew Bible it is necessary to probe matters a little further. It will do no good to tag prophets 'true' or 'false'. That is a mindless activity in which prevailing ideological positions are simply adopted without thought. Prophets are only 'true' or 'false' from some perspective or other. The conditions under which they become one or the other need to be specified. Shared concepts and agreed ideologies play a large part in determining these conditions. Thus in Ezra–Nehemiah, Haggai and Zechariah are good and acceptable prophets because they support the project of Temple building which reflects the ideological values of the producers of Ezra–Nehemiah. Shemaiah and Noadiah are condemned because they are associated with the people who oppose Nehemiah's building enterprise. We can only speculate about why they should be so opposed to the rebuilding of the wall of Jerusalem, but if reasons were required many could be supplied.[7] The lack of shared goals and values determines the differentiation of prophets. Prophets are coopted according to whether they support or oppose a particular position. In the Hebrew Bible the literature of the Second Temple

---

6. On the Ezekiel material, see J. Blenkinsopp, *Ezekiel* (Interpretation; Louisville, KY: John Knox, 1990), pp. 64-72. On the Jeremiah material, see R.P. Carroll, *Jeremiah: A Commentary* (OTL; London: SCM Press, 1986), pp. 449-80.

7. Cf. Blenkinsopp, *History*, pp. 244-46 for a brief discussion of messianic disturbances in the Ezra–Nehemiah period. The many reasons supplied by commentators belong to the *Rezeptionsgeschichte* aspect of biblical studies and are also highly speculative.

period inevitably reflects a pro-Temple bias because, by its very nature, that Bible is a product of Temple ideology. But there is a considerable extra-biblical literature which does not reflect Temple values.[8] Shemaiah and Noadiah may not necessarily be implicated in this alternative set of values, but the denunciation of them by Nehemiah should not be taken as a value-free and innocent rejection of an unsustainable viewpoint.

Coopting the prophets is an inevitable concomitant of prophecy. Taken by itself prophetic utterance can only be believed or rejected. As Winston Churchill once put it, 'It is no use arguing with a prophet; you can only disbelieve him'. Oracular utterances may have persuasive effects, but if the rhetoric or persuasion fails then such utterances will be disbelieved. Where there are many prophets (as there invariably are) prior beliefs and commitments can help to differentiate between prophets. Those who believe in Temple building are going to find ready support in prophets who preach Temple building. Prophets who oppose Temple building (e.g. Isa. 66.1-2?) are unlikely to be coopted by parties in favour of building projects. Whether they are condemned or ignored is a matter of choice. If they cannot be coopted then they serve no useful purpose and may be ignored. The material in Nehemiah 6 on prophets is more complicated because we know nothing about these prophets. The exchange between Shemaiah and Nehemiah (always given in Nehemiah's words) is obscure in the extreme. The most we can say about Shemaiah and Noadiah is that *according to Nehemiah* they were hostile to Nehemiah. That is insufficient information for any historian to work with, although most commentaries appear to be happy to supply further information.

If we move from history to literature, from cool analysis to imaginative evocation, then it is possible to make texts to speak further. We may provoke texts into speech. The silence—some readers may prefer the word 'silencing'—of Noadiah interests me. I see a deconstructive moment here in the text. In what I think of as 'opposing Noadiah'— Noadiah opposes Nehemiah who opposes her opposition, although only Nehemiah's opposition is stated in the text—I catch a momentary glimpse of a situation to which there is more than meets the eye in the text. The egocentric Nehemiah betrays a momentary obsession in his

8.   Qumran and NT literature belong to this category; for a brief treatment of it, see M.A. Knibb, 'The Exile in the Literature of the Intertestamental Period', *HeyJ* 17 (1976), pp. 253-72.

generalized complaint against Tobiah and Sanballat and the prophets. He names a prophet unnecessarily. That is, the figures of Tobiah, Sanballat and the 'rest of the prophets' make his point quite adequately. Entirely adequately you might say. So why mention Noadiah who is otherwise unknown in the text? There is a Noadiah in Ezra 8.33, but there the prophet is male (a son of Binnui; Ezra–Nehemiah seems to favour the Bani–Binnui–Bunni range of names). If we go outside the text we may invent any number of reasons as to why Nehemiah should have singled out Noadiah. If we stick to the letter of the text then it becomes much more difficult to account for the naming of this particular prophet.

Commentators tend to recognize the fact that Noadiah is named or 'comes in for special mention for reasons unknown'.[9] Sometimes they link her with Shemaiah and include her in a blanket condemnation of prophesying for money: for example, 'This group, to whom money was the inspiration for prophecy, included a prophetess, Noadiah'.[10] There may be something to be said for this kind of reasoning, although in my opinion it tends to go beyond the text which simply includes Noadiah among those who were making Nehemiah afraid. Of course there may be less to this matter than meets the eye, but no reader of the Bible ever got anywhere by conceding the principle that the text says less than we imagine. The whole history of the reception of the Bible (biblical *Rezeptionsgeschichte*) is built on the principles of the indeterminacy of meaning in the text and the polysemy of texts. I would therefore like to explore the notion of 'opposing Noadiah' a little further along the lines of my approach to Ezra–Nehemiah in terms of coopting the prophets.

Noadiah is a woman. That in itself speaks volumes. That she is a woman who appears in the Ezra–Nehemiah material speaks further volumes. This is because there are elements of hostility towards women in Ezra–Nehemiah (e.g. Ezra 10.1-44; Neh. 10.28-31). It is

9. Blenkinsopp, *Ezra–Nehemiah*, p. 271.

10. F.C. Holmgren, *Israel Alive Again: A Commentary on the Books of Ezra and Nehemiah* (International Theological Commentary; Grand Rapids: Eerdmans; Edinburgh: The Handsel Press, 1987), p. 118. Mic. 3.11 notwithstanding, I fail to appreciate why so many modern biblical scholars imagine that prophesying or preaching for money invalidates any proclamation. The average Presbyterian minister would be greatly impoverished if their salaries were withheld for fear of impugning their sermons!

not so much a generalized disparagement of women as a denigration of foreign women. Where women in general (always 'in general') are prepared to listen to and follow the ideological instructions associated with Ezra–Nehemiah there is no problem with women (e.g. Ezra 8.3; Neh. 12.43). But where foreignness or opposition is concerned, then the Ezra–Nehemiah literature is opposed to women. In this sense Noadiah must be numbered among the women to be opposed for ideological reasons. She is an ideological enemy. Her existence and her activities (if we knew what they were) are in opposition to Nehemiah.

Opposition to women is not quite a topos in the Hebrew Bible. The opposing of foreign women is a topos, as may be seen in the ideological critique of Jezebel in the Deuteronomistic History and the opposition to foreign wives in Ezra–Nehemiah. Oracular utterances against women (in general perhaps) are to be found at certain points in 'prophetic' literature (e.g. Isa. 3.16–4.11; 32.9-13), but there are insufficient examples of this kind of oracle to presuppose a definite topos of attacking women as such. Women who oppose men where questions of authority are concerned are invariably denounced. Miriam's opposition to Moses is a prime example of this sub-genre (Num. 12). Perhaps Noadiah's opposition to Nehemiah is of this kind. As a prophet, Noadiah would not necessarily be a target for opposition. Prophetesses such as Deborah and Huldah are not criticized in the Bible. Miriam the prophetess is only attacked because she opposed Moses.

Presumably it is because of the clash of authorities that Miriam's opposition to Moses is condemned in the Hebrew Bible. Prophetesses whose work supports the central authorities (e.g. Deborah, Huldah) are never condemned. That being the case, Noadiah's opposition fits the pattern of women prophets who opposed the (male) leadership. In a clash of prophets or of leaders only one figure can be represented as legitimate in the Bible. If Nehemiah is telling the story then Noadiah's opposition to Nehemiah speaks against Noadiah. That is Nehemiah's story and we are reading it. But what if Noadiah had told her story? What if we were not reading the Bible but an alternative bible?

Such questions belong to the utopian world of imaginative literature. They move from the realm of the historical to the poetical and defeat the historian's probe. Of course they may be asked quite legitimately in the world of biblical studies because the Bible belongs to the genre of imaginative literature rather than to history. A bible written by the dissenting voices whose echoes may be heard dimly in the Bible would be a very different book. In such a bible Miriam and Noadiah would have much larger places than they now occupy. Many other dissenting voices, including very many prophetic voices, would also be heard. The mythic structures of such a bible would be very different and our world would itself be quite different. However, it is not necessary to construct such an alternative bible. Interpretation, exegesis and the reading of the text are in the hands of any and all readers of the Bible, so any reading of a text can give voice to the silent ones in the text.

While it is tempting to offer a lengthy speech which would serve as Noadiah's imagined utterance against Nehemiah, it is unnecessary to do so. In drawing the reader's attention to Noadiah's existence and opposition, Nehemiah has undone himself. His overweening egocentricity deconstructs himself. We now know about Noadiah. And we know sufficient about her to be able to imagine her opposition to Nehemiah. Her opposition writes itself. To unpack that densely packed short sentence would be a paper in itself. But to expand on it briefly the following observations may be made. Two facts are given to us by Nehemiah. Opposing Noadiah belongs to the prophets who, according to Nehemiah, are causing fear to Nehemiah. The context of these comments is that of opposition to Nehemiah's building project. So we may deduce from this information the likely facts that Noadiah opposed Nehemiah and did so for reasons not entirely unconnected with the building of the wall of Jerusalem. As Persian governor of the province and as builder of Jerusalem Nehemiah represented the imperial power in the land. Opposition to him must therefore have come from local people who had reason to fear the Persian authorities. Many reasons could be suggested for such fears, including an account of differing ideologies in the Second Temple period. The breaking up of marriages with foreign women (that is local women rather than ideologically correct women perhaps imported from Babylonia, cf. Gen. 24) may have caused serious opposition from the women. Again we can only speculate because the text renders all those women silent—they are not quite invisible because the text refers to them.

Given the behaviour of Ezra and Nehemiah in the biblical text, it would hardly be surprising if a considerable number of women in their Jerusalem were not in open opposition to either leader. Running

through the Hebrew Bible is a very broad strand of female opposition
to powerful males. Indeed, it is difficult to find many stories in the
Bible involving men and women where the women are not severe
critics and opponents of the men. Where biblical narrative is concerned the female is a force defying male control. She may be controlled but often only through force (e.g. the rape of Tamar) or
through religious pressures (e.g. Jephthah's daughter). In Ezra–
Nehemiah the forcible divorce of foreign wives may not have been an
attempt to control the women but a stratagem to limit the membership
of the Temple cult. The theology of Temple membership may have
required a major alienation of women and children or, of course, the
narratives heavily influenced by Deuteronomistic ideology may
represent Ezra and Nehemiah as ideologically correct founders of the
Temple–city cult. In such a situation it is likely that there would have
been opposition to such a controlled and narrowly defined cultic
community. Whether the prophetess Noadiah should be associated
with movements of opposition to such a foreign-controlled (i.e.
Persian) formation of the Jerusalem community must remain open to
question. Whatever she represents, Nehemiah could not coopt her as a
prophet supporting him. Her opposition was such as to warrant him
naming her in one of his many prayers seeking vengeance from the
deity. Opposing Noadiah is all we know about her. To the modern
reader of Ezra–Nehemiah the opposition of Noadiah to Nehemiah is
decidedly a mark in her favour.

Women complicate biblical texts and therefore make them much
more interesting as sites of hermeneutical struggle.[11] In biblical literature associated with the Second Temple period there is a fascinating
development whereby the feminization of language and focus shapes
texts in distinctive ways. Many examples of this phenomenon may be
seen in Isaiah 40–66 and in the book of Jeremiah (especially in
chs. 30–31).[12] This is not the place to explore such textual developments, but I would want to include Noadiah in any such exploration. I
tend to see her (in my mind's eye, that is my imagination) as a strong

11. I touch on this in my 'Textual Strategies and Ideology in the Second Temple
Period', in Davies (ed.), *Second Temple Studies* (see n. 4), pp. 108-24, esp.
pp. 120-24.

12. On the Jeremiah material, see B.A. Bozak, *Life 'Anew': A Literary-
Theological Study of Jer. 30-31* (AnBib, 122; Rome: Pontificio Istituto Biblico,
1991), esp. pp. 155-74.

personality regularly opposing Nehemiah with powerful and denigra-
tory words. As he built that wall and as he laboured to dominate the
whole enterprise week after week, there was always *that woman*
Noadiah within earshot denouncing his imperial ways. Nehemiah's
memoirs give ample evidence of his vanity and his self-vaunting capital 'I' approach to everything. So a strong female voice bawling at
him daily about his vanity and his connivance in imperial domination
of Jerusalem can hardly have endeared her to him. No wonder he
remembered her in his prayers. Opposing Noadiah—how well she
deserved that epithet. Of course this is all a daydream. I have gap-
filled in a most prodigious fashion. Yet I do not think that I have
overstepped the limits set by the text. I have taken Nehemiah's tone
and filled in what he left out. It seems to me patently obvious that
anybody rebuilding Jerusalem in order to make the Temple community secure on behalf of the Persian authorities must have attracted
considerable and justified criticism. It was a project which just
repeated the past and excluded far too many people.[13] If Noadiah did
represent such a viewpoint—there is absolutely no way of knowing
what the grounds of her opposition to Nehemiah were—then in my
opinion she was a pillar of sense. Temple and city building is for
wealthy, powerful strata of society, although the upkeep of such
enterprises will inevitably be funded by taxation of everybody. Again
one may view Noadiah as an opponent of the wealthy, powerful
groups in Jerusalem and, like so many of the so-called classical
prophets, therefore a spokeswoman against such schemes of aggran-
dizement. Her unknown speeches of opposition may be imagined by
reading Amos or Micah 3 or parts of Isaiah 1–11.

I have imagined Noadiah's opposition adequately for readers to get
the drift of my argument. Noadiah will always live on in the text as
'Opposing Noadiah'. Unfortunately her voice cannot be heard because
Nehemiah chose not to let her speak. Others must reimagine her voice
and give it words. Yet it is enough that she opposed Nehemiah. That is
to her eternal credit. She was a prophet who could not be coopted by
Nehemiah. Not all prophets are available for cooption by the powerful. Not all prophetic voices are diluted by canon consciousness,

13. In his chapter on Nehemiah Morton Smith makes a similar point when he
speculates about how the Yahweh-alone party might have developed if they had not
gained control of the Temple; see his *Palestinian Parties and Politics that Shaped the
Old Testament* (London: SCM Press, 1987), pp. 96-112, esp. pp. 111-12.

although it is often the case that opposing voices get marginalized to the extent of not appearing in any canon.[14] For Noadiah will always be a 'false' prophet to those who read the canon of the Hebrew Bible with an insistence on canon consciousness. To read the Bible with the canon in mind—whatever the canon used—is to run the risk of complicity in the ideological values enforced by the canon.[15] Those who insist that 'canon matters' will tend to take Nehemiah at face value and share his opposition to opposing Noadiah.

The feminine has given way to the canonic in my paper so it is time to bring these meditations to a close. Behind the notion of coopting the prophets is a concept of interpretative communities.[16] Canons are the product of communities with shared concepts which determine the formations of canons. Although the Bible has long since escaped from the clutches of such communities, there is still a strong tendency in biblical scholarship for scholars to return to imagined interpretative communities in order to share similar values. The interpretative communities which coopt the prophets Haggai and Zechariah will be groups which do not coopt opposing Noadiah. She belongs to a different and distinctive interpretative community about which we can say very little. And yet the Bible itself is full of warring and opposing voices which can only be silenced by interpretative communities

14. The notion of 'canon consciousness' is I.L. Seeligmann's (see his 'Voraussetzungen der Midrashexegese', in *Congress Volume: Copenhagen 1953* [VTSup, 1; Leiden: Brill, 1953], pp. 150-81). I use it here in order to avoid the later notions of canonical criticism associated with Brevard S. Childs and James A. Sanders. For a discussion of Seeligmann's notion and its bearing on Ezra's work see T.B. Dozeman, *God on the Mountain: A Study of Redaction, Theology and Canon in Exodus 19–24* (SBLMS, 37; Atlanta: Scholars Press, 1989), pp. 156-61, 192-96.

15. Even after all that has been written by Childs and Sanders and about their work, I remain convinced that one of the most perspicacious books on the canon is J. Blenkinsopp's *Prophet and Canon: A Contribution to the Study of Jewish Origins* (University of Notre Dame Center for the Study of Judaism and Christianity in Antiquity, 3; Notre Dame: University of Notre Dame Press, 1977). It beautifully brings out the strong tensions within the canon, especially those caused by prophecy, and refuses to allow any one interpretation of the tradition to be accorded final and definitive status.

16. The notion of 'interpretative communities' is, of course, Stanley Fish's (see his collection of essays, *Is There a Text in this Class? The Authority of Interpretative Communities* [Cambridge, MA: Harvard University Press, 1980]). I rather think that insufficient attention has been paid in the Guild to the influence of such interpretative communities on the shaping of how the biblical text is read.

choosing to privilege one set of voices over another set of voices. If we coopt Haggai and Zechariah we may have to disregard opposing Noadiah. On the other hand, if we coopt Noadiah and attempt to give her (back) a voice, I rather imagine that we shall have to reject Haggai and Zechariah. Or so it seems to me if we insist on reading the Bible in conjunction with a canon-consciousness constructed hermeneutic. I happen to think that canon is irrelevant for reading the Bible because, among many reasons, there is no canon as such. There are only canons (Hebrew, Greek, Christian, Orthodox etc.) and each linguistic level of canon reading enjoins us to a different interpretative community. As we belong to numerous interpretative communities it is not possible to limit ourselves to a univocal viewpoint. Anyone who takes the Bible very seriously would never be so self-limiting as to imagine that canon consciousness necessarily means that there is a particular viewpoint about the Bible which approximates to whatever the various canonizing bodies imagined they were doing. The polysemic diversity of the Bible renders all talk about canon hopelessly inadequate for reading the text.

With these few poor thoughts on opposing Noadiah and the cooption of prophets I offer my heartiest felicitations to Joe Blenkinsopp whom I hold in the highest regard as one of the few 'good guys' and genuine scholars in our Guild of Biblical Studies (Hebrew Bible section).

Part II
WISDOM, SCRIBES AND SCRIBALISM

THOUGHTS ON THE COMPOSITION OF
PROVERBS 10–29

R.N. Whybray*

I

One of the most fascinating developments in the recent study of Prov. 10.1–22.16, 25–29 (henceforward to be referred to as Prov. 10–29) has been the attempt to discover the processes by which this mass of short proverbs[1] came to be compiled and arranged in the order in which they now appear in the Hebrew text.[2] Apart from a general recognition that the material consists of four major collections (10–15; 16.1–22.16; 25–27; 28–29), it was for a long time generally believed that, with few exceptions, there is no evidence at all of any principle governing the present arrangement of the individual proverbs. Whether they were to be regarded as a series of independent

---

*   It is both an honour and a pleasure to participate in this tribute to Professor Blenkinsopp whose many contributions to Old Testament scholarship include a notable study of 'the many faces of wisdom'.

1.   I use this word as a convenient term without prejudice.

2.   Notably those of H.-J. Hermisson, *Studien zur israelitischen Spruchweisheit* (WMANT, 28; Neukirchen–Vluyn: Neukirchener Verlag, 1968), pp. 171-83; O. Plöger, 'Zur Auslegung der Sentenzensammlungen des Proverbienbuches', in *Probleme biblischer Theologie: Gerhard von Rad zum 70. Geburtstag* (ed. H.W. Wolff; Munich: Kaiser Verlag, 1971), pp. 402-16; *idem, Sprüche Salomos (Proverbia)* (BKAT, 17; Neukirchen–Vluyn: Neukirchener Verlag, 1984), *passim*; G.E. Bryce, 'Another Wisdom-"Book" in Proverbs', *JBL* 91 (1972), pp. 145-57; R.N. Whybray, 'Yahweh-Sayings and their Contexts in Proverbs, 10,1–22,16', in M. Gilbert (ed.), *La sagesse de l'Ancien Testament* (BETL, 51; Gembloux: Duculot, 1979), pp. 153-65; T. Hildebrandt, 'Proverbial Pairs: Compositional Units in Proverbs 10–29', *JBL* 107 (1988), pp. 207-24; R.C. Van Leeuwen, *Context and Meaning in Proverbs 25–27* (SBLDS, 96; Atlanta: Scholars Press, 1988); J. Krispenz, *Spruchkompositionen im Buch Proverbia* (Europäische Hochschulschriften, 349; Frankfurt: Peter Lang, 1989).

reflectiöns on life committed to writing by 'learned' scribes whose learning did not, however, include the ability to develop their thoughts at greater length (in contrast to the authors of chs. 1–9), or had been assembled from earlier, possibly oral, sources by 'editors' whose only concern was to make a compendium of traditional proverbs without any thought of creating a unified composition, they remained a purely random collection. This view appeared to be supported by the fact that comparable proverb collections from other parts of the ancient Near East were thought to be equally without any significant principle of arrangement.

Recent studies of Egyptian and Mesopotamian literature have challenged the former consensus about these works,[3] and so have stimulated a new approach to the comparable collections in Proverbs: it can no longer be assumed without further investigation that no principles of arrangement are to be found there. Nevertheless, not all scholars accept the new approach, and a cautious attitude towards the question remains advisable. To assume too easily that compositional patterns are to be found everywhere in these chapters is to run the risk of doing violence to the material, extorting from it evidence which is simply not there. Subjectivism is a serious danger here; this may be illustrated by a comparison of the widely different results obtained by such scholars as Hermisson, Plöger and Krispenz, using similar methods.[4] It would seem that the criteria that have so far been applied to the problem are insufficiently precise; in particular, they permit a great latitude of judgment in determining which points of comparison between one proverb and another are significant and which trivial, which are coincidental and which deliberate. Both in matters of form and of congruity or development of thought, it must frankly be admitted that by the exercise of sufficient ingenuity it is possible to discover

3.   On Sumerian material, see E.I. Gordon, *Sumerian Proverbs* (New York: Greenwood, 1968), p. 19; on Assyrian, W.G. Lambert, *Babylonian Wisdom Literature* (Oxford: Clarendon Press, 1960), pp. 213, 225; on *Ahiqar,* J.M. Lindenberger, *The Aramaic Proverbs of Ahiqar* (Baltimore: The Johns Hopkins University Press, 1983), p. 21; on Egyptian demotic works, M. Lichtheim, *Late Egyptian Wisdom Literature in the International Context* (OBO, 52; Freiburg: Universitätsverlag; Göttingen: Vandenhoeck & Ruprecht, 1983), pp. 63-65, 99-100, 109-16. Van Leeuwen, *Context and Meaning*, pp. 18-19, gives further references.

4.   For example, in ch. 10 Plöger finds connections between vv. 11-13 and 18-21, while Krispenz singles out vv. 13-17 as a group. In ch. 13 we have: Hermisson, vv. 12-19; Krispenz, vv. 15-25.

a 'pattern' or structure embracing almost any of the proverbs which happen to lie side by side. Before I proceed to discuss possible specific methodologies, some general points are in order.

1. What is being discussed is an editorial question. It is important to recognize that with few exceptions each of the proverbs in these collections is in the first place an independent composition which had its origin in circumstances of which we know nothing. If their present arrangement is not purely a random one, various possible editorial intentions must be considered: they may have been placed in their present positions, for example, to assist the understanding of the reader by grouping them according to subject-matter, to assist the hearer by mnemonic aids,[5] to make a comment on one proverb by juxtaposing another which modifies its original meaning, to create a paradox and so promote further thought, or to reconcile different religious perceptions or social attitudes. Some of these procedures will have involved deliberate reinterpretations of the original meaning or purpose of an older proverb or proverbs. But it would be wrong to assume that the editorial intention remained the same at every point.

2. Similarly it should not be assumed that the editors used only one method of composition. It is more probable that they employed a variety of methods, adopting whichever one best suited their purpose.

3. If there is indeed evidence of a significant editorial process in these chapters, it must be recognized that this may have been—and in my opinion almost certainly was—a gradual process. Small groups of proverbs may have been incorporated into larger ones, and these into still larger ones. Some proverbs, or even groups of proverbs, may have acquired a pivotal role, fulfilling a double function by rounding off one group and introducing another, within a new and larger collection. If this was the case, some proverbs are likely to have been interpreted in several different ways at different editorial stages. The complexity of the process may to some extent account for the divergence of scholarly views about the boundaries of particular groups of proverbs.

4. It may be asked what is the point of an investigation into the composition of these chapters of Proverbs. Why cannot each proverb simply be interpreted as the self-contained literary unit which it once was, as has been done by earlier scholars? The answer is that while

---

5.   Mnemonic aids are not confined to 'oral literature'.

each of these small units has its own separate importance, the fact remains that these chapters—and, of course, the whole book of proverbs—now form a single composition: they are the text which has come down to us, and it is ultimately with this 'final form of the text' that we have to deal. Whoever assembled them in their present order intended them to be seen as a whole. If indeed the purpose of the editors was more than simply one of general convenience but was to imprint some kind of message on the mind of the reader, that overall message must be just as important as the many different 'meanings' of the individual proverbs which make up these collections. But that purpose can only be fully understood if something of the process of composition can be grasped.

II

Basically there are only two kinds of clues to editorial intentions in these chapters: connections deliberately contrived between proverbs or groups of proverbs with respect to form or style and those with respect to sense and theme.

Form

The main formal or stylistic devices to be found in these collections of proverbs which attest an intention to arrange them in some kind of order are paronomasia, alliteration and assonance, and key-words (*Stichwörter*). The arrangement of different *syntactical* forms or constructions such as synonymous and antithetical parallelisms, questions, *a fortiori* arguments, comparisons, and so forth, has been used as a criterion, but—apart from the fact that some collections show a predilection for one such form or another—there is little evidence that these distinctions of form played a significant part in the development of *structural* patterns.[6]

Alliteration, assonance and paronomasia in general are, of course, not confined in these proverbs to editorial activity. Indeed, as Boström[7] was the first to point out, they are most frequently to be found within single proverbs, as they are also in the popular proverbs of many peoples. The work of the literary editors in using these

---

6. This is one point at which I differ from Van Leeuwen.
7. G. Boström, *Paronomasi i den äldre hebreiska maschalliteraturen* (LUÅ, 1.23.8; Lund: Gleerup; Leipzig: Otto Harrassowitz, 1928).

phenomena as clamps to fasten one or more proverbs together is, however, very different from the naive delight of the popular proverb-
maker who discovers a connection between sound and sense in a saying
such as בא זדון ויבא קלון ('When pride comes, then comes disgrace',
Prov. 11.2). While in some cases inter-proverbial paronomasia may
go side by side with a connection of sense or theme, more often it
does not. Thus the view that paronomasia necessarily serves a more
significant purpose than either an aesthetic or a mnemonic one is
dubious.

The same is true of the use of key-words. Thus in each of the four
proverbs 15.29-32 the root שמע occurs; but only in two of these
(vv. 31-32) is there any connection of sense: in both cases the reference is to 'hearing'—that is, heeding—admonition. In v. 29 it is
Yahweh who 'hears'; but the connection between his hearing the
prayers of the righteous and the pupil's 'hearing' admonition is a very
remote one, especially as v. 29 is separated from vv. 31-32 by an
entirely different use of שמע in v. 30 in the phrase שמועה טובה, 'good
news'. While it may be assumed that these four verses have been
juxtaposed because they all contain words derived from the root שמע,
it is difficult to see any deeper significance in this. The same applies to
the use of לב in 15.11, 13-15 or 15.28, 30-32. The phenomenon is an
interesting one and was evidently an important factor in the formation
of small groups of proverbs, but it gives no clue to the existence of
any deeper purpose in the mind of the editors.

Theme and Point of View
On this level 'composition' may not have been confined to the ordering of existing proverbs: the question arises whether earlier material
may have been expanded and supplemented by the addition of newly
coined proverbs with the intention of in some way modifying its point
of view. In other words, authorship as well as editorship has to be
considered.

This notion of additional material raises the further question of
the nature of the original units to which additions or expansions may
have been made. Eissfeldt[8] argued that many of the two-line proverbs
were expansions of single-line popular proverbs. This view, which

8. O. Eissfeldt, *Der Maschal im Alten Testament* (BZAW, 24; Giessen:
Töpelmann, 1913).

was contested by Hermisson[9] and rejected by many later scholars including von Rad,[10] has recently been revived by Westermann.[11] The criteria employed by those who espouse this view are partly formal, but not entirely so. There are instances in which a forceful and lively comment on a particular human type is followed by a rather feeble and obviously imitative comment on its opposite in the second line. The existence of a motive-clause following a self-contained saying which was self-explanatory is also a likely candidate for the role of secondary addition, especially if it gives a different twist to what seems to have been the original sense. However, the possibility must be borne in mind that a single person may have first framed an observation in the form of a short, conventional proverb and then himself elaborated or commented on it. Popular proverbs are notoriously easy to imitate.

This article will, however, concentrate on the question of combination of two-line proverbs. On this level there are a few obvious instances of topical grouping. Prov. 16.10-15, in which each proverb with one exception is concerned with the king (or with kings), is a fairly lengthy example of this, but there are many, briefer examples consisting of only two or three proverbs. A shared topic, however, does not necessarily mean a common *point of view*: 16.12, for example, expresses a critical attitude towards kingship which is entirely absent from vv. 10 and 13. Nevertheless, the basis of this grouping is not simply the key-word מלך, 'king'. Whoever assembled this group of proverbs was no doubt well aware of the discrepancies between the different elements in the group, and it may reasonably be supposed that it was his intention to provide food for thought about the nature of kingship. In some instances such an intention is very evident: there can, for example, be no reason why 26.4 and 5 should have been placed together other than to use the device of paradox to provoke reflection on the problem of dealing with fools.

Such methods of composition reveal a capacity on the part of the compilers which goes beyond the encapsulating of a single observation within the bounds of a short proverb. Their interests range beyond

9. *Studien*, pp. 36-64.
10. G. von Rad, *Wisdom in Israel* (London: SCM Press, 1972), p. 26.
11. C. Westermann, *Wurzeln der Weisheit: Die ältesten Sprüche Israels und anderer Völker* (Göttingen: Vandenhoeck & Ruprecht, 1990), pp. 10, 29, 122; cf. also pp. 173-77.

particular issues, and they concern themselves with broader and more complex ones; and in so far as this is so they are engaging in re-interpretation of the proverb material which they are handling. But it has been argued by many scholars that a far more thoroughgoing re-interpretation of the older proverbs has taken place, and that this has been carried out by the addition of new material appropriately couched in the proverb form.

III

It is generally agreed that the compilation of the proverb collections in chs. 10–29 was not the work of a single editor but took place step by step over a long period of time. There are indications that the collections were built up by the combination of smaller groups to form larger ones. The extent to which non-traditional material has been *added* to older proverbs to carry out a major re-interpretation, however, is a matter of dispute, as is also the related problem of the purpose for which this may have been done. On the latter question four main views may be considered. (1) The bulk of the proverbs *were essentially secular in character* ('old wisdom'), and were later supplemented by proverbs which re-interpret them in terms of 'a moralism which derives from Yahwistic piety'.[12] (2) While the older proverbs should not be described as 'secular,' the *incorporation of proverbs which refer to Yahweh* nevertheless represents an intention by later editors to add greater emphasis to a belief that Yahweh controls the whole of life including its smallest details, and makes absolute moral demands. (3) The original proverbs had *no specifically didactic purpose*, but constant references to the importance of submission to instruction as the key to right living indicate an intention to convert them into a series of *educational texts*. (4) Proverbs concerned with abstract or *universal themes* reflect a later and more developed way of thinking than those which deal with concrete, down-to-earth topics.

1. The view that the majority of the proverbs represent an 'old wisdom' which was entirely untouched by 'Yahwistic piety' is no longer tenable. It is based on a distinction between 'secular' and

---

12. W. McKane, *Proverbs: A New Approach* (London: SCM Press; Philadelphia: Westminster Press, 1970), pp. 11-22. For a full account of his concept of 'old wisdom', see his *Prophets and Wise Men* (SBT, 44; London: SCM Press, 1965), esp. pp. 48-54.

'religious' which was unknown in the ancient world. The notion that the ancient Israelites, or indeed any of their neighbours, entertained a view of human life and capacities which ignored the powerful influence of God or the gods is totally erroneous. The argument from silence—that is, that because many of the proverbs in these chapters do not specifically refer to the influence of Yahweh in human affairs their authors were unaware of it or discounted it—is valueless: it is not necessary to indulge in 'God-talk' whenever human problems are discussed, especially in a society in which religious beliefs are held in common and taken for granted.

It is true that McKane did not rely solely for his view on the fact that some proverbs mention Yahweh as the arbiter of human fate while others do not; he also argued, for example, from a supposed change in the meaning of certain terms—e.g. מזמה—from a morally neutral or even approving sense to a condemnatory one as evidence of the growing influence of Yahwistic piety on moral perceptions. This may indeed indicate a difference of moral tone; but this difference is not necessarily a diachronic one, nor was it necessarily due to a change from a 'secular' to a 'religious' way of thinking.[13]

This concept of a secular 'old wisdom' was a consequence of a once widely held view that early Israelite wisdom was in the main a 'school wisdom' composed for the instruction of a class of court officials which had taken as its model the administrative system of Egypt, where empiricism and pragmatism rather than religious beliefs were supposedly the guiding principles. This view has been disproved on two accounts. First, the individual proverbs in Proverbs 10–29 show no sign of a scribal origin or of an interest in administrative affairs; rather, their affinities are with popular or tribal wisdom such as is found among non-literate peoples: they are in fact native Israelite or proto-Israelite products of ordinary people.[14]

13. On the value of such terminological study see von Rad, *Wisdom in Israel*, pp. 12-13.

14. See *inter alia* C. Westermann, 'Weisheit im Sprichwort', in K.-H. Bernhardt (ed.), *Schalom: Studien zu Glaube und Geschichte Israels, Alfred Jepsen zum 70. Geburtstag* (Stuttgart: Calwer Verlag, 1971), pp. 73-85; reprinted in *idem*, *Forschung am Alten Testament: Gesammelte Studien* (TBü, 55; Munich: Chr. Kaiser Verlag, 1974), II, pp. 149-61; *idem*, *Wurzeln der Weisheit*, pp. 9-11, 27-28, 151-77; F.W. Golka, 'Die Königs- und Hofsprüche und der Ursprung der israelitischen Weisheit', *VT* 36 (1986), pp. 13-36. Cf. also R.N. Whybray, *Wealth and Poverty in the Book of Proverbs* (JSOTSup, 99; Sheffield: JSOT Press, 1990). It should be

Secondly, the wisdom of Egypt was itself far from being 'secular' in the sense of having no concern with religious beliefs and practices; and in the later wisdom literature such as the *Wisdom of Ani* and *Amenope* and subsequent works the religious element is particularly prominent.[15] This later literature, more 'popular' in origin than the earlier court-oriented literature, covers roughly the same period as the wisdom literature of Israel. If the individual proverbs in Proverbs 10–29 were 'secular' and uninfluenced by religious considerations, this characteristic can hardly have been derived from Egyptian sources. The Assyrian and Babylonian proverbs which have been preserved more closely resemble those in Proverbs in form than the Egyptian works; but they are too few for an adequate comparison to be made.[16] However, the *Wisdom of Ahiqar*, possibly of Assyrian origin and contemporary with the monarchical period in Israel, recognizes the role of the god Shamash in human affairs. Thus a purely secular proverb literature in Proverbs would be, as far as we can tell, a unique phenomenon in the wisdom literature of the ancient Near East.[17]

2. Nevertheless, there can be no doubt that there are instances in Proverbs 10–29 where the same thought is expressed in two different ways: with and without reference to Yahweh. For example, 13.14 and 14.27 are identical except that in the former it is the teaching of the wise that is a fountain of life, whereas in the latter it is the fear of Yahweh. In 10.4b it is the hand of the diligent that makes rich, whereas in 10.22 it is the blessing of Yahweh. In 14.21b those who

noted that Egyptian wisdom is found mainly in the form of 'instructions' and is admonitory in character, whereas the great majority of the proverbs in Prov. 10–29, like most modern proverbs, are couched in the form of statements about the way the world is. Some of the later Egyptian demotic works—e.g. *Ankhsheshonqy*—are exceptions, but these are 'popular' in character and too late to have influenced Proverbs.

15. This was first pointed out by A. de Buck ('Het religious Karakter der oudste egyptische Wijsheid', *Nieuw Theologisch Tijdschrift* 21 [1932], pp. 322-49). See also H. Brunner, *Altägyptische Weisheit* (Zürich: Artemis, 1988), pp. 33-41.

16. Lambert, *Babylonian Wisdom Literature*, pp. 213, 225.

17. McKane, *Proverbs*, p. 16, discounts the argument from the religious character of Egyptian and other Near Eastern wisdom literature: 'the nature of Old Testament wisdom cannot be determined from such a distance'. But this argument cuts both ways. My own view on 'old wisdom' has been considerably modified since the publication of my 'Yahweh-sayings'.

are kind to the poor are pronounced happy, whereas in 16.20b it is those who trust in Yahweh. In 15.17 it is love which makes a poor meal preferable to a feast where there is hatred, but in the immediately preceding verse it is the fear of Yahweh which is the decisive factor. In 18.11 it is a rich man's wealth which is his strong city, whereas in 18.10 it is the name of Yahweh which is a strong tower. Examples could be multiplied.

Even more striking, and much discussed by scholars, is the double form in which the so-called 'doctrine of retribution'—that is, the belief that the righteous and the wicked will be rewarded according to their deserts—is expressed. While there are innumerable proverbs which assert this belief in an entirely impersonal way (e.g. 11.19, 'He who is steadfast in righteousness will live, but he who pursues evil will die'), a number of proverbs assert that the operation of this principle will be ensured by the direct action of Yahweh.[18] Something like this double phenomenon is found also in Egyptian wisdom literature; but whatever may be its explanation there, it is something which needs to be accounted for in Proverbs.

The view that the 'impersonal' proverbs reflect a belief in the automatic operation of a principle by which righteousness and wickedness somehow produce from within themselves the appropriate consequences, and that consequently the 'Yahweh-proverbs' with their belief in a divine judge are expressing a quite different belief is simply not convincing: the omission of a specific mention of Yahweh does not mean that he was not regarded as having anything to do with the process—there is nothing in these proverbs to suggest this.[19] However, the fact that the matter is expressed in two different ways remains. It is reasonable to suppose that these Yahweh-proverbs—and no doubt other Yahweh-proverbs as well—reflect a feeling on the part of their authors that the personal relationship of Yahweh to human

18. Compare, for example, 10.3 with 13.25; 15.25 with 10.25 and 14.11; 19.17 with 11.7.

19. For this view see esp. K. Koch, 'Gibt es ein Vergeltungsdogma im Alten Testament?', *ZTK* 52 (1955), pp. 1-42, reprinted in K. Koch (ed.), *Um das Prinzip der Vergeltung in Religion und Recht des Alten Testaments* (Wege der Forschung, 125; Darmstadt: Wissenschaftliche Buchgesellschaft, 1972), pp. 130-80. Von Rad, while agreeing with Koch about Israelite belief in 'an effective power inherent both in good and in evil', denied that the proverbs which reflect this belief are in conflict with those which speak of Yahweh as blessing and punishing (*Wisdom in Israel*, pp. 128-29).

affairs needed to be stressed specifically and not simply taken for granted. This feeling may perhaps correspond to the increased sense of nearness to the gods that is found in the Egyptian literature of the New Kingdom. To put this difference in terms of secular versus religious, however, is to misunderstand the matter.

All this suggests that we have to deal with a combination in Proverbs 10–29 of two layers or strata of proverbs. Whether these are to be understood diachronically, with one 'improving' the theology of an earlier one, can only be made clear if the contextual relationship of the two strata is examined. This in turn would only be possible if the proverbs in each stratum could be identified. The obvious place to begin such an investigation would be the Yahweh-proverbs, where identification is a matter of fact and not conjecture.[20]

3. Westermann has recently referred to a group of proverbs in these chapters which, he believes, reflects an educational background, and has suggested that these are late post-exilic additions—or, in some cases, later adaptations of earlier proverbs—which reflect instruction given in schools.[21] There are undoubtedly some proverbs here—not all in admonitory form—which closely resemble the introductory sections of the 'instructions' by father to son which form the greater part of Proverbs 1–9. Three of these (19.20, 27; 27.11) are in admonitory, imperative form; two of them (19.27; 27.11) are addressed to 'my son' and exhort the pupil to pay attention to instruction (שמע מוסר, cf. 1.8; 4.1) or simply to 'become wise' (חכם). All of the proverbs in question employ the same or equivalent terminology as the comparable verses in chs. 1–9.[22] Since in chs. 1–9 the admonition to heed the father's teaching is always followed by the main body of the 'instruction', the question thus arises whether this may also be the case in chs. 10–29: in other words, whether there is evidence of the formation of small—or perhaps longer—groups of proverbs following the admonitory ones, which have at some stage been assembled in order to fulfil—though in a less organized way—something of the function of the more formal instructions of chs. 1–9, thus giving

20. I made a preliminary investigation of the question in 'Yahweh-sayings', but further study is needed. This will be a feature of my forthcoming commentary on Proverbs.

21. *Wurzeln der Weisheit*, esp. pp. 38-40, 107-109, 123.

22. Compare, for example, 10.8, 17; 12.1; 13.1; 19.16 with 1.8; 2.1; 3.1; 4.1, 10, 20; 6.20; 7.1.

the individual proverbs so collected an educational function which they did not originally possess. Such a process would be analogous, in miniature, to the process by which the whole, book of Proverbs has been turned, by the addition of the Prologue in 1.2-7—and indeed of the whole of chs. 1–9—into an educational treatise.

This hypothesis is difficult to assess because the lower limits of such conjectural 'instructions' are not clearly defined. In the case of the instructions in chs. 1–9 these limits are, on the whole, simple to define, despite subsequent expansions in some cases: the instructions either follow one another directly, in which case the introductory verse of one defines the limit of the previous one (e.g. in ch. 4) or are followed by material of a quite different kind (e.g. 3.1-12). Some, though not all of them, conclude with 'summary appraisals' of a generalized kind (e.g. 1.19; 4.18-19). Moreover, each instruction has its own theme, which is sharply defined. In the case of chs. 10–29 there is no single theme, but a variety of assorted proverbs each with its own theme; there is no concluding 'summary appraisal'; and there is no clear break in the character of the succeeding material—or so it seems. But this question has not yet been adequately studied, and the theory deserves further investigation.

4. Finally, it has been supposed, again by Westermann,[23] that a later stratum can be distinguished from an earlier one by its generalizing character. In other words, the earlier proverbs are concerned only with concrete situations, while the later material is more abstract, concerned with the universal rather than the particular: it is, in fact, more 'philosophical'. This seems to me to be an extremely vague and imprecise criterion. While neither a developed philosophical system nor a systematic theology is to be expected here—nor are such to be found in chs. 1–9—there is no reason to deny the ability to reflect on universal problems to the authors of the early proverbs; and in fact reflections of this kind are to be found in some of the oral proverbs of modern non-literate peoples.

Even if it were possible to classify with any certainty every proverb in these chapters according to some system as has been mentioned above, the problem of their composition would not, of course, have been solved. It would still be necessary to account for the particular *arrangement* of material, which has been characterized by many

---

23. *Wurzeln der Weisheit*, esp. pp. 49-50, 130-34, 142-51.

earlier scholars as haphazard. But if it is accepted that the addition of
Yahweh-proverbs and/or instructional headings (categories 2 and 3
above) was made with a purpose, such a haphazard scattering of this
additional material would seem improbable. It is reasonable to
suppose that such additions were intended to serve their purpose *in
their immediate contexts*. Their relative frequency suggests that what
we have to look for is a number of relatively small groups of
proverbs which once stood on their own. No doubt Westermann's
view that these small editorial units were subsequently combined to
form larger ones until the present form of the text was reached is correct; but evidence of the intermediate stages of composition is more
difficult to find, and this task has scarcely been attempted so far. The
search for evidence of relatively small units is the immediate task.[24]

24. I find Van Leeuwen's ambitious search for 'macrostructures' in chs. 25–27,
especially his method of 'structuralist analysis' (*Context and Meaning*, pp. 40-52),
too abstruse to be convincing.

PROHIBITIONS IN PROVERBS AND QOHELETH

James L. Crenshaw

In a recent examination of poverty in the laws of the ancient Near East and of the Bible, Norbert Lohfink[1] lends his voice to earlier claims[2] that Israelite law and wisdom are integrally related. With

---

1. 'Poverty in the Laws of the Ancient Near East and of the Bible', *TS* 52 (1991), pp. 34-50. Lohfink's description of evolving attitudes toward the poor within the several legal codes (Covenant, Deuteronomic and Holiness) rests on structural and linguistic arguments. That is particularly true of his conclusions about Deuteronomy, which he thinks sought to 'create a world in which one can be a stranger, an orphan, or a widow without being poor' (p. 44). Lohfink writes that the authors of the Holiness Code 'tried to bring things back to reality' (p. 47), for the existence of the poor was a fact of daily existence. Deuteronomy's dream of eliminating the poor thus lost out to realistic politics. One feature of Lohfink's investigation of Mesopotamian law codes, the absence of laws about the poor or oppressed despite eloquent rhetoric concerning their well being in the prologues and epilogues, points to the distinctiveness of the biblical legal corpora even though both the Mesopotamian codes and Deuteronomy imagine an ideal society.

2. Most notably, Erhard Gerstenberger, Wolfgang Richter and J.P. Audet. Gerstenberger ('Covenant and Commandment', *JBL* 84 [1965], pp. 49-51) claims that both in form and content legal maxims and wisdom are alike, and the guardians of the precepts are not priests or prophets but fathers, tribal heads, wise men. He also makes the point (*Wesen und Herkunft des apodiktischen Rechts* [WMANT, 20; Neukirchen–Vluyn: Neukirchener Verlag, 1965]) that Israel was not conscious of conflict between wisdom's admonition and legal commands, for wisdom warnings are fundamentally identical with law. W. Richter (*Recht und Ethos: Versuch einer Ortung des weisheitslichen Mahnspruches* [SANT, 15; Munich: Kösel Verlag, 1966]), and Audet ('Origines comparées de la double tradition de la loi et de la sagesse dans le prôche-orient ancien', *International Congress of Orientalists* [Moscow, 1960], I, pp. 352-57]) make the same point. In a discussion of ancient Near Eastern royal ideology Leonidas Kalugila (*The Wise King* [ConBOT, 15; Lund: Gleerup, 1980], p. 37) comments, 'The king was a shepherd, a father and mother of his subjects, taking care of the poor, the widows, the orphans, feeding the hungry, releasing the prisoners, clothing the naked, etc.' Care for widows and orphans is

regard to the emphasis on the poor in the Covenant Code, he remarks that these statutes 'take up well-known themes of traditional Ancient Near Eastern education and royal ideology: to be just and good to the poor in daily life, in business and at court'.[3] Lohfink goes on to compare the general tone of the whole series of laws to Egyptian wisdom texts and prayers. He concludes that these biblical laws arose in a rural area but that the authors were familiar with ancient Near Eastern schools and may even have borrowed specific teachings from them.

Having dismissed the hypothesis of a 'Deuteronomic' reworking of these laws within the Covenant Code,[4] Lohfink is inclined to opt for direct literary borrowing from outside. He insists, however, on the historically embedded nature of the idea of the stranger and the word לחץ with reference to the oppression of a stranger.[5] In his view this verb does not derive from law or wisdom admonition but reflects Israel's particular experience, possibly the result of 'massive migration from the north to the south after the destruction of Samaria'.[6]

R.N. Whybray's analysis in *Wealth and Poverty in the Book of Proverbs*[7] reaches an altogether different conclusion about the social context of the sayings about the poor. After providing a thorough study of the older aphorisms in 10.1–22.16 and 25–29, he writes that 'there is nothing in them to suggest that they were composed as tribal law or to form part of a system of education'.[8] Whybray rejects the

mentioned in the Ugaritic Dan'el text (*ydn dn 'almnt / ytpt tpt ytm*; 'He decides the case of the widow, he judges the suit of the orphan').

3.   'Poverty in the Laws', p. 40.

4.   'Poverty in the Laws', p. 39. He therefore cannot explain wisdom influence as mediated through Deuteronomy, which Moshe Weinfeld in *Deuteronomy and the Deuteronomic School* (Oxford: Oxford University Press, 1972) attributes to ancient sages. If Lohfink's theory is correct that Deuteronomy changes 'the structures of society so as to provide support for those groups which, for very different reasons, are not in a position to live off their own land' (p. 44), the attempt to reorganize society fits badly into ancient wisdom, which endeavored to sustain the status quo. Even such radical sages as the authors of Job and Qoheleth did not propose a new social order, despite the injustice they witnessed.

5.   'Poverty in the Laws', p. 42. Lohfink thinks the Covenant Code marks the origin of the traditional group of *personae miserae,* the stranger, the orphan, the widow (p. 40).

6.   'Poverty in the Laws', p. 41.

7.   JSOTSup, 99; Sheffield: JSOT Press, 1990.

8.   *Wealth and Poverty,* p. 74. Whybray concludes that the instructions in 1–9, 22.17–24.22, 30.1-9, 31.10-31 derive from different circles entirely from the

view that the form of these sayings demonstrates a literary culture, for African folk proverbs have many of the same characteristics that in the Bible have led some interpreters to argue for 'literary' formation.[9]

In the debate over the accuracy of the claim that wisdom and law shared a common origin in the ancient clan, Lohfink clearly belongs to the camp in which Joseph Blenkinsopp has pitched his tent. Blenkinsopp's view finds expression in *Wisdom and Law in the Old Testament*,[10] where he suggests that casuistic law closely resembled aphoristic wisdom, whereas apodictic law bore a striking resemblance to instructions.[11] His understanding of wisdom as an attempt 'to bring human conduct into line with a cosmic law of regularity and order observable in the sequence of seasons, the movements of the heavenly bodies and the like'[12] made a comparison between law and wisdom a logical consequence. His definition of wisdom as living in conformity

working class responsible for the sentences in 10.1–22.16; 25–29; 24.23-34 (*sic*); 30 and miscellaneous sayings in 1–9. The authors of the first two instructions belonged to the upper class and wrote for students, some of whom may have been preparing for responsibilities at the royal court. Two of these instructions, 31.1-9, 31.10-31, reflect the views of those persons who have already reached the top of the social ladder. Whybray (*Wealth and Poverty*, p. 116) identifies four social strata in Proverbs: officials of the court, members of the educated urban society, prosperous farmers, and small farmers earning a precarious living.

9. Laurent Naré (*Proverbs salomoniens et proverbs mossi* [Publications Universitaires Européennes; Frankfurt: Peter Lang, 1986]) compares Prov. 25–29 and African proverbs. The chief proponent of the literary character of canonical proverbs is Hans-Jürgen Hermisson (*Studien zur israelitischen Spruchweisheit* [WMANT, 28; Neukirchen–Vluyn: Neukirchener Verlag, 1968]).

10. Oxford: Oxford University Press, 1983.

11. Blenkinsopp writes, 'If, as noted above, case law is in some respects comparable with proverbial wisdom, categoric law exemplified in the decalogue has analogies with the admonitions and instructions of the sages' (*Wisdom and Law*, p. 81). The distinction made by Claus Westermann ('Weisheit im Sprichwort,' in K.H. Bernhardt [ed.], *Schalom: Studien zu Glaube und Geschichte Israel, Alfred Jepsen zum 70. Geburtstag* [Arbeiten zur Theologie, 46; Stuttgart: Calwer Verlag, 1971], pp. 73-85) between sayings, which originated among ordinary people and were circulated orally, and admonitions, which arose in educational circles, might accommodate this understanding of two types of laws. Westermann (*Forschungsgeschichte zur Weisheitsliteratur 1950–1990* [Arbeiten zur Theologie, 71; Stuttgart: Calwer Verlag, 1991], p. 17) thinks of sayings as universal, while the admonitions are specific to a particular people.

12. *Wisdom and Law*, p. 19.

with the law of nature[13] strengthened that logic considerably.

In light of Claus Westermann's observations in *Wurzeln der Weisheit*[14] that the older proverbial sayings never refer to relationships within the larger clan nor do they champion such a family structure,[15] perhaps we should think instead of the nuclear family unit. Far too much has already been made of the clan ethos as a wisdom locus for the summons to pay attention, with misleading conclusions that link prophets closely with the sapiential tradition.[16] Nevertheless, a family setting for law and wisdom may still be proposed, the authoritative father being the promulgator of both types of command.[17]

13. *Wisdom and Law*, p. 19. Blenkinsopp (p. 28) notices that the same pattern, imperative or prohibition with motivation, occurs in the *Instruction of Amenemopet* and in the Decalogue, as well as in other biblical legislation.

14. Göttingen: Vandenhoeck & Ruprecht, 1990.

15. *Wurzeln*, pp. 35-36. He writes: 'Eine über die Familie (Vater–Mutter–Kind) hinausreichende grössere familiäre Gemeinschaftsform "Sippe" dommt in der Proverbien niemals, in keinem Spruch vor; niemals wird das Denken oder das Handeln auf eine grössere Gemeinschaftsform, niemals auf weitere Verwandte bezogen' (p. 35). The second reason to consider *Sippenethos* problematic is: 'Mit "Sippe" kann nur eine familiär strukturierte Gemeinschaftsform gemeint sein. Von der Familie aber, von Vorgängen in der Familie, von Verhältnissen zwischen Familiengliedern oder von familiären Problemen handeln die Sprüche nur äusserst wenig, sie spielen eine grössere Rolle fast nur im Bereich der Erziehung' (pp. 35-36). Arguments from silence are never entirely satisfactory, a fact that interpreters who study the problem of schools in ancient Israel have come to appreciate. In Westermann's view the world of the oldest proverbs is the simple village, and their language is that of daily discourse. R.N. Whybray ('The Social World of the Wisdom Writers', in R.E. Clements [ed.], *The World of Ancient Israel* [Cambridge: Cambridge University Press, 1989], pp. 227-50) writes that 'Israelite tribal wisdom is a somewhat shadowy postulate' (p. 233).

16. Hans Walter Wolff has argued repeatedly that the prophetic appeal for a hearing originated in an educational setting of the wise. In itself a dubious claim, this hypothesis has led Wolff to posit wisdom influence on several minor prophets (Hosea, Amos, Micah, Joel, Jonah). On Joel 1.2-3, for example, he writes (*Joel and Amos* [Philadelphia: Fortress Press, 1977], p. 20): 'The book's opening employs in v. 2a the ancient "call to receive instruction" (*Lehreröffnungsruf*), a form especially popular in wisdom circles, used to arouse attentiveness'.

17. Gerstenberger, 'Covenant and Commandment', p. 51. Philip Johannes Nel (*The Structure and Ethos of the Wisdom Admonitions in Proverbs* [BZAW, 158; Berlin: de Gruyter, 1982], p. 89) concludes that the authority of wisdom is intrinsic (i.e. rests in its truth) and therefore does not depend on an authority figure such as a father or an institution like the family. On this problem, see my 'Wisdom and

Space does not permit me to evaluate the strength or weakness of the argument about law and wisdom. Instead, I shall address a more modest task—to provide some data that ought to precede such discussions. In short, how do the proverbial sayings express prohibitions? The assumption that a common origin issues in similarity of form makes such comparative information desirable, indeed essential. I shall leave to specialists in Israelite law the further task of applying these data to the several legal codes within the Bible.

1. *Prohibitions in the Book of Proverbs*

As one might expect, most of the prohibitions are found in instructions; in them the huge diversity of form immediately comes to mind. Warnings and negatively stated admonitions using direct address are expressed in many different ways, as the following examples demonstrate.

1. Either בני or בנים accompanied by one or two jussives with אל, stated either synonymously or antithetically (3.1, 11; 5.7; 6.20; 24.21);
2. a conditional clause introduced by אם and followed by a single jussive with אל (1.10);
3. a jussive without any explicit reference to sons, but with implicit address to them (3.7, 25, 27-31; 4.6, 14, 21, 27; 5.8; 6.25; 7.25; 8.33; 9.8; 20.13, 19, 22; 22.22, 24, 26, 28; 23.3, 4, 6, 10, 13, 17, 20, 31; 24.1, 15, 17, 19, 28-29; 25.6; 26.4; 27.1; 30.6-8, 10; 31.3);
4. the mention of objects first, then a jussive with or without a suffix (3.3; 23.23; 27.10);
5. an imperative followed by a single or multiple jussives (3.5; 4.5, 13, 15; 6.3-4; 23.22-23);
6. ועתה and vocative בנים plus imperative and לי with accompanying jussive (5.7);
7. an imperative and antithetic jussive (23.23);
8. a verbless warning (31.4); and
9. a relative clause as the object followed by a jussive (25.7b-8) or a participle followed by a jussive (26.24-25).

Authority: Sapiential Rhetoric and its Warrants', *Congress Volume Vienna 1980* (VTSup, 32; Leiden: Brill, 1981), pp. 10-29.

A striking example of indirect address or impersonal speech, Prov. 28.17, lacks אם although its conditional nature appears likely. In one instance, 20.19, לא with the imperfect occurs where it cannot be explained as a verb that prefers לא to אל inasmuch as the same form, תתערב, is negated by אל in 24.21. Occasionally, a motive clause has a prohibition (4.2).

The motive clause is equally varied; at least eleven ways of expressing motivation can be detected:

1. כי in the same verse or the next one (1.8-9; 3.1-2, 25-26; 4.21-22; 7.25-26; 22.22-23; 23.9, 10-11, 17-18, 20-21; 24.1-2, 15-16, 19-20, 21-22; 25.6-7; 26.25; 27.1);
2. כי at the end of a series (3.5, 7, 12; 4.5, 6, 13-16; 23.6-7);
3. כי plus כן (1.16-19) or כי and antithesis (3.31-32; 6.26);
4. ו copulative (3.3-4, 21-22, 28, 29; 20.22);
5. ב *temporalis* (3.27) within an infinitive construct;
6. adverbial אם (3.30) and conditional (22.26-27);
7. פן (9.8; 20.13; 22.24-25; 24.17-18; 25.8-10; 26.4, 5; 30.6, 8-10; 31.3-5);
8. פן and פ, followed by ו and ו (5.7-10);
9. אשרי with כי (8.33-35);
10. כי in the sense of when (23.13);
11. a summary statement (23.31).

The motivation is conspicuously absent in 4.27; 6.4-5; 22.28; 23.22-23; 24.28-29. A preference for פ over כי is observable in instructions attributed to Agur and to Lemuel's mother, but פ also occurs in sayings where one does not expect to find them (25.9-10; 26.4-5). Verbal forms show decided preference for *qal* and *piel*, although *hiphil* forms occur often, with an occasional *niphal* and *hithpael*.

2. Prohibitions in Qoheleth

Within Qoheleth eight, possibly nine, varieties of prohibition indicate that later wisdom retained stylistic fluidity akin to earlier instructions.

1. אל with the jussive plus ל and the infinitive, a dative of administration and a motive clause introduced by כי (5.1[2], 3[4]);
2. אל plus ואל and jussives, followed by a question with למה as introductory particle (5.5[6]; 7.16-17);

3. אל with the jussive plus a motive clause introduced by כי (7.9-10);

4. אל plus ואל and jussives followed by a motive clause with כי (8.2-3; cf. 10.20);

5. אל with jussive but without an immediate motive clause (9.8; cf. כי in 9.9);

6. a conditional clause introduced by אם, followed by אל and a jussive, with a motive clause beginning with כי (5.7; 10.4);

7. אל with a jussive followed by לא and the imperfect, coupled with a motive clause and כי (7.21-22);

8. an imperative plus אל with a jussive, followed by a motive clause with כי (11.6);

9. טוב followed by a relative and לא with an imperfect, plus partitive מן (5.4[5]).

The diversity in Qoheleth extends beyond form to syntax, grammar, topic and semantic field. No single form appears to be normative, either in quantity or in aesthetic appeal. Warning or admonition, vetitive, and motive clause comprise essential components, although ambiguity persists with regard to the formal or functional nature of these categories.[18]

Armed with this information about the actual variety of prohibitions in proverbial wisdom, interpreters should be able to assess claims about similarities between law and wisdom. One significant test case exists within Proverbs itself, although its resolution alone will not settle the argument.

Prov. 22.28 is one of those rare sayings with multiple variants (23.10-11; Deut. 19.14; 27.17; cf. Job 24.2). No motive occurs in Prov. 22.28, only a terse warning (אל תסג גבול עולם אשר עשו אבותיך = 'Do not remove the age-old boundary that your ancestors set up'). The Egyptian parallel from the *Instruction of Amenemope* adds a religious justification for the prohibition, which *ANET* omits ('Do not carry off the landmark at the boundaries of the arable land...nor encroach upon the boundaries of the widow'). Loss of land meant exclusion from the divine promise, and violation of established order

---

18. The trail was laid out by unknown authors of earlier sayings, but Ben Sira made it familiar territory. I have discussed his use of an ancient debate form in 'The Problem of Theodicy in Sirach', *JBL* 94 (1975), pp. 47-64.

was a serious offense. As is well known, respect for boundaries was not unique to the Egyptians and Israelites, for the Greeks praised Zeus as protector of borders and the Romans honored Terminus in an annual festival.[19] Within Proverbs itself, 15.25 asserts that YHWH is committed to maintaining widows' boundary stones, a belief presupposed also by the passage from *Amenemopet* cited above (but with a different deity, of course; cf. Deut 32.8; Ps. 74.17).

In Prov. 23.10 the oft-proposed change of עולם to אלמנה improves the symmetry;[20] the motive clause in the next verse describes YHWH as the one accepting social responsibility for the nearest of kin and argues a case within the judicial system. In early times the office of גאל functioned, among other things, in cases of blood revenge occasioned by murder or serious sexual offenses.[21] The clause, 'He will plead their case against you' recalls Prov. 22.23, 'For YHWH will plead their case' which is further reinforced by assurance that the deity will despoil the despoilers. Here the victims of oppression belong to the ranks of the marginalized (the poor, דל, and helpless, עני).[22] In this particular case the injustice occurred precisely in the place where justice was supposed to be carried out (בשער, 'in the gate'). Presumably the agent of this miscarriage of justice was a bribe, for which practice the sayings provide ample evidence. To curb such abuse of power and wealth reflected, for example, in Job 24.2, an epithet describing YHWH as 'father of the fatherless, champion of the widow', came into existence (Ps 68.5[6]; cf. Exod. 22.21-22; Job 10.13).

Differences between Prov. 22.28 and Deut. 19.14 discredit the attempt to relate the two texts in any way other than subject matter: לא

19. C.H. Toy, *The Book of Proverbs* (ICC; New York: Charles Scribner's Sons, 1902), p. 427.

20. The versions offer no evidence that the translators read אלמנה, but the parallel from *Amenemopet* and the frequent biblical association of widows and orphans (Exod. 22.21; Deut. 10.18; Pss. 68.6; 146.9; Isa. 1.17; Jer. 7.6; 22.3) favour this emendation (cf. O. Plöger, *Sprüche Salomos [Proverbia]* [BKAT, 17; Neukirchen–Vluyn: Neukirchener Verlag, 1981], p. 272).

21. H. Ringgren, 'גָּאַל ga'al, גֹּאֵל go'el, גְּאֻלָּה ge'ullah', *TDOT*, II, pp. 350-55 and J.J. Stamm, 'גאל g'l erlösen', *Theologisches Handwörterbuch zum Alten Testament* (Munich: Chr. Kaiser Verlag, 1978), cols. 383-94.

22. On the understanding of poverty as a sign of divine displeasure, see my essay entitled 'Poverty and Punishment in the Book of Proverbs', in the United Methodist ministry journal, *Quarterly Review*, 9.3 (1989), pp. 30-43.

with imperfect, רעך instead of עולם (or אלמנה), ראשנים for גבלו, אבותיך for עשו and typical Deuteronomic rhetoric ('in the inheritance which you will hold in the land YHWH your god gives you to possess'). The only point of similarity occurs in the two words תסיג גבול. The ancient curse in Deut. 27.17 (ארור מסיג גבול רעהו) is closer to the other legal text, Deut. 19.14, than to the passages from Proverbs. In the curse against one who removes a neighbor's boundary mark the participle occurs rather than the imperfect, the oath particle functions as negation, and רעהו has a third-person singular suffix instead of second-person, for indirect address characterizes the genre of curse (cf. Job 3.4, 6, 7, 9-10). Such differences among these texts exclude direct dependence, and the functional use of the curse as a prohibition implies that maxims may have played a similar role.

Some evidence supports the claim that positively stated maxims occasionally amounted to prohibitions. Prov. 3.7a has the usual pro-hibitive form (אל תהי חכם בעיניך), but the folly of this inordinate pride is condemned in proverbial sayings such as דרך אויל ישר בעיניו (12.15)[23] and 'Do you see a person wise in his own eyes? There is more hope for a fool than for him' (26.12). The emphasis falls on reluctant students who think they already have all the answers and therefore do not need to learn from superiors.[24] All three texts aim at a single goal—to effect an openness to instruction. Functionally, all three are identical, despite their differences in syntax.

Another type of prohibition in Proverbs complicates the attempt to correlate law and wisdom. In three instances אל תאמר occurs; one of these legislates speech, while two of them place constraints on thought

---

23. Otto Plöger (*Sprüche Salomos*, p. 151) writes that the fool establishes his own standard, refusing to hear advice from wiser individuals. The scandalous stories in Judg. 19–21 describe chaotic circumstances resulting from a society ruled by independent judgments at odds with any sense of obligation to the community at large. These stories serve as a powerful apology for kingship ('In those days there was no king in Israel; everyone did what suited him', איש הישר בעיניו יעשה, Judg. 21.25). According to Prov. 21.2 the fool has plenty of company, for human beings generally set their own standards, although YHWH weighs hearts (כל דרך איש ישר בעיניו ותכן לבות יהוה).

24. I have examined 'Resistance to Learning in Ancient Egypt and Israel' in a plenary address presented at the national meeting of the Catholic Biblical Association in Los Angeles, August 10-13, 1991. This paper, part of a larger work to be published later, deals with the conclusion to *Ani, Papyrus Insinger* and Ben Sira, among other texts.

itself. The first, 3.28, issues a warning against requiring a debtor to grovel at the creditor's feet; for such delay in advancing a loan only lowers borrowers' self-respect. The second verse, 20.22, cautions against repaying evil deeds in kind and urges patience made possible by a conviction that YHWH will provide the desired retribution. In the third instance, 24.29, a warning against enforcing the principle of *lex talionis* seems to presuppose divine response for the purpose of punishing offenders in due time.[25] The same sentiment underlies *Ahiqar* 79 ('My enemies will die, but not by my sword'), which also leaves the matter of instrumentality open. The belief in the inevitable consequence of an evil deed, the conviction that the deity will punish villainy, and the knowledge that everyone must die make this saying richly ambiguous in one sense but absolutely certain in yet another sense.[26]

This survey of prohibitions in Proverbs and Qoheleth indicates the rich diversity of ancient sapiential speech. Preliminary examination suggests that similar variety characterizes prohibitions in Job and Sirach, but the data must await future study. In a few instances where identical prohibitions exist in law and wisdom, the differences of expression stand out. At the very least, those interpreters who identify wisdom and law as a common phenomenon will need to explain the sharp divergencies. Why would fathers choose such distinct language if both law and wisdom derive from family paraenesis? And why are most of the prohibitions found in instructions which originated in educational circles? Perhaps an adequate explanation can be found, but the question should not be ignored. As Westermann's history of research in wisdom literature during the years from 1950 to 1990 makes abundantly clear, scholars have yet to resolve the issue of wisdom's origins, whether oral or literary, and locus, whether family or school. Until further clarity is achieved on these crucial matters, claims about a common origin of law and wisdom must remain highly suggestive but at the same time equally problematic.

25. William McKane (*Proverbs* [Philadelphia: Westminster Press, 1970], pp. 574-75) calls attention to the Babylonian 'Precepts and Admonitions': 'Do not return evil to the man who disputes with you. Requite with kindness your evil-doer. Maintain justice to your enemy. Smile on your adversary'. McKane resists any theological reading of Prov. 24.28.

26. J.M. Lindenberger, *The Aramaic Proverbs of Ahiqar* (Baltimore: The Johns Hopkins University Press, 1983), p. 178.

PATTERNS IN PSALMS 25 AND 34

David Noel Freedman

This paper will point out certain unusual features that Psalms 25 and
34 have in common and suggest that these coincidences can hardly be
the result of chance. The commonalities should therefore be regarded
as part of a planned, rather intricate, poetic structure. A brief run-
down of these features follows.

1. As is generally known, Psalms 25 and 34 have the form of alphabetic acrostics in which each poetic unit begins with a different letter
of the alphabet, beginning with the letter *aleph* and following the usual
order, ending with *taw*. A minor variation which occurs in other
alphabetic acrostic poems may be observed in Psalm 34. It has been
suggested that the lines beginning with *ayin* and *pe* (vv. 16-17) should
be reversed because of sense requirements, that is, v. 16 (beginning
with עיני יהוה) seems to fit better with v. 18 (beginning with צעקו)
while v. 17 (beginning with פני יהוה) seems to go better with v. 15
(beginning with סור מרע). This alternate order of *ayin* and *pe* is
attested elsewhere, particularly in the alphabetic acrostic poems of
Lamentations (cf. Lam. 2.16-17 and 3.46-51; also 4.16-17). While the
change may be justified, whichever sequence we adopt will be well
within the range of actual usage in the biblical group of acrostic
poems. Hence the possibility of a deliberate interlocking arrangement
of these lines, departing from normal narrative prose style, should not
be excluded. Other minor and presumably inadvertent deviations from
the norm should also be noted. In Ps. 25.1-2 the official verse
division violates the alphabetic order by placing the word אלהי at the
beginning of v. 2 instead of at the end of v. 1 . This error should be
corrected by beginning the second line of the poem with the next
word, בך, which conforms to the alphabetic pattern. In v. 18 of the
same psalm we would expect, and the acrostic form would require, a
word beginning with the letter *qoph* at the start of the line, whereas in

fact, the word ראה is in that position. Since the identical word occurs at the beginning of v. 19 which conforms to the alphabetic expectation, it seems clear that an error has occurred at the beginning of v. 18, which we may describe as anticipatory vertical dittography—the scribe mistakenly copied the first word of the *resh*-line when he meant to copy the first word of the *qoph*-line. What the original initial word of the *qoph*-line may have been is not entirely clear, but the suggestion (*BHS*) that it was קשׁב is as good as any. No similar minor lapses occur in Psalm 34.

2. Much more significantly, Psalm 25 entirely omits the *waw*-line. While suggestions have been made to recover or restore such a line by detaching the third colon of the *he*-line, emending the text slightly (by adding a *waw* at the beginning of the colon), and thereby supposedly restoring the original pattern of the poem, at best such a procedure is a makeshift—no textual evidence supports such an emendation. Furthermore, the resulting hypothetical *waw*-line is abnormally short (only one colon) and does not stand well by itself. It is much better to leave this colon where it is, a complement to the previous two cola of the *he*-verse as the MT has it. The clinching argument for leaving the text as it is and recognizing that the *waw*-line has been omitted on purpose comes from Psalm 34, where the *waw*-line is likewise absent. Psalm 34 not only omits one of the expected lines of the alphabetic acrostic poem, it omits the same line that is missing in Psalm 25. Any explanation of the phenomenon in either poem must take into account the same phenomenon in the other poem, so an ad hoc line of reasoning that might serve to explain the omission in one poem as inadvertent must also be applied to the other poem. It is going beyond the bounds of probability to suppose that the omission of a line, the same line, in both poems which have other features in common, resulted from coincidence or inadvertence. While we may not be able to give an adequate explanation of why this particular line was omitted, I think we must operate with the supposition that the omission was deliberate in both cases. The omission constitutes a deviation from the normal arrangement, but it also belongs to a larger consideration or configuration.

3. Yet another significant correspondence or correlation occurs between these two poems. As though to compensate for the omission of one of the internal lines of the acrostic poems (the *waw*-line) at the end of each psalm, an additional line is appended after the *taw*-line,

normally itself the last line. While in principle such a line could begin
with any letter, it is remarkable and impressive that in both cases the
line begins with the same letter, constituting a second *pe*-line. The
initial word in both cases derives from the same root פדה (the imperative verb in Ps. 25.22, פְּדֵה, and the masculine singular active participle in Ps. 34.23, פּוֹדֶה). If these phenomena had turned up in only one
psalm, we might wonder about accidental omissions and possible
inadvertencies, but when there are two psalms with so many identical
points in common, it is clear that a deliberate program of alteration
and adaptation has taken place in both cases. Whether or not we can
explain the underlying reasons or the overall objectives or purpose of
such treatment, we must recognize that the procedures are deliberate
and accept these altered psalms as belonging to a specific subcategory
of the larger class of alphabetic acrostic poems in the Bible.

4. The simplest general solution to these curiosities is that the added
line at the end of each poem serves as compensation for the omitted
line in the body of each poem. It would appear that the added line was
intended to make up for the omission of a line in the regular sequence,
thereby retaining the normal and normative 22-line total for poems of
this type: alphabetic acrostics. Alternatively and better, we could say
that one of the internal lines of the poem has been omitted in order to
allow for or to accommodate the addition of a final closing line. There
is a very reasonable explanation for the supernumerary *pe*-line, the
letter itself being part of and contributing to the interpretation. As
expounded by Patrick Skehan, the initial *pe* of the last line of the
poem was chosen deliberately in order to complete a combination with
two other letters, namely, the *aleph* at the beginning of the first line,
and the *lamedh* at the beginning of the twelfth or middle line of the
poem.[1] These three letters in turn spell the word *aleph*, which stands
for the whole alphabet (just as the combination of the first two letters
stands for the whole sequence in Greek or English).[2] This little added
twist serves to reinforce the special character of the poem in its alphabetic patterning. It also adjusts the structure of the poem to provide a
23-line arrangement, which thereby provides not only a first and last,

1. P.W. Skehan, 'The Structure of the Song of Moses in Deuteronomy (32:1-
43)', in *Studies in Israelite Poetry and Wisdom* (CBQMS, 1; Washington: The
Catholic Biblical Association of America, 1971), pp. 74-75.
2. Cf. M.D. Coogan, 'Alphabets and Elements', *BASOR* 216 (1974), pp. 61-
63; more recently, '*LP, "To Be an Abecedarian"', *JAOS* 110 (1990), p. 322.

but also a distinctive middle line, which the ordinary 22-line pattern would lack.

This last consideration raises a new question about these two psalms—asymmetry results from the loss of the *waw*-line in each poem. This omission reduces the overall total to 22 lines, and therefore strictly speaking, the *lamedh*-line is not in fact the twelfth line but the eleventh, and the mathematical precision of the super-imposed pattern is somewhat marred. We may recognize, therefore, that the poet has created or allowed to persist a certain tension or inconsistency in trying to merge two patterns and to retain some features of the 22-line pattern while augmenting the poem to a 23-line pattern. In fact, the recognition of this apparent imbalance leads to further investigation of the phenomenon and to the acquisition of additional data bearing on a more comprehensive resolution to the remaining problems. In the end, however, why the *waw*-line was omitted in each instance may remain a mystery.

5. According to my analysis of the two psalms, the purpose of the poet regarding structure was twofold. On the surface, at least, he intended to maintain the appearance of a normal 22-line alphabetic acrostic poem, albeit with two obvious alterations in the regular sequence of the letters of the alphabet: the omission of one line (the *waw*-line in both poems) and the addition of a line at the end after the last line of the normal sequence (in both cases the added line begins with the same letter, *pe*). In both cases, therefore, the *waw*-line has been dropped and a second *pe* line has been added at the end. On the one hand, the poet seems to have been at some pains to maintain the same profile for these poems as obtains for other poems with the normal sequence of the 22-letters of the Hebrew alphabet. On the other hand, these two poems share and exhibit other features that point to a 23-line structure, rendering these poems distinct from the other more normal set in various ways. In summary, while the poet(s) in both cases arranged their psalms to have 22-lines or alphabetic units, they also intended to project a larger or 23-line format. Surprisingly, both of these features appear in the poems as they have come down to us.

If we take a closer look at Psalm 25, we note that, while most of the lines are characteristically balanced with two half-lines or cola each (there are 20 of these), two lines uncharacteristically have an additional colon, making them tricola. Respectively vv. 5 and 7 (the *he*-line and the *ḥet*-line) in effect bracket the missing *waw*-line (although not exactly, as the *zayin*-line [v. 6] intervenes). While scholars in the past, and some still in the present, regard such tricola lines as contrary to the requirements of Hebrew poetry and systematically eliminate one of the three cola in such lines in order to restore the original structure of the poem, that is an outmoded procedure. We now recognize that the occurrence and presence of tricola in biblical poetry is a frequent and, almost always, deliberate creation of the poet. The widespread occurrence of this phenomenon in Ugaritic poetry has especially persuaded most scholars that the phenomenon is deeply rooted in Northwest Semitic literary conventions. Therefore its widespread occurrence in biblical poetry is no accident and certainly not a persistent and repeated error to be corrected by excision or any other kind of manipulation. It thereby becomes apparent that the purpose of these two tricola in Psalm 25 is precisely to make up for the deficiency caused by the omission of the *waw*-line. Immediately before the omission and almost immediately after it, and within the context of the first half of the poem, the addition of two cola, or the equivalent of one bicolon line, has made up for the deficiency created by the omission. The validity of this contention is borne out by the obvious way in which the number of cola for the poem as a whole, namely 46, equals 23 bicola or lines, while at the same time being restricted to 22 actual lines. A complete description of the poem would have to include both phenomena: the 22 actual lines and the 46 actual cola. The poet has combined these somewhat dissonant elements in the manner indicated: the poem consists of 20 lines of bicola and 2 lines of tricola, making a total of 22 lines and 46 cola. Furthermore, both of the additional cola occur in the first half of the poem, thereby balancing the different major segments of the poem:

Part I: vv. 1-10	10 lines	22 cola
Middle line: v. 11	1 line	2 cola
Part II: vv. 12-22	11 lines	22 cola
Total	22 lines	46 cola

To bring out the augmented alphabetic indicator, the first and last lines or verses could be isolated, and the following table produced:

First line: v. 1	1 line	2 cola
Part I: vv. 2-10	9 lines	20 cola
Middle line: v. 11	1 line	2 cola
Part II: vv. 12-21	10 lines	20 cola
Last line: v. 22	1 line	2 cola
Total	22 lines	46 cola

At one and the same time, the poem conforms to the standard pattern of 22 lines but equally gives the impression of an augmented alphabetic acrostic with an additional line appended at the end of the poem. Now we turn to a more precise count of words and syllables to show that the underlying pattern of this poem is the larger or augmented, rather than the normal one.

As I have shown elsewhere, the standard alphabetic acrostic poem has 22 lines or bicola, with an average or normative line length of 16 syllables, making a total for the poem of 352 syllables.[3] These numbers hold up well for the alphabetic acrostic psalms and poems in the Bible, along with a number of other poems of identical or similar structure which do not preserve or contain the alphabetic sequence (for example, Lam. 5 and Ps. 33).[4] In the case of Psalm 25, however, although the line total is the same (22), there are 46 cola (instead of the expected 44) and the syllable count is substantially higher than the normal and expected 352. In fact, while we must allow for some uncertainty in reproducing the actual pronunciation at the time of composition and also for some freedom on the part of the poet in matching words with metrical requirements, the total number of syllables for Psalm 25 could range from 363 to 382. The reason for the relatively wide range is the frequent and repeated occurrence of the second masc. sing. pronominal suffix which is almost always written as ךָ-, but in the MT, at least, is often vocalized as ךָ- rather than the shorter form ךְ-. While the spelling and the vocalization diverge throughout the MT, the existence of the two forms, side by side can be demonstrated. While it may be possible to trace some evolution in the history of this form, originally ךָ-, it may well have lost the final vowel in certain situations and under certain

---

3.   D.N. Freedman, 'Acrostic Poems in the Hebrew Bible: Alphabetic and Otherwise', *CBQ* 48 (1986), pp. 408-31, especially the tables, pp. 417-18; 424-28. An earlier, more provisional study appeared in my 'Acrostics and Metrics in Hebrew Poetry', *HTR* 65 (1972), pp. 367-92, esp. p. 392.

4.   See D.N. Freedman, 'Acrostic Poems in the Hebrew Bible'.

circumstances. The survival of the longer form, especially in poetry, however, can be assumed. At the same time, the shorter form must have permeated the language so that in any given case it would be difficult to decide which form the author intended. The spelling in the manuscripts of the Masoretic tradition favors the short form, while the vocalization favors the longer. Many of the Dead Sea Scrolls confirm that the longer form was widespread—the so-called Qumran spelling, ‑כה, confirms the presence and pronunciation of the final vowel. Just what the poet intended in each case would be very difficult to determine, so we may leave the matter at this point and approach the question from the point of view of symmetry and structure. In Psalm 25 the suffixed forms occur as follows: vv. 1, 2, 3, 4 (twice), 5 (twice), 6 (twice), 7 (twice), 11 (twice: שמך and סלחת, where we have the comparable second masc. sing. perfect form of the verb, mostly written ‑ת but occasionally ‑תה in the MT), 20, 21, for a total of 15 of these variable forms. The remaining instances of variable pronunciation and syllable-count occur where the MT elides a syllable in its vocalization and produces a lower count than would have obtained in classical pronunciation. The chances are that the older, longer pronunciation prevailed when the poem was written, but we must also allow for the poet to contract or condense words according to need or desire, and the MT offers a clue here as to how that might have been done. In my count, I do not include the numerous and uniform instances in which the MT expands the pronunciation of typical words, for example, segolate formations, in conjunction with laryngeals, and so forth. There is no basis for these modifications in any ancient source, and they can be regarded as later and secondary additions to the text.

Given the numerous converging structural features of the two psalms, I conclude that the expected number of syllables for each poem as a whole would be 368 (that is, 46 cola × 8 syllables = 368), which is clearly within the range noted above for Psalm 25 (363 to 382). If we suppose that the four Masoretic contractions (in vv. 7a, 9b, 14a, 18b) do not reflect the pronunciation at the time when the poem was composed and that we should therefore adopt the older and more original longer syllable count, the total would be 367. We could, then, suppose that none of the suffixed forms (second masc. sing. pronominal suffix) was given the long pronunciation, while the single case of the second masc. sing. perfect verb would have had the longer count. This would add one more to the total, and it would come out exactly at 368. I make no claim that this is the technique the poet employed, or that the poem was actually counted out in this fashion. I simply suggest one plausible way in which the syllables could be counted to reflect the structure of the poem. As in the poetry of all languages and cultures, minor variations or deviations from the norm are only to be expected, but here we are very close to the mark. Regardless of the precise representation, I think it is clear that the text of Psalm 25, as it has come down to us, is an example of an augmented or enhanced alphabetic acrostic poem. The additional or second *pe*-line was seen to be a plus, an extra line, with its own special significance for the enhanced structure, a signature or seal stamped on the original, as already discussed. The omission of the *waw*-line in this poem is thus seen to be a separate matter, although part of the overall schema; but its loss is already compensated for by the addition of a third colon to the bicola in vv. 5 and 7, thus bringing the number of cola in the first half of the poem to 22 to match the 22 cola of the second half, and making a total of 44 before we reach the appended line at the end of the poem. The overall syllable count, which is a lot closer to 368 than to the expected 352 for the normal 22-line acrostic poem, supports this interpretation of these curious phenomena, and as I have shown, the number 368 fits the poem quite reasonably.

Turning now to Psalm 34, we find a different arrangement and strategy for conforming to the metrical or quantitative norms or requirements of this type of poem. The basic features are the same as in the case of Psalm 25. Therefore I am predisposed to consider the second *pe*-line as an addendum or augmentation to the poem, while the loss of the *waw*-line will be compensated internally, that is, within the alphabetic structure of the poem as a whole. Furthermore, we would expect the deficiency to be made up within the same half of the poem, as in the case of Psalm 25. In other words, while a line has been left out, nothing in fact is missing. In the case of Psalm 25, the missing bicolon was replaced by a third colon in each of two nearby lines; the poet of Psalm 34 does not employ that strategy, perhaps because it may have seemed a little too obvious and simple. Perhaps the same poet wished to employ a more subtle or intricate technique and not leave easy traces to follow. In any case, no cola have been added in this poem, and we have only 44 cola for the 22 lines extant. At the same time, the poem belongs to the augmentation group, as can be shown by matching the two poems and counting both words and syllables. The two poems are almost identical in length by whichever counting system used, and that can hardly be accidental either:

	Words	Syllables	
Psalm 25	158	363-382	(368)
Psalm 34	157	369-373	(371)

Given all the matching points between the two psalms, it seems clear that they were also designed to be of equal length, something that does not just happen accidentally. Furthermore, the length, as we have seen in the case of Psalm 25, corresponds to the pattern for an augmented or enhanced alphabetic acrostic poem, namely the 23-line or 46-cola type. In the case of Psalm 25, the 22-line, 44-cola, standard type has been expanded through the addition of two cola to existing lines, whereas in Psalm 34 the enhancement is spread over the whole poem by the addition of words and syllables here and there to achieve the desired totals of words and syllables. Thus Psalm 34 has a range from a minimum of 369 syllables to a maximum of 373, according to my count, which fits well within the range for Psalm 25 (363 to 382). If the count in Psalm 34 is adjusted along the same lines as for Psalm 25, we would come out with 371 (restoring the syllables elided by the Masoretes in vv. 8, 10, while opting for the short form of the second masc. sing. pronominal suffix in v. 14 [twice]). This total is slightly higher than that for Psalm 25, and the latter total may be too low. If we averaged the minima and maxima for both psalms we would have slightly different numbers: 372.5 for Psalm 25 and 371 for Psalm 34. I think the numbers are close enough, however they are calculated, to show that the poems share the same pattern and structure. In the case of Psalm 34 the poet had a choice between the numbers 368, which was the norm for the 23-line, 46-cola, augmented acrostic poem, and 374, which would have been the norm for a 22-line, 44-cola acrostic poem augmented by adding a single syllable to each line, for a total of 17 syllables per line instead of 16 (which is essentially what this poet did). The resultant number, 371, is a compromise between the two norms (the average of 368 and 374). When we add in the special features of these alphabetic acrostic psalms, including the omission of the *waw*-line, and the addition of the second *pe*-line, it is clear that the poems have been created out of the same basic mold. But in reaching a common goal, the poet or poets proceeded along somewhat different paths and pursued different tactics. In the one case (Ps. 25), the poet simply added two cola to other lines of the poem to make up the desired total of 46 cola and 368 syllables, while in the other case (Ps. 34), the poet judiciously added enough syllables to the 22-line, 44-cola poem, to reach the same goal.

Postscript

In the accompanying charts, I have given syllable and accent counts for both poems. Regarding the number and distribution of the accents, I have followed the MT almost slavishly, but here and there indicated alternate possibilities based on Masoretic usage in similar situations. As is generally known, there is considerable flexibility and leeway in the Masoretic accentual system, with the same or similar words receiving or not receiving accents (depending in part on whether they are connected through *maqqeph*, in which case the first word of the pair often loses an expected accent). Then there is the somewhat arbitrary use of the *metheg* which may be regarded as a secondary accent. The same particles, such as כי, ל, and so on, may stand alone and have an accent or be tied to the following word and each lose its accent; or in such cases the *metheg* may be used. So precision in the matter of recovering the plan of the original poet can hardly be expected or attained. Nevertheless, and especially because the accentual approach remains dominant in this field, it is worthwhile to record the results, which agree overall and quite emphatically with the basic argument presented here. If I am right in supposing that the basic pattern is a 23-line, 46-colon poem in both cases, then we would expect a total of 138 accents, corresponding to the 23 lines at 6 accents per line, or 46 cola at 3 accents per colon (these being balanced lines of 3 + 3 = 6 accents each). In the case of Psalm 25 there are 46 cola and a total of 138 accents, precisely as expected, although not distributed exactly evenly among the lines and cola (the principle of compensation seems to be at work here; that is, if one line or colon has more than the expected number of accents, another line or colon will have fewer, and vice versa). In Psalm 34, with only 44 cola, the total number of accents nevertheless ranges between 133 and 139, so the results are not much different. It would not be difficult to reach a total of 138, which in any case seems to be the target number.[5]

5. One remaining alphabetic acrostic psalm has some common and different features when compared with the two psalms under consideration in this paper. One of the internal lines has been omitted from Ps. 145, although it is not the *waw*-line, as in the case of Pss. 25 and 34, but the *nun*-line, for which there is no other precedent. Other manuscripts (from Cave XI of Qumran) and versions, supply a *nun*-line to make up for the apparent loss. In the light of our findings about the two psalms discussed in this paper, however, it is possible that the omission was deliberate. Furthermore, while Ps. 145 has only 21 lines, there is considerable evidence of augmentation, although there is no second *pe*-line at the end of the psalm. The number of words is less than the total for Pss. 25 and 34, 150 against 158 and 157, but the number of syllables is very close to the totals for the two earlier psalms: a range from 371 to 395 compared with 363 to 382 for Psalm 25 and 369 to 373 for Ps. 34. Applying the same general rules to Ps. 145 that we applied to the other psalms, we arrive at a total of 374 syllables for Ps. 145 (counting certain syllables that are elided in the MT, but also selecting the short form of the 2nd masc. sing. pronominal suffix against the MT vocalization), compared with totals of 368 for Ps. 25 and 371 for Ps. 34. A preliminary judgment would be that in Ps. 145 the poet uses the same basic mold of the augmented alphabetic acrostic poem, but has departed even more radically from the pattern observed in the two other psalms. Thus the poet has dispensed not only with one of the internal lines of the poem (though a different line from the one omitted in the other poems), but also with the added external *pe*-line observed in the other two poems. At the same time, syllables were added throughout. The author especially made up for the deficiency in the half of the poem in which one line was omitted, so that the 10 lines of the second half more than match the 11 lines of the first half, a circumstance already observed in both of the other poems. There is a family connection, although the resemblance between the third psalm and the other two has been attenuated. It is more like a second cousin, whereas the other two are more like siblings, but hardly twins.

Psalm 25

	Syllables					Accents		
A	B	C	Total	*Verse*	A	B	C	Total
4	7		11	**1**	2	3		5
8	8		16	**2**	3	3		6
8	9		17	**3**	4	3		7
9	8		17	**4**	3	2		5
13	8	8	29	**5**	3	4	3	10
11	6		17	**6**	3	3		6
13	8	6	27	**7**	4	2	3	9
6	9		15	**8**	2	4		6
8	9		17	**9**	3	3		6
9	11		20	**10**	4	3		7
Sub-Total 89	83	14	186	**1-10**	31	30	6	67
6	11		17	**11**	3	4		7
8	7		15	**12**	4	3		7
6	6		12	**13**	3	3		6
7	8		15	**14**	3	2		5
7	8		15	**15**	3	5		8
8	8		16	**16**	2	4		6
8	9		17	**17**	3	2		5
8	8		16	**18**	3	2		5
8	9		17	**19**	3	3		6
9	8		17	**20**	3	4		7
7	4		11	**21**	2	2		4
Sub-Total 82	86		168	**11-21**	32	34		66
9	5		14	**22**	3	2		5
Sub-Total 89	83	14	186	**1-10**	31	30	6	67
Sub-Total 82	86	14	182	**11-22**	32	34	5	71
Totals 171	169	28	368		63	64	11	138

Psalm 34

	Syllables					Accents	
A	*B*	*Total*	**Verse**	*A*	*B*		*Total*
10	8	18	**2**	3	3		6
8	10	18	**3**	3	3		6
8	9	17	**4**	3	3		6
10	11	21	**5**	3	3		6
9	8	17	**6**	3	2		5
10	9	19	**7**	4	3		7
6	11	17	**8**	3	3		6
9	7	16	**9**	4	3		7
9	8	17	**10**	3	3		6
9	12	21	**11**	3	4		7
Sub-total 88	93	181	**2-11**	32	30		62
7	8	15	**12**	3	3		6
8	7	15	**13**	3	4		7
7	9	16	**14**	3	3		6
7	8	15	**15**	3	3		6
8	7	15	**16**	3	2		5
8	7	15	**17**	4	3		7
8	9	17	**18**	3	3		6
9	8	17	**19**	4	3		7
6	10	16	**20**	3	3		6
6	9	15	**21**	2	4		6
7	9	16	**22**	3	3		6
Sub-total 81	91	172	**12-22**	34	34		68
8	10	18	**23**	4	4		8
Totals 177	194	371		70	68		138

Psalm 145

	Syllables					Accents		
	A	B	Total	Verse	A	B	Total
	9	12	21	**1**	3	4	7
	7	12	19	**2**	2	4	6
	10	7	17	**3**	4	3	7
	8	8	16	**4**	4	2	6
	6	10	16	**5**	3	3	6
	10	10	20	**6**	3	2	5
	7	8	15	**7**	3	2	5
	7	7	14	**8**	3	4	7
	5	8	13	**9**	3	3	6
	7	9	16	**10**	3	2	5
	8	9	17	**11**	3	2	5
Sub-total	84	100	184	**1-11**	34	31	65
	13	8	21	**12**	4	3	7
	9	9	18	**13**	3	3	6
	10	9	19	**14**	4	3	7
	9	13	22	**15**	3	5	8
	6	8	14	**16**	3	3	6
	9	7	16	**17**	4	3	7
	9	11	20	**18**	4	4	8
	7	11	18	**19**	3	4	7
	9	9	18	**20**	4	3	7
	9	15	24	**21**	4	6	10
Sub-total	90	100	190	**12-21**	36	37	73
Totals	174	200	374		70	68	138

EZRA AND QOHELETH MANUSCRIPTS FROM QUMRAN (4QEZRA, 4QQOHᴬ, ᴮ)

Eugene Ulrich

The books of Ezra and Qoheleth have been favorite biblical books for Joseph Blenkinsopp over the years.[1] Neither Ezra nor Qoheleth, however, were extensively preserved among the manuscripts discovered at Qumran. Out of all the MSS of these books which must have been copied in antiquity, only one of Ezra and two of Qoheleth have surviving fragments. Since the order of the biblical books dictates that these Ezra and Qoheleth MSS will be published only in the last of the biblical volumes in the series *Discoveries in the Judaean Desert*, it seems both a fitting tribute in honor of my colleague Professor Blenkinsopp, and a service to scholars interested in the Qumran biblical MSS, to provide preliminary editions of these MSS here. The purpose of this paper, accordingly, is to present editions of 4QEzra, 4QQohelethᵃ and 4QQohelethᵇ, and to begin to reflect on what these small MSS teach us.[2] In the latter regard focus will especially be on proposing a means of classifying variants between textual witnesses, a means which illumines the level at which so-called 'higher criticism' and 'lower criticism' intersect.

---

1. J. Blenkinsopp, *Ezra–Nehemiah: A Commentary* (OTL; Philadelphia: Westminster Press, 1988); 'A Theological Reading of Ezra–Nehemiah', *Proceedings of the Irish Biblical Association* 12 (1989), pp. 26-36; 'The Mission of Udjahorresnet and those of Ezra and Nehemiah', *JBL* 106 (1987), pp. 409-21; and *Wisdom and Law in the Old Testament* (London: Oxford University Press, 1983).
2. I thank Peter W. Flint and Robert A. Kugler for their help in producing these editions and for insightful contributions to the discussion which follows.

4QEzra

(PLATE 1)

Introduction

The leather of the 4QEzra scroll is thin, tan, well-prepared and polished. The darkening and contraction in the bottom right and left corners of frg. 3 appear to be the result of moisture. The largest fragment (frg. 3) measures about 5.4 cm at its highest, top to bottom, and 5.5 cm at its widest point. Fragments 1 and 2, as the photograph reveals, are considerably smaller. There is irregular spacing visible especially in frg. 3; the distance between the tops of lines varies from 0.6 to 0.8 cm.

The manuscript is written in a formal hand from the late Hasmonaean period or the transition into the Herodian period, with similarities to the scripts of 4QSam[a] and 4QDan[a].[3] According to Cross's typological schema, it would thus date to the middle of the first century BCE.[4] The formation of letters is fairly consistent, though they are quite small; Cross describes them as 'minuscule'. The number of letters per line in frgs. 1 and 2 ranges from 65 to 70; in frg. 3 the number is consistently somewhat over 70 letters per line. The resulting average line length can be estimated at about 10.5 cm.

The text preserves Ezra 4.2-6, 9-11 and 5.17–6.5. Parallels with 1 Esdras are:

4QEzra	1 Esdras	4QEzra	1 Esdras
4.2	5.66	6.1	6.22a
4.3	5.67-68	6.2	6.22b
4.4	5.69	6.3	6.23-24a
4.5	5.70	6.4	6.24b
5.17	6.20-21	6.5	6.25

The orthography is similar to that in 𝔐, although the MS displays correct forms twice, highlighting phonetic-orthographic lapses in 𝔐:

3. See F.M. Cross, 'A New Qumran Biblical Fragment Related to the Original Hebrew Underlying the Septuagint', *BASOR* 132 (1953), pp. 15-26; and E. Ulrich, 'Daniel Manuscripts from Qumran. Part 1: A Preliminary Edition of 4QDan[a]', *BASOR* 268 (1987), pp. 17-37.

4. See F.M. Cross, 'The Development of the Jewish Scripts', in *The Bible and the Ancient Near East: Essays in Honor of William Foxwell Albright* (ed. G.E. Wright; Garden City, NY: Doubleday, 1961), p. 138, fig. 2, ll. 3 and 4.

נהרא in frg. 2 line 3 (Ezra 4.10) versus נהרה in ℳ; and מדינתא in frg. 3 line 4 (Ezra 6.2) versus מדינתה in ℳ.

Variants are listed for those instances where the scroll is extant and there is disagreement among the four textual witnesses: 4QEzra, ℳ, 𝕲 Ezra, and 1 Esdras.

Museum location: Rockefeller Museum, Inventory Number 1124. Photograph numbers: Palestine Archaeological Museum 43.089; 41.301, 42.638.

Frg. 1 Ezra 4.2-6 [2-5 // 1 Esd. 5.66-70]

[ככם נדרוש ל[אל]היכם ולא אנחנו זבחים מימי אסר חדן מלך אשור המעלה אתנו]	1
[פה ³ויאמר] להם ז[רבבל וישוע ושאר ראשי האבות לישראל לא לכם ולנו לבנות]	2
[בית לאלהינו]כי אנ֯ח֯נו יחד נבנה ליהוה אלהי ישראל כאשר צונו המלך כורש מלך]	3
[פרס ⁴ויהי עם ה]ארץ מ֯[רפים ידי עם יהודה ומבלהים אותם לבנות ⁵וסכרים]	4
[עליהם יועצים ל]הפר עצתם֯ כל ימי כורש מלך פרס ועד מלכות דריוש מלך פרס]	5
[⁶ובמלכות אחשורוש בתח]ל֯ת מלכו֯ת֯ו	6

Variant

4.2 (1)   ל[אל]היכם ℳ] τω θεω υμων 𝕲; του κυριου υμων 1 Esd. 5.66

Frg. 2 Ezra 4.9-11

[ספרא ושאר כנ[תה]ו[ן]ד֯י֯נ֯יא ואפרסתכיא טרפליא אפרסיא ארכוי בבליא]	1
[שושנכיא דהוא ע[למא ¹⁰ושאר אמ֯]א די הגלי אסנפר רבא ויקירא והותב המו]	2
[בקריה די שמרין]ושאר עבר נהרא וכענ֯ת֯ ¹¹דנה פרשגן אגרתא די שלחו עלוהי]	3
[על ארתחששתא מ[ל]כא]ע֯ב֯ד֯י֯ך אנש עבר] נהרה וכענת ¹²	4

Frg. 3 Ezra 5.17–6.5 [// 1 Esd. 6.20-25]

הן איתי די מן]	]o[¹⁷]	1
[כורש מלכא שים טעם למבנא ב]ת אלהא דך ב֯[ירו]שלם ורעות מלכא על דנה ישלח עלינא]		2
[¹⁶·¹באדרן דריוש מלכא שם ט[עם ובקר בבית ספ]ריא די גנזיא מהחתין תמה בבבל ²והשתכח]		3
[באחמתא בבירתא די במדי]מ֯ד֯ינתא מגלה חדה [ו]כ֯ן כת֯[יב בגוה דכרונה ³בשנת חדה לכורש]		4
[מלכא כורש מלכא שם טע]ם֯ בית אלהא בירושלם ית[ב]נא יתבנא אתר די דבחין דבחין]		5
[ואשוהי מסובלין רום]ה֯ אמ֯[י]ן שתין פ֯ת֯יה אמין שתין ⁴נ֯ד֯ב֯כ֯י֯ן די[ן] אבן גלל תלתא]		6
[ונדבך די אע חדת ונפקה]א֯ מן בית מלכא תתי֯ה֯ב ⁵ואף מאני בי[ת אלהא די דהבה]		7
[וכספא די נבוכדנצר הנפק]מ֯ן היכלא די בירושלם והיבלו לב[בל יהתיבון ויהך]		8
[להיכלא די בירושלם לאהרה]ו֯ת֯ח֯ת֯ ב֯ב֯ית אלהא vacat o]ooכ	9

Line 7 (6.4) תת֯יהב. It is difficult to determine whether the third letter is *yod* or *waw*; the form could be תתוהב, showing the historical root, but cf. the *yod* in the first בית in line 5.

142   *Priests, Prophets and Scribes*

Variants

6.1 (3)   וּבְקֹר 𝕲 (και επεσκεψατο)] ובקרו 𝔐; επισκεψασθαι 1 Esd. 6.22

6.2 (4)   בְּמָדִי[אֹ 𝔐 (חה-; see Introduction)] της Μηδων πολεως 𝕲; τη εν Μηδια χωρα 1 Esd. 6.22

6.4 (7)   תחיהב מלכא ביה מן 𝔐 𝕲] δοθηναι εκ του οικου Κυρου του βασιλεως 1 Esd. 6.24

6.5 (8)   והיבלו] והיבל 𝔐 𝕲 (και εκομισεν) 1 Esd. 6.25 (και απηνεγκεν)

6.5 (9)   אלהא בבית זהחת 𝔐] ου ετεθη εν οικω του θεου 𝕲; οπως τεθη εκει 1 Esd. 6.25

4QQoheleth^a

(PLATE 2)

Introduction

This scroll is one of only two manuscripts found at Qumran containing text from the book of Qoheleth, or Ecclesiastes, and was published preliminarily by J. Muilenburg.[5] The extant manuscript preserves portions of Qoheleth 5.13-17; 6.1?, 3-8, 12; 7.1-10, 19-20. The largest fragment (frg. 1) measures 17.2 cm across the top margin, has a maximum height of 6.2 cm, and contains the remains of three contiguous columns. A second fragment (frg. 6) measures 9.3 cm along its bottom margin.

The leather is thin, well-prepared and creamy tan in color. Deterioriation is evident in several places (for example, ll. 13–14 of col. II). Random dots are scattered over the fragments; for instance, in col. I 4 one dot is within the *he* of זמֹ[and another lies above the *waw* of לו. The top margin of c. 1.4 cm is preserved on frg. 1, and the bottom margin of c. 1.3 cm, measured from the ruling of the last line, is extant on frg. 6 (ignoring הבל towards the right edge). Right and left margins are preserved between each of the three columns, measuring c. 1.0 cm between cols. I and II, and c. 0.8 cm between cols. II and III. The width of col. II measures c. 11.1 cm, and the height of the original inscribed column may be estimated at c. 12.1 cm. The total height of the manuscript would thus have been about 14.9 cm.

The horizontal ruling of the manuscript is still visible, and the distance between the lines of script varies from 0.5 to 0.9 cm. There were probably 20 lines per column, although the scribe inserted some omitted text in the top margin of col. II, and הבל is written in the

5.   'A Qoheleth Scroll from Qumran', *BASOR* 135 (1954), pp. 20–28.

bottom margin of col. II. The number of letters (including spaces between words) per line ranges from 30 to 42.

The manuscript is inscribed in an archaic semiformal hand, which is spacious and elegant, and is dated by F.M. Cross at approximately 175–150 BCE.

Orthography

The manuscript contains several types of orthographic differences from 𝔐. Most of these involve the presence of *waw* where 𝔐 lacks it.[6]

Line	Qoh	Qoh^a	𝔐	Line	Qoh	Qoh^a	𝔐
I 7	5.17	בכול	בכל	II 4	6.6	הכול	הכל
II 1	6.4	ובחושך 1°	ובחשך 1°	II 4	6.7	כול	כל
II 1sup	6.4	ובחושך 2°	ובחשך 2°	II 5	6.7	לוא	לא
II 2	6.5	לוא	לא	II 15	7.2	כול	כל
II 2	6.5	ולוא	ולא	II 16	7.3	משחוק	משחק
II 4	6.6	לוא	לא	II 18	7.5	לשמוע	לשמע
II 4	6.6	הלוא	הלא	II 20	7.6	שחוק	שחק

One word appears in two orthographic forms:

5.14 (I 1)　　כיא (note כאשר 𝔐) but כי in 6.4 and 7.6

Once *he* is written where 𝔐 correctly has *aleph*, and once a word appears without the *aleph* found in 𝔐:

6.4 (II 1)　　בה [בא 𝔐
7.8 (III 3)　　מרשיתו [מראשיתו 𝔐

On two occasions the fuller orthography allows for only one interpretation of a word which is otherwise ambiguous on the basis of the 𝔐 consonants alone:

6.5 (II 2)　　נחת [נוחת 𝔐 [variant or orthography?]
7.5 (II 18)　　נערת [נערות 𝔐 [variant or orthography?]

The scribe made several errors, erasures and insertions into the text. These will be described in the notes.

---

6. Cf. Muilenburg, 'A Qoheleth Scroll', pp. 24-26, and the literature cited there.

Museum location: Department of Antiquities of Jordan, Amman.
Photograph numbers: Palestine Archaeological Museum 43.092;
40.580 [frg. 7], 40.602, 40.607, 40.615, 40.967, 42.005, 42.638.

Col. I: Frg. 1 i Qoh. 5.13-17

top margin

1   בעינין רע והוליד בן ואין בידו מאו]מֹה ¹⁴כיא[

2   יצא מבטן אמו ערום ישוב ללכת]כשבא[

3   ומאומה לא ישא בעמלו שילך בי]דֹו ¹⁵גם זה[

4   רעה חולה כול עמת שבא כן ילך]וֹמה יתרון לו[

5   שיעמל לרוח ¹⁶גם כול ימיו בחשך   כעס°[

6   הרבה וחליו וקצף ¹⁷הנה אשר ראי]תֹ[י] אֹנֹי טוב[

7   אשר יפה לאכול ולשתות ולראות טו]בֹה בכול עמלו[

8   שיעמל תחת השמש מספר ימי חיו]אשֹר נֹתֹן לו[

Both a top and a left margin are preserved for this column. Random
spots dot the surface; the most confusing one appears within the *he* of
וֹמה[in line 4.

Line 4 (5.15). An ink-mark lies above the *waw* of לו.

Line 5 (5.16) ‏כעס°[ ]. The *kaph* appears to be written over some
other letter (ר?), and ink from a previous letter is visible before it.
There was probably no *lamedh* in the preceding word (cf. יאכל 𝔐),
since enough of the leather apparently remains that the top of a
lamedh would be visible had it originally been there (cf. לו in line 8
below).

Line 7 (5.17). A hole follows the *waw* of עמלו.

Variants

5.14 (1)   כיא] כאשר 𝔐𝔊(καθως)
5.15 (3)   גם 𝔐^{ed. J. ben Chayyim}; cf. 7.6] וגם 𝔐𝔊(και γε)

Frg. 2 Qoh. 6.1?

(1)   ]   ורבה הי]א על הֹ]אדם ²   [

Line 1 (5.17). The penultimate letter may be *lamedh* written over
daleth; cf. the *lamedh*s in כול (col. II 15) and כקול (II 19). However,
it is not certain whether this fragment has been placed correctly. If it
does belong here, it would have been near the bottom of col. I.

Col. II: Frgs. 1 ii, 3–6 i Qoh. 6.3-8, 12–7.6

top margin

f. 1   הלך ובחושך שמו

אמרתי טוב הנפל ממנו ⁴כי בהבל בה ובחושך   1

שמו יכסה ⁵גם שמש לוא ראה [ו]לוא ידע נחת לזה   2

מזה ⁶ואם לוא חיה אלף שנים פעמים וטובה   3

לוא ראה הלוא אל מקום אחד הכול הולך ⁷כול   4

עמל האדם לפיהו וגם הנפש לוא תמל[א]   5

⁸כמה יותר לחכם מ[ן] הכסיל מה לעני יודע[6

∘∘ל∘∘ ∘ל[ ] החיים ⁹טוב מראה עינים מהלך נפש]   7

[גם זה הבל ורעות רוח ¹⁰מה שהיה כבר נקרא]   8

[שמו ונודע אשר הוא אדם ולא יוכל לדין עם]   9

[שהתקיף ממנו ¹¹כי יש דברים הרבה מרבים]   10

[הבל מה יתר לאדם ¹²כי מי יודע מה טוב לאדם]   11

f. 3, 4   בחיים[   ]∘[ ]שמ יג[יד לאדם]   12

f. 5   [מה יהיה אחרי תחת השמ[ש ⁷·¹טוב שם]∘[ ]ן[∘]   13

[טוב ויום המות מיום הו[לדו ²טוב ללכת אל בית   14

f. 6   [אבל מלכת אל בית ש[מחה] באשר ה[ו]אה כול סו[ף   15

[האדם והחי יתן]∘∘ל לבו ³טוב כעס משחוק   16

[כי ברע פנים יי[טב לב ⁴לב חכמים בית אבל   17

[ולב כסילים]∘בית שמחה ⁵טוב לשמע גערות   18

[חכם מ[לשמ̇ע ////////]שיר כסילים ⁶כי כקול   19

[הסירים ת[ח]ת הסיר כן שחוק הכסיל גם זה   20

[הבל   ]

bottom margin

The entire top margin, as well as parts of the other three margins, are preserved for this column.

Lines 1–2 (6.4). The scribe seems to have written שמו immediately after ובחושך 1°, thus omitting הלך ובחושך 2° by parablepsis. Realizing his error, he proceeded to erase שמו in line 2 and to insert הלך ובחושך שמו above line 1 and extending beyond the left margin. The mark following שמו has the appearance and possible function of a parenthesis. The parallelism and lack of textual disturbance in 𝔐 for this verse indicate that this is a simple scribal correction of an error, rather than an intentional emendation in order to produce conformity with another reading.

Line 7 (6.8). The reading of this line is problematic. The tops of two clear *lamedh*s (the second possibly erased), about 2 cm apart, are clearly visible early in the line; however, this configuration does not match 𝔐 (להלך נגד) for these words. Line 7 may therefore contain the remains of a variant reading, part of which may have been erased.

Line 12 (6.12). The reading of 𝕸 for this line is בחיים מספר ימי חיי הבלו ויעשם כצל אשר מי יגיד לאדם, but that is too long for this line. Perhaps the MS had a shorter reading or had one more line than the transcription indicates. At any rate, the extant letters disagree with 𝕸.

Line 17 (7.3). יי.[טבלב. The scribe did not divide between the words.

Line 18 (7.4). בית°. A small ink trace of the letter prior to *beth* remains on the surface of the leather. The large dark spot and the two small spots above are not on the writing surface of the leather.

Line 19 (7.5). Two corrections appear to have been made here. First, the scribe seems to have written מלמוע and then altered it to מלשמוע via the supralinear insertion of ש (see variant). Secondly, a word originally preceded שיר but was erased, leaving a space of c. 2cm.

Line 20sub (7.6). Space for about 10 letters would have preceded הבל; this may signify a longer text than גם זה\והבל, an erasure (thus Muilenburg), or possibly a defect in the leather. The position of הבל in the bottom margin indicates that the scribe probably intended to avoid writing the end of a section at the top of the next column.

Variants

6.3 (1) הנפל הנפל] ממנו 𝕸𝕲; note 3[a–a] in *BHS* seems incorrect, although the lack of a critical edition for the LXX of Qoheleth precludes final judgment on this issue.

6.4 (1sup) הלך] ילך 𝕸; πορευεται 𝕲

6.5 (2) נחת] נוחת 𝕸𝕲 [variant or orthography?]

6.6 (3) ואלו] ואם לוא 𝕸 (cf. Est. 7.4); και ει 𝕲

6.8 (6) כי מה] כמה 𝕸𝕲

6.12 (12) אשר מי יגיד (εν σκια 𝕲)] [°[ ] שם י]נֿ[יד 𝕸 𝕲 ויעשם כצל (see note)

7.2 (15) משׁה] מחה[ש 𝕸ms ; cf. v. 4 et Est. 7.4] 𝕸𝕲

7.4 (17) בית] בבית 1° 𝕸 𝕲

7.5 (18) נערות] נערת 𝕸 𝕲(επιτιμησιν) [variant or orthography?]

7.5 (19) מאיש שמע 𝕸 𝕲] מלשמע*;corr] מלמוע

7.6 (20) וגם 𝕸 𝕲(και γε)] גם 𝕸ed. J. ben Chayyim

Col. III: Frgs. 1 iii, 6 ii, 7   Qoh. 7.7-10, 19-20

top margin

f. 1

[כי העשק יהולל⁷] ////////////////////////   1

[חכם ויעוה]את לב מתנה ⁸טוב אחרית דבר]   2

[מרשיתו]טוב ארך רוח מגבה רוח ⁹אל תבהל]   3

[ברוח]ך לכעוס כי כעס בחיק כסילים ינוח]   4

[¹⁰א]ל [תאמר מה היה שהימים הראשנים היו]   5

[11 lines missing]

f. 6

[   ]◦   17

f. 7

[ה]חכמה]תעזר ◦◦   מעשרה שליטים]   18

[ש]היו] בעיר ²⁰כי אדם אין צדיק בארץ]   19

[ש]יע]שה טוב ו]לא יחטא   20

bottom margin

Part of the top, bottom and right margins are preserved for this column. Fragment 7, included in the photograph published by Muilenburg in 1954 but not on the more recent photographs, has been restored in the one used for this edition.

Line 1 (7.6fin-7init). Several words were originally written but seem to have been erased. Most commentators have sought to correct 𝔐 at this point, whether by emendation or by inserting additional text. Two previous proposals are: (1) טוב מעט בצדקה מרב תבואות בלא משפט 'Better is little with righteousness than great revenues with injustice' (cf. Prov. 16.8); and (2) טוב מלא כף בצדקה ממלא חפנים בעשק 'Better is the filling of the hand with righteousness than the filling of both hands with oppression' (cf. *BHS* note 6a-a and Qoh. 4.6).

Line 18 (7.19). The first letter may be *he*. The first dark spot at the right margin is the bottom tip of the right leg. At the left edge of the fragment is the juncture of the horizontal stroke with the angled top of the left leg. But the middle dark spot is off the surface of the leather, caught in the cellulose tape, and thus not part of the letter. To the left of תעזר are traces of two uncertain letters (𝔐 has לחכם).

Line 20 (7.20). The first letter cannot form *aleph* (cf. 𝔐 אשר) or *ayin* in this hand; see variant.

Variants

7.7 (2)	ויעוה [ויאבד 𝔐 𝔊(απολλυσι)
7.19 (18)	תעזר 𝔐mss 𝔊(βοηθησει)] העז 𝔐
7.19 (19)	ש]היו] [אשר היו 𝔐
7.20 (20)	ש]יע]שה [אשר יעשה 𝔐

4QQoheleth*ᵇ*

(PLATE 1)

Introduction

Only two fragments survive from this manuscript. The leather is thin and friable, now dark brown to black, and decayed. There are few samples of letters for classifying the script, but it shares characteristics of late Hasmonaean and some early Herodian hands, and thus can be dated around the middle of the first century BCE, though possibly as late as the early first century CE.

Two instances of orthography fuller than that in 𝔐 are found in what remains of this manuscript:

1.10 (1)	𝔐 לעלמים] לעולמים
1.11 (2)	𝔐 לו] לוא

Museum location: Rockefeller Museum, Inventory Number 1117.
Photograph numbers: Palestine Archaeological Museum 43.090; 42.005, 42.635.

Frgs. 1–2 Qoh. 1.10-14 (15?)

f. 1	כ[ב]ר היה לעולמים] אשר היה מלפנו ¹¹אין[	1
	[זכרון לראשנים וגם לאחרי]ם שיהיו לוא יהיה] להם זכרון[	2
	[עם שיהיו לאחרנה ¹²אני ק]הלת הייתי מל[ך על ישראל בירושלם[	3
f. 2	[¹³ונתתי א]ת לבי לדרוש [ולתור בחכמה ע]ל[ו] כל אשר נעשה תחת]	5
	[השמים הוא]ענין רע נתן [אלהים לבני האדם לענות בו ¹⁴ראיתי את כל]	6
	[המעשים]אשר נעשו תח[ת[	7
[	]גב[ן	8
[	] ∘[	9

Line 8 (1.15?). There can be little doubt about the *gimel-beth* below נעשו of line 7. The text found in 𝔐 has no *gimel* in the vicinity; the nearest is in הגדלתי (v. 16), but this is precluded by the *beth* and would also require far greater space than the fragment allows.

Variants

1.14 (7)	𝔐 שנעשו] אשר נעשו
1.15? (8)	[גב[ן] aliter 𝔐 (see note)

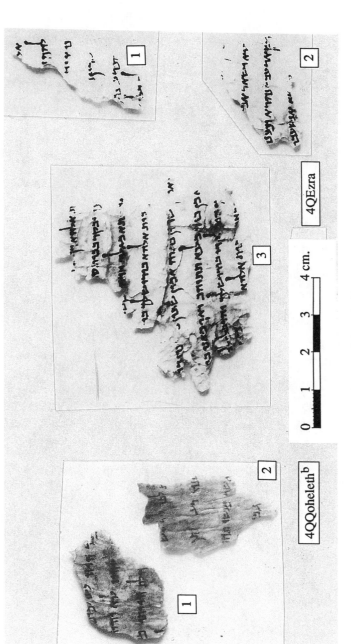

Plate 1. *4QEzra 4QQoheleth^b*

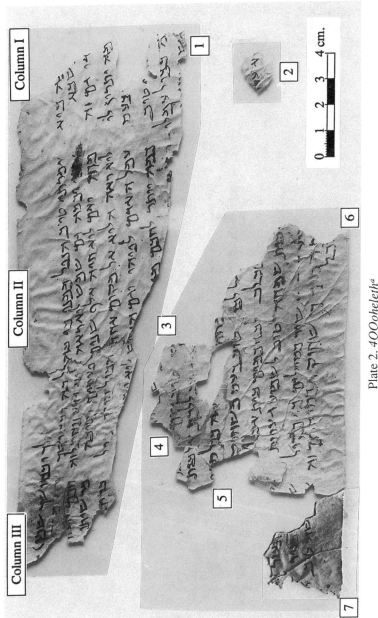

Plate 2. *4QQoheleth[a]*

Literary Activity in the Second Temple Period

The study of these manuscripts can lead in many directions. Here I would like to discuss classification of some types of literary or scribal activity that characterized the late Second Temple period. A generous array of types of activity exercised by the learned scribes can be documented and illustrated by the use of new material from the Judaean Desert, though the clues have long been available in the MT and the versions. For example, examination of the types of variants found in MSS in the Massoretic tradition, MSS from the Judaean Desert, and MSS of the versions shows that scribes could copy existing texts exactly when they wished to do so, but that they could also develop texts in a variety of ways, in fact even according to identifiable categories.

Some MSS, such as 4QEzra, show that certain scribes at times set about copying a traditional form of a text and did so exactly, or at least as accurately as human nature would allow. Other manuscripts, however, such as 4QpaleoExod[m], show that scribes sometimes exercised the creative role of literary editor. In this case, some scribe produced a revised and expanded literary edition of the traditional text of Exodus. Between these two poles[7] there were many types of activity. With respect to revised editions, there were various types that can be described (see below).

To describe this array of literary activity it will be helpful to sort the kinds of textual variations observable in MSS according to three classifications that have been becoming increasingly clear: (1) orthographic differences, (2) individual variant readings, and (3) variant editions of works.[8]

1. Orthography

Orthographic differences can be described as different ways to spell a word, each of which is correct or at least understandable, with no dif-

7. Works displaying greater literary creativity beyond the pole represented by 4QpaleoExod[m] (e.g. the *pesharim*, 1QapGen, pap4QParaExod gr, 4QPentPar[a-d], 4QpsDan ar[a-c]) move outside the category normally termed biblical MSS.

8. See my, 'Pluriformity in the Biblical Text, Text Groups, and Questions of Canon', in *Proceedings of the International Congress on the Dead Sea Scrolls— Madrid, 18–21 March 1991* (ed. J. Trebolle Barrera and L. Vegas Montaner; STDJ, 10; Madrid: Universidad Complutense; Leiden: Brill, 1992), pp. 23-41, esp. pp. 29-37.

ference in meaning involved. Closer inspection can distinguish various subclassifications. One is characterized by the simple addition of *matres lectionis* as an aid to pronunciation. More often than not this results in no change in meaning. For example, note כול and לוא in 4QQohᵃ. On occasion, however, the use of *matres lectionis* is helpful from the perspective of historical grammar, indicating a shift in a scribal tradition's approach to the manner of signaling short and long vowels.

A second subclassification involves the insertion of *matres lectionis* as signs of interpretation on the part of the scribe (e.g. expanding לשמע to indicate לשמוע versus לשׁמע). 4QQohᵃ provides illustrations of this type: see נוחת for נחת in 𝔐 at 6.5, and גערות for גערת in 𝔐 at 7.5.

A third phenomenon entails the use of short versus long suffixes (e.g. ך- versus כה-, or ה- versus חה-). This is properly a morphological phenomenon, but in editions of Qumran MSS it can for practical reasons be included with orthographic differences since no change of meaning is involved. Neither the Ezra nor the Qoheleth MSS exhibit such variation, though it is useful to note it for general consideration.

A fourth subclassification involves the historically correct *mater lectionis* versus an incorrect, if understandable, one. I have noted above that 4QEzra twice displays correct forms in contrast to 𝔐: נהרא versus נהרה (Ezra 4.10), and מדינתא versus מדינתה (Ezra 6.2).

The significance of orthographic differences appears at first blush to be rather small. They do, however, contribute to the determination of textual history. For example, insofar as the expanded use of *matres lectionis* characterizes especially the later Second Temple period, the consistent appearance of full spellings in a MS helps to date it.[9] Moreover, when one discovers the addition of *matres lectionis* in a MS tradition which is then consistently followed in subsequent MSS, such orthographic evidence aids in the stemmatic ordering, both diachronically with respect to chronological age and synchronically with respect to family groups. For example, once a text with לשמע has been vocalized as לשׁומע, whether that interpretation is intentionally aimed at precluding לשמוע or is unintentional, any subsequent MS copied or translated from it will necessarily be aligned with the MS family which reads לשׁומע. Other unrelated MSS can, of course, independently

---

9. It should be remembered that this is simply a tendency. Manuscripts with expanded use of *matres lectionis* can, of course, be earlier than those without; for example, an early exemplar with fuller orthography can be older than a late exemplar copied exactly from a MS with sparse use of *matres lectionis*.

introduce לשמע, but other features will demonstrate its unrelatedness.

2. *Individual Variant Readings*

The category of individual variant readings serves as the routine category in which most textual variants are initially considered and as the focus of most text-critical discussion. This is as it normally should be, unless there is a reason to classify them otherwise.

The individual variant readings of 4QEzra and 4QQoh[a-b] are listed in the 'variants' section of the editions above. With but one exception they display little that is new or significant. 4QEzra again simply demonstrates that the Massoretic *textus receptus* of each of the books has been very faithfully preserved from one of the plural forms of the text which circulated in the Second Temple period. 4QQoh[a-b] demonstrate, as do MSS generally, apparently minor but occasional individual textual variants from what later became the traditional text.

The present discussion, however, attempts to bring added clarity by removing from this category both those types of variation between texts which have little bearing on the meaning of the text (orthographic differences) and those which have a larger, overarching influence on the text (variant editions).

3. *Variant Editions of Biblical Books or Passages*

Sometimes the variants of one textual form of a scriptural book or passage are not simply haphazard but form a coherent pattern, coalescing to constitute a variant literary edition of that book or passage.[10] The one exceptional aspect of the 4QEzra variants alluded to above is the fact that the readings in 1 Esdras, when seen as a whole, demonstrate a consistent pattern which transcends the level of individual variants and constitutes an intentionally different form of the work.

Elsewhere I have described an array of variant editions of biblical books and passages.[11] The book of Exodus was edited during the

10. It is not necessary that all textual variants in a certain MS consistently show signs of affiliation with the intentional pattern that constitutes the variant edition. Once the edition has been generated, each MS witness to that edition begins its own trajectory which will often include errors, additions, readings influenced by other text groups, etc. In such cases, some textual variants will exhibit the defining features of the variant edition, but others will appear anomalous.

11. 'The Canonical Process, Textual Criticism, and Latter Stages in the Composition of the Bible', in *Sha'arei Talmon: Studies in the Bible, Qumran, and the*

Second Temple period in such a way that a noticeably expanded edition—a form of which we had known in the Samaritan Pentateuch—was produced.[12] The David–Goliath episode in 1 Samuel 17–18 appears in one sufficient and coherent narrative in the LXX and in a second, conflate narrative in the MT. Similarly, the book of Jeremiah appears in one literary edition in the LXX and in a secondary, expanded edition in the MT. Recently it has been demonstrated that the Old Greek version of Daniel 4–6 and the Aramaic version in the MT are two differently developed editions of an earlier, but no longer extant, common core version of those narratives.[13] It may also be that beside the edition of the book of Psalms as it appears in the MT there were other expanded editions of the Psalter, as was earlier suggested by James Sanders concerning 11QPs[a].[14]

It appears that this was the normal manner in which the books that became our scriptures were composed and reached their developed forms. It was a process, a continuous process that could be called a sequence of revised editions of traditional material. The 'final' forms of the books as we know them resulted not so much because the formation process was completed, but because the process just suddenly froze or was terminated. It is possible that either the First Revolt against Rome, or the Second Revolt, or the escalating threat of Christianity, or a combination of these, put a sudden end to the era of the compositional growth of the Hebrew scriptures. The discussion concerning whether the final selections of texts by the Samaritans, the Rabbis and the early Christians was arbitrary or accidental or polemical, as opposed to being based on textual character or textual

Ancient Near East Presented to Shemaryahu Talmon (ed. M. Fishbane and E. Tov with W. Fields; Winona Lake, IN: Eisenbrauns, 1992), pp. 267-91, esp. pp. 276-87.

12. 4QpaleoExod[m], however, displays the major expansions witnessed by the Samaritan Pentateuch but apparently lacks the few specifically Samaritan theological features. This variant edition, therefore, was at home in Jewish circles prior to being adopted by the Samaritans. See DJD 9, and J. E. Sanderson, *An Exodus Scroll from Qumran: 4QpaleoExod[m] and the Samaritan Tradition* (HSS, 30; Atlanta: Scholars Press, 1986).

13. See D.O. Wenthe, 'The Old Greek Translation of Daniel 1–6' (unpublished PhD dissertation, University of Notre Dame, 1991).

14. See J.A. Sanders, 'The Qumran Psalms Scroll (11QPs[a]) Reviewed', in *On Language, Culture, and Religion: In Honor of Eugene A. Nida* (The Hague: Mouton, 1974), pp. 79-99, and the forthcoming dissertation of Peter W. Flint on 'The Psalters at Qumran'.

superiority, appears to merit further research.[15] Might we, for example, as we enter the third millennium have enough data and clarity to write commentaries which seriously analyse and incorporate the growth of texts within the communities that gradually produced them? The examples described above constitute various samples within the single category of 'revised edition'. But the book of Ezra may point us to a further category of scribal creativity. The following chart indicates in general the relationship between the contents of the MT of Ezra and those of 1 Esdras:

1 Esdras	*Chronicles–Ezra–Nehemiah*
1	2 Chron. 35; 36
2.1-15	Ezra 1
2.16-30	Ezra 4.7-24
3.1–5.6	[not in MT]
5.7-73	Ezra 2.1–4.5
6; 7	Ezra 5; 6
8.1–9.36	Ezra 7–10
9.37-55	Neh. 7.72–8.12

When one begins to study the interrelationship between Ezra and 1 Esdras, such charts appear useful. The impression received, however, can lead to a conclusion that 1 Esdras is a secondary work, drawing upon the completed Chronicles, Ezra and Nehemiah. But, as James VanderKam notes in his contribution above, 1 Esdras is not an amalgam of these three *books*.[16] It remains to be demonstrated whether the compiler of 1 Esdras excerpted from those completed books, or whether the latter in their traditional form are not the product of one or more literary editors drawing from the source(s) used independently by 1 Esdras.[17]

The purpose of this paper, however, is not to analyse and solve the

15. See my 'Pluriformity in the Biblical Text'.

16. See the essay by J.C. VanderKam, 'Ezra–Nehemiah or Ezra and Nehemiah', in this volume.

17. Since the oldest witness to Ezra/1 Esdras used to be Josephus, who used 1 Esdras for his narrative in the *Jewish Antiquities*, one valuable factor offered by 4QEzra is that it now provides yet earlier witness to the other form, viz. the MT of Ezra. Since both 4QEzra and Josephus, however, postdate the composition of both Ezra and 1 Esdras, a conceivable claim that 4QEzra establishes the compositional priority of the MT of Ezra would be as baseless as an earlier claim would have been that Josephus establishes the priority of 1 Esdras.

problem of the literary relationship between 1 Esdras and MT Ezra, but to provide more data than has been hitherto available and to suggest some clarified categories to help chart that task. If 1 Esdras turned out to be secondary to the form in the MT, then it would be classified as a text composed mostly of excerpts from known, related works. In that case it could be compared to the David–Goliath episode, insofar as 1 Esdras, like the MT version of 1 Samuel 17–18, added blocks of material from one source to augment a narrative that could, and already did, stand on its own.

The Ezra/1 Esdras example, however, might represent a fourth level of variation, wherein the difference is no longer like that found in Jeremiah (shorter and expanded texts) or in the David and Goliath story (two parallel traditions of the same story conflated), but amounts to a new version altogether, though dependent on its predecessor.

Some questions raised by these MSS, but which must await another opportunity or another hand, are:

1. Specifically, what is the relationship between 1 Esdras and 𝔐𝔊Ezra? In order to solve this problem a joint study is necessary that combines a rigorous and detailed textual analysis with a rigorous and detailed literary analysis.[18]

2. Canonically, are 1 Esdras and 𝔐𝔊Ezra still close enough to constitute an example of what I have termed 'variant editions' of the same biblical book, or is the development of one too distant from the other? In this discussion, two things should be remembered: first, the variant editions of Exodus, Samuel, Jeremiah, (Psalms?) and Daniel did function as alternate forms of the same canonical book; and secondly, some canonical lists include only one form of Ezra/1 Esdras, while some lists include both.

3. With regard to Bible translation, what are the criteria for deciding which form of the text is to be translated as 'The Holy Bible'? It

---

18. See R. Klein, 'New Evidence for an Old Recension of Reigns', *HTR* 60 (1967), pp. 93-105; 'Supplements in the Paralipomena: A Rejoinder', *HTR* 61 (1968), pp. 492-95; 'Old Readings in 1 Esdras: The List of Returnees from Babylon [Ezra 2/Nehemiah 7]', *HTR* 62 (1969), p. 107; J.D. Shenkel, 'A Comparative Study of the Synoptic Parallels in 1 Paralipomena and I-II Kings', *HTR* 62 (1969), pp. 63-86; and L.C. Allen, 'Further Thoughts on an Old Recension of Reigns in Paralipomena', *HTR* 61 (1968), pp. 483-91; *The Greek Chronicles. I. The Translator's Craft* (VTSup, 25; Leiden: Brill, 1974); *idem, The Greek Chronicles. II. Textual Criticism* (VTSup, 27; Leiden: Brill, 1974).

should not go unnoticed that, in the array of variant editions described above, the assortment of texts collected into the Massoretic *textus receptus* sometimes contains the earlier, sometimes a parallel, sometimes the later, edition of a particular book. As we continue to discover the richness and patterns that constitute the history of the composition and growth of the sacred literature that formed the scriptures of Second Temple and Rabbinic Judaism and early Christianity, how should decisions concerning the textual basis for translation be made?[19] Sometimes the form of the text to be translated is selected on the basis of confessional allegiance, often it is selected through the path of least resistance ('the Massoretic Text unless it is corrupt or difficult'). The issues are not simple; a defense can be made for the former; one wonders about the latter.

19. Some of these issues are discussed in my 'Double Literary Editions of Biblical Narratives and Reflections on Determining the Form to be Translated', in *Perspectives on the Hebrew Bible: Essays in Honor of Walter J. Harrelson* (ed. J.L. Crenshaw; Macon, GA: Mercer University Press, 1988 [= *Perspectives in Religious Studies* 15.4 (1988), pp. 101-16]), pp. 101-16.

WISDOM HIDDEN AND REVEALED
ACCORDING TO BARUCH (BARUCH 3.9–4.4)

Walter Harrelson

1. *Introductory Remarks*

a. *The Character of the Poem*
The poem on Wisdom in the book of Baruch brings together five
distinct and important biblical themes. While all of the themes are
developed in other biblical texts, some of them more fully and more
elegantly than in Baruch, the Baruch poem brings them together with
power and with sensitivity, producing a unified document of significant literary merit and religious discernment. The five themes are:
(1) Israel is in exile because of the people's abandonment of Wisdom;
(2) no mortal can find the path to Wisdom; (3) Wisdom was present
with God at the creation (see 3.32-34); (4) God has conferred the gift
of Wisdom upon Israel; and (5) that gift is identical with Torah.

The first theme is new. While earlier texts see wisdom as a fruit of
obedience to Torah (Deut. 4.6; Pss. 19.7 [MT 19.8]; 119.98), no earlier
text, I believe, explicitly connects the Babylonian exile with Israel's
forsaking the fountain of wisdom (Bar. 3.12). The second theme
clearly draws upon Job 28, where the hiddenness of Wisdom is vividly
portrayed. The author of Baruch uses the Job 28 theme in distinctive
ways, but is without doubt dependent upon the text from Job. For the
third theme, the author makes use of Prov. 8.22-31, which describes
Wisdom as present with God at the creation and an active participant
in the process—either as assisting in the task, or as a delighted and
enthusiastic bystander, or both (Prov. 8.30-31). The same theme is
found in Sirach 1 and 24, although significantly elaborated in the
latter chapter. The fourth theme also appears in Sirach 24, and the fifth
theme first finds explicit statement in Sirach 24. Thus there can be no
doubt that, as scholars have long noted, Baruch's poem on wisdom is

heavily dependent for its thought upon earlier writers and thinkers.[1]

The more elaborate presentation of Wisdom found in Wisdom of Solomon 7–9 does not seem to have been a direct source for Baruch. The notion of Wisdom as an emanation of the Godhead, present in history as the semi-divine Guide of the entire course of Israel's pilgrimage, offers a broader perspective on Wisdom than that found in Baruch's specific identification of Wisdom and Torah. Since Sirach is dated to the early second century BCE, while Wisdom of Solomon is generally assigned to the middle or late first century BCE, we may suppose that our author composed the poem on Wisdom at some point in the late second or the early first century BCE. The other two parts of the book, and the book itself, probably belong to the same general period, and all three parts may have been produced in Palestine.[2]

b. *The Poem's Purpose*

The purpose of the poem on Wisdom seems to have been to under-score the need for the people of God to recognize two realities at once. The first is that the Torah offers to an embattled community all the guidance for life that the community needs. Torah is nothing less than the first of God's creations, Wisdom herself, rich in glory and mystery, full of life and guidance for Israel now and always. The second is the fact that God's Torah, identified as it is with Wisdom, has within it such secret recesses that its interpretation is a task never completed. Indeed, Torah arises out of the mystery of the Creation itself. God alone knows the way to Wisdom in its fullness; and in a certain sense, God has things to learn from this mystery that is Wisdom. I will speculate below as to the likely social and religious setting of such a poem in the late second or the early first century BCE.

Exposition of the five themes and of this purpose of the Wisdom poem will be attempted below. I will make some use of the old Ethiopic (Ge'ez) version of Baruch. Several early manuscripts of Baruch are now available in the Ethiopian Manuscript Microfilm Library of Addis Ababa, microfilm copies of which are on hand at the Hill Monastic Manuscript Library at St. John's University in Collegeville,

---

1. A thorough textual study containing many fine exegetical insights is D.G. Burke, *The Poetry of Baruch: A Reconstruction and Analysis of the Original Hebrew Text of Baruch 3.9–5.9* (SBLSCS, 10; Chico, CA: Scholars Press, 1982).

2. See the fine summary of evidence on the date, place and purpose of composition by Burke, *The Poetry of Baruch*, pp. 26-32.

Minnesota.[3] The Ethiopic version of Baruch may be of help in understanding some of the difficult readings in the poem, simply on the basis of its way of making sense, in a Semitic language, of the presumed Hebrew or the preserved Greek or Syriac text.

2. *Translation of the Poem from Ethiopic (Ge'ez)*

A translation of the Ethiopic text follows. A comparison with the LXX indicates that the Ethiopic must have been made from the LXX, although there are several interesting departures from the Greek text. A transliteration of the Ge'ez text is given below in the Appendix.

a. *Exile Due to Israel's Rejection of Wisdom (3.9-14)*

3.9 Hear, O Israel, the commandment of life;
        listen to the counsel of Wisdom.
10 Why, O Israel, is it,
        why is it that you are found in a strange land,
11 grow old in an alien country,
        are polluted among corpses,
        and counted among those in Sheol?
12 You have abandoned the fountain of life.
13 If you had walked in the way of God,
        you would have remained at peace forever.
14 Learn where there is Wisdom,
        and where there is strength;
    where there is counsel and knowledge,
        and where there is life
        for length of days;
    and where there is light
        for the eyes, and peace.

b. *The Way to Wisdom is Hidden (3.15-21)*

15 Who has found out her place?
        Who has entered into her storehouses?
    Where are the leaders of the nations,
16   those who exercised rule over the beasts

---

3.   Among the oldest of the available manuscripts is EMML (Ethiopian Manuscript Microfilm Library) 2080. See f. 115a-116a. The manuscript dates to the thirteenth to fifteenth century. I am grateful to Dr Getatchew Haile and Dr Julian G. Plante of the Hill Monastic Manuscript Library for making available a photocopy of the relevant pages.

of the wilderness,
17   and amused themselves with the birds of heaven?
those who hoarded up silver and gold
        in which mortals place their trust,
and there is therefore no limit
        to their acquisition.
18   For they built up silver, and were watchful,
        and one is not able to fashion their works.
19   They have vanished, and gone down into Sheol,
        and others have arisen in their place.
20   Their offspring[4] have seen the light (of day),
        and have settled in the earth;
but the way of wisdom they did not learn,
21   or discover her path.
Their children did not accept her;
        they have gone far from their way.

c. *Even the Wisest of Nations are Ignorant of Wisdom (3.22-23)*

22   Canaan has not heard (of her),
        and Temona has not seen (her).
23   The Hagarites search for wisdom on the earth,
        the traders of Maryan and Teman;
those who tell tales of her (by her?),
        and those who seek knowledge.
But the way of wisdom they do not know;
        they do not remember (it).

d. *The Greatest of the Ancients Lacked Wisdom (3.24-28)*

24   O Israel, how great is the house of God!
        How vast his territory!
25   It is great, and beyond enumeration,
        and as for its height, there is no measure of it.
26   Those of renown were born there,
        those of great wealth, from ancient times;
        huge in stature, skillful in warfare.
27   God did not choose them,
        and did not give them the path to instruction.
28   And they perished, because they did not have Wisdom;
        they were blotted out because of their presumption.

4.   Literally, 'the young'.

e. *God Alone Knows the Hidden Path to Wisdom (3.29-36)*

29   Who has ascended to heaven and taken her
         and brought her down from the clouds?
30   Who has crossed the ocean and found her,
         and offered fine (lit. 'red') gold for her?
31   There is no one who knows her way,
         none who can boast of her path.
32   The One who knows all knows her (or 'it', i.e., her path),
         and it is by wisdom that he has discovered her;
     the One who created the world forever,
         the One who filled it with sheep and cattle.
33   He sends out his light, and it goes;
         he calls to it, and it obeys him with fear.
34   The stars shine forth in their times,
         and they sing aloud to one another.
35   He calls to them, and they say, 'We are coming!'
         They shine for their Maker with joy.
36   He is our Lord, for there is no other;
         there is no one who is like Him.

f. *God Revealed Wisdom to Israel (3.37-38)*

37   He found out the entire way of Wisdom,
         gave it[5] to his servant Jacob,
         to Israel, his beloved one.
38   And then she appeared on earth,
         and became like a mortal one.

g. *Wisdom Identified as God's Torah (4.1-4)*

4.1 This is the book of the commandment of God,
         the Law that is for all time.
     All those who safeguard her will live,
         while those who abandon her will die.
2   Turn back, O Jacob, hold fast;
         and walk in her light!
3   Do not give your glory to another;
         your best gifts to another people.
4   We are set apart, O Israel,
         for what is known to be pleasing to our Lord
             lies upon us!

---

5.   Masculine singular, and thus referring to 'way'.

3. *Commentary*

I shall now proceed with some observations on each section of the poem, calling attention to significant differences between the Ethiopic and the Greek and offering comments as to the meaning and import of the poem.

a. *Exile Due to Israel's Rejection of Wisdom*

This section is very close to the Greek. The Ethiopic reads 'fountain of life', (3.12) rather than 'fountain of wisdom'. Prov. 18.4 has 'fountain of wisdom', as does 2 Esd. 14.47, but the LXX text of Prov. 18.4 reads 'fountain of life'. Probably, as Burke points out[6], we have evidence for an alternate Hebrew text tradition, since there are manuscripts that read what appears to be a conflate text, 'life and wisdom'.

The central affirmation of this section is that the Babylonian exile has come upon the people of God because of their rejection of Wisdom. While we know that the author will shortly identify Wisdom with the Torah, the use of Wisdom in place of the divine commandments (as in the classical prophets and in the Deuteronomic tradition) to account for the Babylonian exile must have some particular weight. Our author, in all probability, wishes to affirm at the start that Wisdom is not simply to be identified with what the scholars/teachers of wisdom pass along to their pupils. Wisdom is to be comprehended as that whole sweep of divine guidance for Israel in history that displays God's love for this particular people—a point to be registered more explicitly later on. In addition, the author is probably influenced by the increase in the authority of the wise that develops in the later stages of postexilic life, as prophecy is becoming Scripture and living prophets are losing influence with the populace.

b. *The Way to Wisdom is Hidden*

Here too the Ge'ez text is very close to the Greek. In v. 18, the Ethiopic text has a very interesting rendering of the difficult text. The NRSV reads, 'those who schemed to get silver, and were anxious, / but there is no trace of their works'. Burke reads, 'Those who schemed for silver and were anxious, / and whose deeds were beyond

---

6. *The Poetry of Baruch*, p. 83.

discovery'. The Ge'ez version stresses their building up silver, becoming anxious, and making objects that cannot be duplicated or understood. The Ethiopic probably was translated from the LXX text available to us, but the translators understood the text to mean that those who amassed silver were metalsmiths who made their objects (idols?), carefully protected their secrets, and thereby prevented anyone from being able to duplicate their creations.

c. *Even the Wisest of Nations Are Ignorant of Wisdom*
This section in Ethiopic presents no significant departures from the Greek text. Verse 22 is stated actively: Canaan (i.e., the Phoenician cities of Tyre and Sidon, known for their wisdom [Ezek. 28]), and Temona (i.e., Teman) have neither seen nor heard of Wisdom.

The section applies the common theme (Job 38–41; Isa. 40.12-31, etc.) that God's ways and deeds are beyond human comprehension to the inaccessibility of Wisdom by even the wisest of mortals. Even those whose wisdom is world-renowned cannot claim to know Wisdom's location. Since, however, Wisdom is being connected with God's Torah, this use of the hiddeness of Wisdom underscores the graciousness of God in conferring the gift of Wisdom upon Israel.

d. *The Greatest of the Ancients Lacked Wisdom*
Not only was Wisdom inaccessible to the wise of the world, it also was not granted even to the most powerful and gifted of the world's ancients. As a result, the giants and the persons of renown came to their end without having attained their goals. There seems to be a clear allusion to the offspring of the heavenly beings and women of earth, the warriors of renown of Gen. 6.1-4.

Two themes are only loosely related in this section. The vastness of God's creation apparently reminds the poet of the huge stature and massive prowess of the giants of early times, the Nephilim. Not even these specially endowed beings possessed Wisdom or had the capacity to search it out. They may have had knowledge of heavenly secrets (as in *1 En.* 6–8), but even so, they did not have access to Wisdom.

The use of the expression 'house of God' to refer to the entire universe is unprecedented in earlier Jewish literature but is known from the Greek world and from Philo.[7]

---

7.   See the references in Burke, *The Poetry of Baruch*, p. 127, nn. 76-77.

e. *God Alone Knows the Hidden Path to Wisdom*

The giants or heavenly beings cannot ascend to the heavens and take possession of Wisdom. It is only the one who knows all things who knows Wisdom, knows her location, knows the path that leads to her home. The poet's use of imagery showing the mastery of the Creator-deity over all that has been called into being skirts the path of suggesting some mysterious connection between the God of creativity and fertility, and hidden Wisdom (vv. 32-35). Especially suggestive is the use of the verb 'to know' for God's knowledge, not just of the path leading to Wisdom, but of Wisdom herself. The Ethiopic uses the same verb 'to know' in both parts of v. 32a, not the verb 'to see' in the first instance and 'to know' in the second, as in the Greek. It seems clear that the author is hinting at the collaboration of the deity and Wisdom in the bringing forth of the special glories of the Creation: the world itself, its animal life, the light and the stars. The poet, while dependent upon Job 28 and theophany poems such as Ps. 104.1-9, goes much further. It is Wisdom herself who reveals the way that the deity must traverse to reach her hidden location. And vv. 34-35 remind one of the bridegroom Sun who leaves his chamber in the east and romps across the heavens (Ps. 19.4b-6, [5b-7 MT]) after the bridal night.

f. *God Revealed Wisdom to Israel*

If we take the Ethiopic rendering at face value, it goes far toward portraying Wisdom as a heavenly being. The expression *wa-kona kama sab'* can only be translated, 'and became like a human being', or, as I have rendered it, 'like a mortal one'. Wisdom is not only a personified being, she is one whom the deity has come to know completely, and who has appeared as a mortal among mortals. Many interpreters have understood the text to be a modification by Christian editors, thereby causing the text to support the Incarnation. But it is certainly not a Christian incarnational text in its Ethiopic reading, for the portrayal is of a divine or semi-divine being who, intimately known by the deity, now has her place within the human community as well.

g. *Wisdom Identified as God's Torah*

As in Sir. 24.23-29, so also in Baruch the identification of Wisdom and God's Torah is affirmed. And in both texts, the portrayal is such an intimate one that again one thinks of lovers. The community of Israel is to safeguard and protect Wisdom/Torah as a husband protects and guards a wife. Jacob is admonished not to give his glory to another (see Isa. 42.8; 48.11)—an image of faithful relations between husband and wife, referring in Second Isaiah to God's faithfulness to bride Israel, but here underscoring the need for Jacob to be faithful to the bond that binds him to Torah/Wisdom in a marriage covenant.

The closing line of the Ethiopic version of the poem is striking. The translation uses a preposition with pronominal suffix rather than a form of the verb 'to know', as in the Greek. The result is a translation that reads, literally, 'for what is recognized to be pleasing to our Lord is upon us'. The translator may have in view male circumcision as a sign of the covenant bond, a sign that is placed upon the male and remains with him always. In any event, it is Torah/Wisdom that is God's precious gift to Israel, the gift of God's most beloved companion.

4. *The Wisdom Poem in Perspective*

Baruch's treatment of Wisdom is significant largely because of the remarkably fine way in which the theme of Job 28 and one of the two themes of Sirach 24 are brought together. The result is a literary and theological achievement of remarkable power and finesse. Baruch's use of Sirach 24 is particularly interesting. Very little remains of the connection of Wisdom with the Creation. That part of the tradition, so central for Proverbs 8 and Sirach, is only hinted at in 3.32b-34, as the author makes what is essentially another point altogether regarding the intimate bond uniting God and Wisdom.

Yet, Baruch develops the hiddenness of Wisdom theme in a distinctive way, drawing a conclusion from that theme quite different from that of the author of Job 28. Baruch's view is more closely akin to that expressed in Sir. 24.23-29. The Job text registers the utter unknowability of Wisdom, except insofar as one is devoted to God and to God's ways. Wisdom is a reality known only to the deity, and reserved by the deity; Wisdom is imparted to human beings on God's terms alone, as one submits to the will of God and accepts what God sees fit to impart to mortals from the hidden treasure house of Wisdom. Viewed in this light, Job 28 fits rather well into the overall theme of the poetic sections of the book of Job, including the speeches from the whirlwind[8] and Job's responses to those speeches.

The author of Baruch's wisdom poem, however, registers another

8.   The author uses language and imagery from Job 38 in particular.

theme—related to the Joban theme, to be sure, but distinct from it. Baruch's point is that Wisdom is a special, reserved, utterly inaccessible reality, not available to any of God's creatures, not even the wisest, the most powerful, the most diligent. God alone was able to search out the path to Wisdom. God did so in order to make a gift of this hidden treasure to the elect people of God. Wisdom is a gift of love to God's beloved people Israel. The author offers an alternative statement about the content of God's love for Israel, to that presented, say, in Exod. 19.3-6. What is the special treasure (Hebrew סְגֻלָּה) promised Israel there? Our author answers: Wisdom herself is the special gift to the people of God. And Wisdom is God's companion in love, God's delight. Baruch has contributed markedly, I believe, to a growing understanding within the community of Israel of just how central the notion of Wisdom is for the faith of Israel.

We may then speculate that our author wishes to have readers recognize the extent to which God's gift of Torah is also the gift of divine Wisdom, a Wisdom at once hidden and revealed. Those interpreters of Torah who want to stress only the esoteric dimensions of Wisdom need to recognize that God has given the Torah in human words, accessible for all to hear and ponder. But those interpreters of Torah who wish to insist that God's Torah/Wisdom is plain and straightforward, evident and obvious in its meaning for the common life, need to be reminded that this gift remains accessible in its full meaning, power and glory to God alone. None can claim to have understood all (see also Sir. 24.28-29).

But perhaps even more importantly, the author wants to help register the sheer mystery and beauty of God's Wisdom/Torah in order to preserve it from the banality of flat interpretation and bourgeois application so widely represented in some of the schools of wisdom and perhaps also in some of the houses of Torah-study. If so, we can have sympathy with the author's purpose, for the effort to hold before a religious community this double dimension of a revelatory tradition is always needful. Interpreters who delight in the effort and find companionship with both of the partners—Wisdom/Torah and deity too—are fortunate indeed. They owe a debt to the unknown author of the wisdom poem assigned to Jeremiah's companion Baruch.

List of Works Consulted

Bible. Ethiopic. 1915. (Asmara) (ed. Fr. Francesco da Bassano; Asmara: Franciscan Press, 1919–26); American Theological Library Association Board of Microtext edition, Book No. 517.

Burke, D.G., *The Poetry of Baruch: A Reconstruction and Analysis of the Original Hebrew Text of Baruch 3.9–5.9* (SBLSCS, 10; Chico, CA: Scholars Press, 1982).

A Catalogue of Ethiopian Manuscripts Microfilmed for the Ethiopian Manuscript Microfilm Library and for the Hill Monastic Manuscript Library, Collegeville V-VI (Catalogue by Getatchew Haile, Checklist by William F. Macomber; Collegeville, MN: St. John's Abbey and University, 1981, 1982).

Gunneweg, H.J., *Das Buch Baruch* (JSHRZ, III.2; Gütersloh: Gütersloher Verlagshaus; Gerd Mohn, 1975), pp. 165-81.

Churton, W.R., 'Baruch', *The Old Testament: The Apocryphal Books* (London: SPCK, 1889).

Leslau, W., *Comparative Dictionary of Ge'ez (Classical Ethiopic)* (Wiesbaden: Otto Harrassowitz, 1987).

Tov, E., (ed. and trans.), *The Book of Baruch* (SBLTT, Pseudepigrapha Series, 8; Missoula, MT: Scholars Press, 1975).

Appendix

THE WISDOM POEM OF ETHIOPIC BARUCH

Transliteration[9]

Chapter 3

9   *semā' 'esrā 'ēl te'zāza ḥeywat*
      wa-'aṣme' mekara ṭebab.

10   *ment we'etu 'esrā ' ēl*
      wa-la-ment westa beḥēra ḍarr hallo.

11   *wa-balya ba-beḥēra nakir*
      wa-rakʷsa mesla 'abdent[10]
      wa-taxʷallaqʷa mesla 'ella westa si'ol.

---

9.   I am using the Ge'ez text from the Asmara Bible, with comparisons with EMML 2080 and two other EMML texts: 1763 and 2082. The critical text of Augustus Dillmann (*Veteris Testamenti Aethiopici, Tomus Quintus, Libri Apocryphi* [Berlin: Asher & Socios, 1894], pp. 3-4) offers a very fragmentary text. Catalogue information on the three EMML manuscripts appears in the two catalogue volumes listed in the bibliography: No. 1763 in Vol. V; Nos. 2080 and 2082 in Vol. VI.

10.   Verse 11 is missing entirely to this point in Dillmann; Dillmann has only the next line for his v. 11.

12   *wa-xadaga naq'ā ḥeywat.*

13   *sobahu ḥorka fenota 'egzi' abḥēr*
      'em-nabarka la-'ālam ba-salām.

14   *tamahhar 'aytē we' etu ṭebab*
      wa-'aytē we' etu xāyl
    'aytē mekar[11] *wa-'a'mero*
      wa-'aytē we' etu ḥayew
      la-nawwāxa mawā'el
    wa-'aytē we' etu berhāna
      'a'yent wa-salām.

15   *mannu rakaba beḥērā*
      wa-mannu bo' a westa mazāgebtihā

16   *'aytē 'emuntu malā'ekta 'aḥzāb*
      'ella qannayewwomu la-'arāwita gadām

17   *wa-yetwānayewwomu 'a'wāfa*[12] *samāy*[13]
      wa-'ella yezaggeb berura wa-warqa
    za-botu yet' ammanu sab'
      wa-'albonu 'enka wassan la-'aṭreyotomu.

18   *'esma 'ella yenaddequ berura yetaggehu*
      wa-'albo 'enka faṭarā la-gebromu.

19   *xalqu wa-waradu si'ola*[14]
      wa-tanše'u heyyantēhomu kāle'ān.

20   *wa-re'yu berhāna ne'usān*
      wa-nabaru westa medromu
    wa-la-fenota[15] *ṭebab-sa 'i-yā'maru*

21   *wa-'ašarā-hi 'i-rakabu.*
      wa-'i-tawakafewwā daqiqomu
      wa-reḥqu 'em-fenotomu.

22   *wa-'i-sam'u Kana'ān*
      wa-'i-re'yu[16] *Tēmonā.*

23   *wa-daqiqa 'agār-hi 'ella xašašewwā*
      la-tebab diba medr.[17]
    nagādeyāna Maryām wa-Tēmān
      'ella yezzāwe'u bāti
    wa-'ella yaxaššešewwo la-'a'mero
    wa-la-fenota ṭebab-sa 'i-yā'marewwo
    wa-'i-hi tazakkaru.

11. Dillmann reads *wa' aytē we' etu mekar.*
12. Dillmann reads *watatwānayewwomu la-'a'wāfa.*
13. The next five lines are missing in Dillmann (through v. 18).
14. Or one could read *si'ol.*
15. Dillmann: *wa-fenota.*
16. Reading with Dillmann; Asmara lacks the negation.
17. Dillmann lacks the next five lines (to v. 24).

170   *Priests, Prophets and Scribes*

24 *'esrā'ēl 'efo 'ābiy bēta 'egzi' abhēr*
    wa-nawwāx behēru!
25 *'ābiy we' etu wa-' albo māxlaqt*[18]
    wa-lā'lu-hi 'albo masfart.[19]
26 *heyya hallawu za-yesammeyu*
    yārbehaweyān 'ella 'em-tekāt
    nawwāxān qomomu
    wa-' ella ya' ammeru qatela.
27 *'i-xarayomu 'egzi' abhēr la-' ellu*
    wa-' i-wahabomu fenota tagšaṣ.
28 *wa-māsanu 'esma 'albomu ṭebab*
    ṭaf'u ba-taxbelotomu.
29 *mannu za-'arga samāya wa-naš'ā*
    wa-' awradā 'emenna dammanāt
30 *mannu 'adawa bāhra wa-rakabā*
    wa-' amṣe'ā ba-warq qayeh
31 *wa' albo za-ya' ammer fenotā*
    wa-za-yehēleyo la-' ašarā.
32 *za-kʷello ya' ammer ya' ammerā*
    wa-rakabā ba-tebab.
    za-faṭarā la-medr la-'ālam
    wa-za-mal'ā 'abāge'ā wa-' ensesā[20]
33 *wa-yefēnu berhāno wa-yahawwer*
    za-yeṣēwe'o wa-yet' ēzazo ba-ferhāt.[21]
34 *wa-kawākebt-ni yābarrehu*
    ba-gizēhomu wa-yetfēšehu.
35 *wa-yeṣēwe'omu wa-yebelu maṣā'na*
    wa-' abrehu lotu la-za-gabromu ba-tefšeht.[22]
36 *we' etu 'amlākena 'esma 'albo bā'ed*
    za-yemassel kiyāhu.
37 *we' etu rakabā la-kʷellā fenota tebab*
    wa-wahabo la-yā'qob qʷel'ēhu
    wa-la-' esrā' ēl fequru.
38 *wa-' emze 'astar' aya diba*[23] *medr*
    wa-kona kama sab'

18. Dillmann has only *'albo māxlaqta* for this line.
19. Dillmann reads the last word as *masfarta.* All of vv. 26-28 are missing in Dillmann.
20. This entire line is missing in Dillmann.
21. This entire line also is missing in Dillmann.
22. This entire line is missing in Dillmann.
23. Dillmann has *westa.*

Chapter 4

1   *ze-we'etu maṣḥafa te'zāzu la-'egzi'abḥēr*
      wa-ḥegg[24] *za-la-'ālam*
      kʷellomu 'ella yaʿaqqebewwā yaḥayyewu
      wa-'ella-sa yaxaddegewwā yemawwetu.

2   *tamayaṭ yāʿqob*
      'axaz wa-ḥur ba-berhānā.

3   *'i-tahab la-bā'ed kebraka*
      za-yexēyesaka la-kāle' ḥezb.

4   *beḍuʿān neḥna 'esrā'ēl*
      'esma taʿawqa šemratu la-'amlākena lā'elēna.

---

24. Dillmann reads *wāyaḥayyewu*.

Part III

EARLY JUDAISM AND ITS ENVIRONMENT

THE PERCEPTION OF 'THINGS' AND THEIR PRODUCTION IN THE OLD TESTAMENT HISTORICAL WRITINGS

Joel P. Weinberg

A very attractive feature of J. Blenkinsopp's work is the diversity and variety of his research. This feature facilitates participation in a volume of this kind, because it is little labour to find a subject that corresponds to the interests of the honoree. At the same time, it complicates the task in making it difficult to find a subject not discussed by him in the wide area of Old Testament studies! I hope that the selected subject avoids this embarrassment. It is a pleasure to dedicate these notes to J. Blenkinsopp, whom I appreciate very much as a scholar and a gentleman.

An essential feature of the ancient scientific-logical thinking, the classical notion,[1] perceives a 'thing' as a creation of humanity which substantially differs from its creator, the human. It acknowledges the discrepancy and separation between humanity as creator and 'thing' as creation. According to Democritus (*Diod.* 1.81ff.), humanity differs from animals mainly by living in its own created environment, in the so-called 'second nature'. Centuries later, Augustine (*De civitate Dei* 11.16) expressed the opinion that all 'things' must be evaluated according to their position and role in the universe, to their benefit for humanity, and the sensual pleasure caused by them. But such a perception of 'thing' was not something permanent and constant in the classical world-model. In an earlier period, the identity and unity of humanity with inanimate things was acknowledged: a 'thing' was correspondingly perceived as an embodiment of all the surrounding

---

1. H. and H.A. Frankfort, 'Myth and Reality', in *The Intellectual Adventure of Ancient Man: An Essay on Speculative Thought in the Ancient Near East* (Chicago: University of Chicago Press, 1946), pp. 3-27; J.P. Veynberg (Weinberg), *Chelovek v kuljture drevnevo Blizhnevo Vostoka* (Man in Ancient Near East Culture) (Moscow: Nauka, 1986), pp. 44-52.

world.[2] Such a perception of 'thing' is evident, for example, in the Homeric poems which perceive gods and humans, animals and things as phenomena which are qualitatively uniform, differing from one another only by the amount and distribution of this uniform quality in each of them.[3]

The recognition of the unity and identity of human and thing, creator and creation, evidently prevailed in all mythological world-models and world-pictures. Accordingly, for a person who thought mythologically, a thing was not valued so much for its utility, its usefulness (although this aspect must not be ignored), but mainly for continuing and supplementing the existence and essence of the person. If a thing is perceived as isolated and distant from humanity, then its use, its necessity or otherwise, determines its importance and role for humanity. But if a thing is perceived as something continuing and supplementing humanity, then its importance and role are determined by etiquette, the question of 'must have' and/or 'must be'. Each 'good person' must produce, and have, 'good things' or vice versa.[4]

Which of these two different perceptions of 'thing' and 'production' prevails in Old Testament historical writings? The following table records the results of a linguistic-statistical analysis of words denoting 'things' and 'production' in the main Old Testament historical writings and notes the quota (as percentages) of such words in the respective vocabularies.

The data demonstrate that things and their production occupy a noticeable and, in the course of time, relatively stable space in the world-view of Old Testament historical writings. Such an evident interest on the part of the Old Testament historians in things corresponds with the recognition of material well-being which was so essential for the Near Eastern, Israelite mentality, as a necessary precondition and important component to live a 'good', 'happy' life.[5] This interest confirms the observation of B. Halpern that 'from David through Hezekiah Chronicles regards and bestows abundance as a

2. O.M. Frejdenberg, *Mif i literatura drevnosti* (Myth and ancient literature) (Moscow: Nauka, 1978), pp. 63, 98.
3. I.V. Stalj, *Chudozhestvennyj mir gomerovskova eposa* (The artistic world of the Homeric poems) (Moscow, 1983), p. 156.
4. Vejnberg, *Chelovek*, pp. 74-84.
5. Vejnberg, *Chelovek*, pp. 174-76.

mark of divine favor'.[6] At the same time, however, it must be stressed that a diachronic view reveals a gradual diminution in vocabulary relating to things in Old Testamental historical writings. Reaching its lowest point in the book of Ezra–Nehemiah, this may reflect the economic difficulties that occurred in the emerging postexilic community (Neh. 1.3-11; 5.1-19 etc.). It also concurs with the gradual transition from a more mythological mode of thinking that is favourable to 'things' towards scientific-logical thought, which as a rule is less interested in things.

Words denoting 'things' and 'production' (%)

Phenomena	JE		D History		Ezra–Neh.		Chron.	
Agriculture:								
Farming	4.1		3.8		3.4		2.7	
Cattle-breeding	2.4	6.5	3.0	6.8	2.4	5.8	3.0	5.7
Handicraft:								
Metallurgy	2.1		2.8		1.0		2.2	
Building	1.5		1.6		0.7		1.4	
Weaving	1.3		1.6		0.0		0.7	
Other	0.5	5.4	0.2	6.2	0.2	1.9	0.7	5.0
Transport	1.0		1.5		0.8		1.0	
Commerce:								
Trade	0.6		0.4		0.9		0.4	
Usury	0.7		0.4		0.2		0.4	
Units of measure	2.0	3.3	1.6	2.4	2.1	3.2	1.8	2.6
Consumption:								
House	1.8		3.5		3.4		3.6	
Utensils	3.3		3.4		1.7		3.3	
Clothing	2.1		2.2		1.5		0.7	
Adornment	1.4		0.6		0.2		0.7	
Nourishment	2.8		2.5		2.3		2.2	
Possessions, Property	1.4	12.8	0.8	13.0	1.7	10.8	1.5	12.0
Total		29.0		29.9		22.5		26.3

In contrast to mythological world-models and world-views where special attention is paid to specific, mythologically and sacrally signifi-

6.   B. Halpern, 'Sacred History and Ideology: Chronicles' Thematic Structure–Indications of an Earlier Source', in R.E. Friedman (ed.), *The Creation of Sacred Literature: Composition and Redaction of the Biblical Text* (Berkeley: University of California Press, 1981), p. 40.

cant things, the world-views of Old Testament historical writings display an almost complete and exhaustive systematic enumeration and/or description of things and their production in Palestine. This systematic attitude discloses another essential peculiarity of the perception of things in Old Testament historical writings, namely its evident urban orientation. Indeed, the ratio between words primarily denoting urban things and their production and words denoting rural things and their production equals 9.7:5.4 in JE; 10.1:6.8 in the Deuteronomistic History; 7.6:5.7 in Chronicles; and 5.9:5.8 in Ezra–Nehemiah. The last data confirm the reliability of this analysis, because they conform exactly with the real economic and social conditions in the early postexilic community.[7] This predominant urban orientation in the realm of things corresponds with R. Alter's observation that 'though biblical poetry abounds in pastoral, agricultural, topographical, and meteorological images, the manufacturing processes of ancient Near Eastern urban culture are frequently enlisted by the poets'[8]—the more, let us add, by the historians.

Mythological thought focuses its attention first and foremost on the creation of things, on the productive activity of humanity. The data in the table, on the contrary, show that it was the consumption and distribution of things that held the interest of the Old Testament historians and their audience much more than their production. Similarly, the units of measure—bath, shekel and others, which are often mentioned in Old Testament historical writings—belong to the realm of consumption and distribution and coincide with the available archaeological and epigraphical data from Palestine.[9] This again demonstrates the reliability of the Old Testament historians and their striving for authentic information; that is, their historicism. Nevertheless, this assertion must not be overestimated. The Chronicler, for

7.   J.P. Weinberg, 'Demographische Notizen zur Geschichte der nachexilischen Gemeinde in Juda', *Klio* 54 (1972), pp. 54-58; A. Lemaire, 'Populations et territoires de la Palestine à l'époque perse', *Transeuphratène* 3 (1990), pp. 32-45; J. Sapin, 'Recherches sur les resources et les fonctions économiques du secteur de Ono à l'époque perse', *Transeuphratène* 4 (1991), pp. 55-59.

8.   R. Alter, 'The Characteristics of Ancient Hebrew Poetry', in R. Alter and F. Kermode (eds.), *The Literary Guide to the Bible* (Cambridge, MA: Belknap Press, 1987), p. 617.

9.   A.F. Rainey, 'Royal Weights and Measures', *BASOR* 179 (1965), pp. 34-36; S. Yeivin, 'Weights and Measures of Varying Standards in the Bible', *PEQ* 101 (1969), pp. 63-68.

example, mentions anachronistically the Persian coin, the daric
(אדרכנים), in his story of David (1 Chron. 29.7) and repeats nearly
verbatim the Deuteronomist's story about David's purchase of the
threshing-floor of Arauna (1 Chron. 21.18-26 = 2 Sam. 24.18-25),
but radically changes the price paid from the 50 silver shekels mentioned in his *Vorlage* to 500 gold shekels, a change that corresponds to
the augmentation of prices in the Persian period.

This observation leads to the main question about the perception of
things by the Old Testament historians. The mythological world-view
arranges things in a clear-cut hierarchical order, the top of which is
usually maintained by gold as the substance of deity and the incarnation of supreme goodness, the symbol and synonym of solidity and
durability.[10] In all Old Testament historical writings, gold (זהב) is a
keyword mentioned by the Deuteronomist and the Chronicler mainly
in connection with the Temple of Jerusalem and its utensils (1 Kgs
6.20, 21; 7.48 etc.; 1 Chron. 29.2-7; 2 Chron. 2.6 etc.); that is, in
connection with the realm of the sacred. Therefore both historians
consider Rehoboam's enforced substitution of copper shields for
Solomon's gold shields (1 Kgs 14.26-27 = 2 Chron. 12.9-10) as
reducing the 'goodness', the 'positivity' of the new king. It is evident,
therefore, that the world-pictures of the Old Testament historians preserve some relics of a mythological perception of gold. This conclusion, however, must not be generalized. The Chronicler, for example,
persistently underlines the fact that the gold utensils in the Temple of
Jerusalem are 'hand-made' (1 Chron. 22.14; 2 Chron. 2.6 etc.),
lessening the sacrality of gold. He further mentions gold in a purely
profane sense in connection with trade, tribute or booty (1 Chron.
18.7, 10; 2 Chron. 21.3 etc.).

An analogous tendency appears in the usage by Old Testament
historians, especially the Chronicler, of another keyword, שדה. This
word has many meanings: open country, open field; fields, domain (of
a city); arable land, plot of land, field (of an individual). It also commonly implicates distinct and significant mythological allusions as
well, such as 'place of birth and/or death' (Gen. 25.10; 49.30;
Josh. 24.32 etc.). But such sacral allusions are completely absent in
Chronicles. In all of its eleven occurrences, שדה has only the meaning

10. Vejnberg, *Chelovek*, p. 79.

'arable land, field' as a thing or result of human productivity (1 Chron. 27.26, 27 etc.).

It is easy to multiply arguments, but the above suffices to conclude that Old Testament historical writings perceive things and their production in a demythologized and desacralized way. Although some relics of a mythological apprehension of things endure, especially in the earlier works of the Yahwist and Elohist and the Deuteronomist, Old Testament historical writings consistently portray things as phenomena distant and separated from humanity, a human creation which therefore can and does play a considerable role in the historical activity of humanity.

In Near Eastern historical writings of the middle first millennium BCE, things can be seen to play three roles. The first embraces the productivity of humans. It is remarkable that the Yahwist and Elohist thought it necessary to include within the patriarchal narrative detailed descriptions of the cattle-breeding farms and other forms of production by Abraham, Laban and other personages (Gen. 13.1-7; 29.1-10 etc.), while the Deuteronomist, with evident pleasure, describes not only the economic activities of such 'good' rulers as Solomon, Hezekiah and others (1 Kgs 5.6 ff.; 2 Kgs 20.13 ff. etc.), but the large farms of such private persons as Nabal and Barzillai as well (1 Sam. 25; 2 Sam. 17.27-29). Chronicles, especially, pays great attention to the productive economic activity of citizens and kings, mainly in its own special literary material, thus proving the significance of this issue for the historian and his audience.[11] With evident delight the Chronicler describes the abundance of things surrounding David (1 Chron. 27.25-31), and the brisk and enterprising productive activity of King Uzziah (2 Chron. 26.9-10) and others.

A second aspect of the role of things in human historical activity is consumption, the distribution and redistribution of things through booty and tribute, trade and usury. This aspect attracts the attention of the Yahwist and Elohist (Gen. 14.11-12 etc.), and especially the Deuteronomist, who carefully records the booty taken by Saul (1 Sam. 15.9 etc.), by David (2 Sam. 8.6-8 etc.) and so on. The Chronicler, however, considered these lists and descriptions to be insufficient and therefore supplemented the Deuteronomistic Jehoshaphat story by a description of the tribute paid to this king (2 Chron. 17.10-11) and the

11. J.P. Weinberg, 'Das Eigengut in den Chronikbüchern', *OLP* 10 (1979), pp. 161-81.

Asa story by a description of the booty taken (2 Chron. 14.13-14).

In both these roles, things function mainly as the outcome of human historical activity. In contrast, the third role points to things operating as subjects, as a power, a factor of active influence on persons, communities and human historical activity. Arms and armaments of war most obviously display this role and the Near Eastern historians, including the Old Testament historians and their classical colleagues and contemporaries,[12] pay much attention to this issue. The Deuteronomist not only offers a detailed description of the arms of Goliath (1 Sam. 17.4-7.) and David (1 Sam. 17.38), but also accentuates the significant role of David's arms for his victory. The Chronicler not only describes the strongholds built by King Uzziah and the armaments of his soldiers (2 Chron. 26.13-15), but is also convinced that these things furthered his reputation, for 'his fame spread far and wide, for he was miraculously assisted until he became strong' (v. 15).

But Near Eastern historical thought did not restrict itself to the self-evident connection between things and arms on the one hand and war and its outcome on the other, but sometimes points to a deeper, more essential influence of things on the historical activity of humanity. A remarkable example is the use of the word 'riches' (עשׁר) in Chronicles. The Chronicler mentions this word much more frequently than his predecessor, the Deuteronomist—eight times as against twice—but mainly (seven times in all: 1 Chron. 29.12, 28; 2 Chron. 1.11, 12; 17.5 etc.) in connection with the religiously and ideologically important word כבוד (weight, burden, possessions; appearance, splendour, magnificence; distinction, respect, mark of honour of humanity; splendour, magnificence, authority of God).[13] This connection expresses something extremely positive. For example, the Chronicler supplements the concluding formula in the David story by mentioning the king's 'wealth and honour' (עשׁר וכבוד, 1 Chron. 29.28). He not only enumerates the 'many gifts' brought to Hezekiah (2 Chron. 32.23), but also emphasizes that 'Hezekiah became very

12. H. Wilsdorf, 'Antike Auffassungen von den Einwirkungen der τέχνη und der φύσις auf die Geschichte', *Klio* 66 (1984), pp. 432 ff.

13. I.I. Efros, *Ancient Jewish Philosophy: A Study in Metaphysics and Ethics* (Detroit: Wayne University Press, 1964), pp. 7ff.; T.N.D. Mettinger, *The Dethronement of Sabaoth: Studies in the Shem and Kabod Theologies* (ConBOT, 18; Lund: Gleerup, 1982), pp. 80 ff. etc.

rich and respected; he provided for himself treasure houses for his silver, gold, precious stones, spices, shields, and all kinds of desirable things; and storage places for the produce of grain, must and oil, and stalls for all kinds of cattle and pens for the flock. He also provided cities for himself, in addition to an abundance in the form of sheep and cattle, because Elohim gave him a very great abundance of wealth' (2 Chron. 32.27-29).

In sum, things take up a relatively large space in the world-view of the Old Testament historians. They and their production are perceived mainly as demythologized and desacralized, separated from humanity, exerting a substantial influence on human historical activity.

THE PHASES OF HUMAN LIFE IN
MESOPOTAMIAN AND JEWISH SOURCES

Moshe Weinfeld

Mesopotamian as well as Jewish sources characterize various stages of advancing age. Similar in form and content, an analysis and comparison of these sources suggest fruitful cultural interchange between Mesopotamia and Israel.[1] I shall begin by commenting on the Akkadian text and compare it to analogous or related biblical traditions. Later I shall enhance the comparative study by adducing rabbinic passages.

Phases of Human Life in Sultantepe Tablet #400
and the Biblical Tradition

A diverse collection of cuneiform texts, the Sultantepe Tablets, was discovered in Northern Mesopotamia in 1951–52. Amidst various literary, astrological, medical (and other) tablets, O. Gurney classifies one text as 'a learned compendium of theological and other equivalences'.[2] It contains the following passage:[3]

---

1. For a technical delineation of the 'ages of man' in an Egyptian source of the Ptolemaic period, cf. M. Lichtheim, *Ancient Egyptian Literature*. III. *The Late Period* (Berkeley: University of California Press, 1980), p. 199. This passages tries to determine the peak of Life (= 60): 'the life that approaches the peak, two thirds of it are lost'. See A. Malamat, 'Longevity: Biblical Concepts and Some Ancient Near Eastern Parallels', in *Vorträge gehalten auf der 28. Rencontre Assyriologique Internationale in Wien, 6.-10. Juli 1981* (ed. H. Hunger and M. Hirsch; AfO Beiheft 19; Vienna: Rencontre Assyriologique Internationale, 1982).

2. Line 1 reads AD.HA[L U]M.ME.A, 'scribal mysteries'; see O.R. Gurney, *The Sultantepe Tablets* (Occasional Publications of the British Institute of Archaeology at Ankara, 7; London: British Institute of Archaeology at Ankara, 1964), II, p. 20.

3. O.R. Gurney and P. Hulin, *The Sultantepe Tablets*, No. 400 Rev. ll. 45ff. The text is translated in *CAD*, L, *littūtu*, p. 220; also by J. Nougayrol, 'Notes

Forty [years mean] prime of life (*lalûtum*)
Fifty [years mean] short life (*ūmū kurūtu*)
Sixty [years mean] mature age (*metlūtu*)[4]
Seventy [years mean] long life (*ūmū arkūtu*)
Eighty [years mean] old age (*šībūtu*)
Ninety [years mean] might (*littūtu*).[5]

The vocabulary and conceptuality from this Akkadian list find occasional parallels within the biblical materials.

Forty—Desire (lalûtum)

The Akkadian root *lalû* denotes both desire and that which is desired.[6] At the age of forty, one has most likely attained one's desire; that is, has exhausted one's abilities and fulfilled self-expectations. *lalû* thus also refers to the 'prime of life';[7] this sense is especially pronounced in contexts dealing with death before one's time: *ina lališu imât*, 'will die in his prime'.[8]

חמדה is seemingly the appropriate biblical term to compare to this Akkadian term. Like *lalûtum*, חמדה refers to the object of desire as well as to desire itself.[9] 2 Chron. 21.20 may imply that forty is the age of חמדה. King Jehoram of Judah dies of a severe illness at the age of forty; he 'passed on בלא חמדה'. Apparently the phrase indicates that Jehoram died without having obtained his life's ambitions, before satiating his appetitie. In Ehrlich's paraphrase of the rabbinic dictum, the king 'quit the world without his desire in his hand'.[10]

---

brèves', *RA* 62 (1968), p. 96.

4. Cf. *CAD*, M II, p. 45. A possible alternative reading would be *mētellūtu* 'excellence'; see R. Borger, 'Review of *The Interpretation of Dreams in the Ancient Near East* by Leo Oppenheim', *AfO* 18 (1958), p. 416, applied by A. Malamat, 'Longevity', p. 221.

5. See below.

6. See *CAD*, L, *lalû*, pp. 49-51.

7. *CAD*, L, p. 50, 3; see also p. 220; Nougayrol, 'Notes': 'la fleur de l'âge', p. 96.

8. *CAD*, L, pp. 50-51.

9. See BDB, p. 326.

10. A. Ehrlich, *Mikrâ ki-Pheschutô* (Berlin: Poppelauer, 1900), p. 461. The rabbinic phrase is אין אדם יוצא מן העולם וחצי תאותו ידו (*Eccl. R.* 1.14).

Fifty—Short Life (ūmū kurû)
The age of fifty is one of 'brief days' or brevity of life. This statement indicates that the list here discusses the tragic nature of an early demise more than the quality of life at fifty.

Sixty—Maturity (metlūtu)
Sixty is the age of maturity.[11] Here the text seems to deal only with life at sixty, not with death, as in the text quoted below.

Seventy—Long Life (ūmū arkūtu)
The definition of seventy years as 'long days', that is, length of life, is natural enough. Within the biblical tradition, the well-known passage from Ps. 90.10, 'The span of our life is seventy years', would likewise indicate that seventy is a 'long life', that is, a life lived to its expected length. The biblical tradition, just as the Mesopotamian text, deepens the significance of 'the length of days'. Both reflect the widespread concept that wisdom is a function of age: the older one is, the wiser. For instance in Job 12.12-13 maturity accompanies the 'length of days' (ארך ימים):

> Is wisdom in the aged
> And understanding in length of days?
> With Him are wisdom and might;
> Counsel and understanding are His.

Wisdom, understanding and counsel, here attributed to God, are the qualities needed for maturity. Such passages as Prov. 8.14-16 and Isa. 11.2 express the same idea. Compare also Job 32.7: '...Let age speak, let advanced years declare wisdom'.

Eighty—Extreme Old Age (šibūtu)[12]

Ninety—Might (littūtu)
littūtu originates from the root *le'ŭ* indicating strength, ability; thus *litu* denotes might, victory.[13] The parallel Hebrew term would be

---

11. Nougayrol, 'Notes': 'l'âge avancé', p. 96.
12. Nougayrol, 'Notes': 'la vieillesse', p. 96. To distinguish *šībūtu* (Hebrew שׂיבה) from the Hebrew זקנה, 'old age', I have adopted 'extreme old age' for *šībūtu-*שׂיבה throughout.
13. Hence, while both *CAD* and Nougayrol render 'extreme old age', I have used this for *šībūtu-*שׂיבה (see n. 12) and preferred 'might' for *littūtu*.

גבורות. Just as *litu* on royal tombs indicates the heroic deeds of the kings enshrined within,[14] so the Israelite kings' chronicles record their גבורות, their mighty deeds and victories (see, for example, 1 Kgs 15.23; 16.5, 27; 2 Kgs 14.28).[15] It is thus natural that the Bible uses גבורות, like *littūtu* in the text under discussion, in connection with advanced years. The well-known verse from Ps. 90.10 comes immediately to mind:

> The span of our life is seventy years,
> given the strength (בגבורת), eighty years.[16]

The obvious difference is that גבורות in the Bible characterizes the age of eighty, whereas *littūtu* in the Mesopotamian text pertains to the age of ninety, with *šībūtu*, 'extreme old age' given as the definition of life at eighty. We shall return to this discrepancy below.

Another biblical passage is equally instructive. In Ps. 71.9 the poet pleads for God not to forsake him in old age (לעת זקנה). He goes on to petition (v. 16):

> Let me come with might (בגברות)[17]; O Lord God,
> celebrating Your beneficence, Yours alone.

The psalmist desires to reach an advanced age in order to recount God's mighty deeds.[18] As he goes on to say (vv. 17-18):

> You have let me experience it, God, from my youth;
> Until now I have proclaimed Your wondrous deeds,
> and even in hoary old age (זקנה ושיבה)
> do not forsake me, God,
> until I proclaim Your strength to the next generation.[19]

---

14. See *CAD*, L, p. 222, 2[1].

15. Just as the Hebrew גבורות derives from גבר = man (see Jer. 51.30), that is, manliness, the Hittite royal annals are called *pišnadar* (LU - natar)—'deeds of men'; see H.G. Güterbock, 'Hittite Historiography', in *History, Historiography and Interpretation* (ed. H. Tadmor and M. Weinfeld; Jerusalem: Magnes, 1983), p. 31. Compare as well the 'virtues' of the Roman Caesars. To the Akkadian *ana littūtu kašadu* (*CAD*, L, p. 220), compare Hebrew בא/הגיע לגבורות.

16. The translation is from *The Book of Psalms—A New Translation* (Philadelphia: The Jewish Publication Society of America, 1972) prepared by M. Greenberg, J. Greenfield and N. Sarna.

17. אבוא בגברות; the JPS translation (see n. 16) offers 'Let me reach old age' as an alternative translation, preferring 'I come with praise of Your mighty acts'.

18. Thus taken correctly by A. Ehrlich, *Die Psalmen* (Berlin: M. Poppelauer, 1905), p. 164.

19. Translation from Greenberg *et al.*, *Psalms—A New Translation*.

Here too, then, גבורה refers to the might which characterizes, indeed is a precondition for, זקנה ושיבה—extreme old age. It is therefore not surprising to note that the corresponding Akkadian terms are juxtaposed in a common Mesopotamian prayer motif, the petition that the god grant long life (*ūmešu līriku*), enjoyment, happiness (*lalû*), and extreme old age (*littūtu*); that is, the attainment of maximum capacity until advanced age.[20]

Phases of Human Life in rabbinic Literature

While the biblical tradition contains echoes of the conceptuality and vocabulary of the phases of human life in Mesopotamian sources, rabbinic literature possesses even more striking parallels. Beginning with the Mishnah, the rabbis carried on an active discourse concerning the phases of human life, a discourse which developed into various traditions.

The Mishnah contains an extensive list describing the phases of human life. *Ab.* 5.21 reads as follows:[21]

1   At five years [the age is reached] for [the study of] the Bible,
2   at ten [the age is reached] for the Mishnah,
3   at thirteen [the age is reached] for [the fulfilment of] the commandments,
4   at fifteen [the age is reached] for the Talmud,
5   at eighteen [the age is reached] for the bride-chamber,
6   at twenty [the age is reached] for seeking [a livelihood],
7   at thirty [the age is reached] for strength (לכח),
8   at forty [the age is reached] for understanding (לבינה),
9   at fifty [the age is reached] for counsel (לעצה),
10 at sixty [the age is reached] for old age (לזקנה),
11 at seventy [the age is reached] for extreme old age (לשיבה),
12 at eighty [the age is reached] for might (לגבורה)
13 at ninety [the age is reached] for bending over,[22]
14 at a hundred, he is as if he had already died and gone from the world.

---

20. For references, see *CAD*, L, p. 50, 2b.

21. The translation is my own; cf. H. Danby, *The Mishnah* (Oxford: Oxford University Press, 1933), and the many English renditions of *Abot*.

22. לשוח. See commentaries; apparently a reference to the aged man's bent-over walk, or to the image of the ninety-year old as 'bending over' the grave.

While this passage is a later addition to the tractate[23] and alternative talmudic traditions are to be found,[24] the Mishnah is a two-part summary of the various phases of human life in its given form. Lines 1-5 are prescriptive: they offer instruction as to the proper age for each educational stage in the passage through childhood and determine eighteen as the right age for marriage. Lines 6-14 covering the ages 20–100 are not didactic but speculative; their purpose is to reflect on what is peculiar to, or characteristic of, life at various ages. While the first portion of the Mishnah determines precise ages for each phase of learning, the latter section is arranged schematically according to decimal intervals. Only the second part of the Mishnah bears affinity to the Sultantepe passage insofar as it deals with the quality of life at various levels of advancing age.

Rabbinic literature also discusses a further aspect of the Sultantepe passage, the nature of death at various ages. The following schema is found in *y. Bikk.* 2.1 (64c):

1   One who dies at fifty years old, dies by *hikkārēt* (בהכרת). . .[25]
at sixty, [he dies] the death referred to in the Torah,[26]
at seventy, a death of love,[27]
at eighty, a death of old-age (זקנה).[28]

23. See J.N. Epstein, *Mavo Lenusah Hamishnah* (Jerusalem: Magnes, 1964), p. 978; the tractate originally ends with the prayer contained in the preceding paragraph.

24. The amora Abaye, quoting his mother's dictum, 'At *six* [the age is reached] for [the study of] the Bible, at ten for the Mishnah, and at thirteen for fasting' (*b. Ket.* 50a), apparently was not familiar with the tradition given in the Mishnah, see C. Albeck, *Mishnah* (Jerusalem: Dvir, 1959), IV, p. 351.

25. הכרת (below: כרת), that is, 'cutting off', is the rabbinic term for death as a result of crimes whose penalty is given in the Torah as 'that soul shall be cut off from its people'; the assumption is that death by הכרת is meted out by God at an early age. See S.E. Löwenstamm, 'Karet. Hikkaret', in *Encyclopedia Mikrait*, IV, pp. 330-32.

26. That is, sixty is an average life-span. The amoraic discussion derives this in two fashions: first from the Israelites who lived out the length of their natural lives in the wilderness, calculating their death at age 60; second on the basis of the *gematria* of בכלח in Job 5.26 (בכלח = 60).

27. חבה, interestingly deduced from Ps. 90.10a.

28. Variously deduced from Ps. 90.10b and 2 Sam. 19.36.

Two parallel passages differ somewhat from the above:

2   If one dies at fifty years old, this is death by *kārēt* (כרת). . .
    at sixty, this is death at the hand of God. . .[29]
    at seventy, extreme old age (שׂיבה)
    at eighty, might (גבורה)[30] (*b. M. Qat.* 28a)

3   If one dies under fifty years old, he dies by *hikkārēt* (בהכרת). . .
    If one dies at sixty years old, this is the death referred to in the
       Torah. . .
    If one dies at seventy years old, this is a death of love,
    He who dies at eighty years, this is a death of might (גבורה) (*Şem.* 3.8).[31]

Several comparisons suggest themselves. First, just as the Akkadian term *lalūtum*, used in the sense of 'prime of life, vigour' in the Sultantepe passage, also implies 'wealth, riches',[32] so does the Hebrew כח, used in *Abot*.[33] The traditions differ, however, in their placement of the concept. Whereas the Mesopotamiah *lalūtum* and biblical חמדה are assigned to the age of forty, the Mishnaic כח is attributed to the age of thirty.

The Mesopotamian notion that fifty years is a 'short life' (*ūmū kurû*) corresponds to the rabbinic definition of death at fifty (or before) as death by כרת. Indeed, the Akkadian *karû* is the semantic equivalent of Hebrew כרת/קצר, and the Akkadian expression *napišta kurrû* recalls the biblical כרת נפשׁ.[34]

Sixty is given in Sultantepe as mature age. This is most closely paralleled by *Abot*'s description of an age of counsel (עצה), once again moved down in the Mishnah by ten years to fifty. In the ancient Near East, as has been shown, עצה refers to a form of authority,[35] thus

---

29. That is, death before one's time meted out by God for a capital offence in instances when the death penalty was for some reason not carried out by the court. See n. 25.

30. The latter two both deduced from Ps. 90.10.

31. M. Higger, *Treatise Semahot* (New York: Debay Rabanan, 1931), p. 113.

32. *CAD*, L, p. 50, 2[1].

33. See Prov. 5.10: פן ישׂבעו זרים כחך; also Ezra 2.69. On כח as wealth, possessions in Second Temple period writings, see my remarks in 'They should bring all of their Mind, all of their strength, and all of their wealth into the community of God' (1QSa. 12), *Te'uda*. II. *Bible Studies* (ed. B. Uffenheimer; Y.M. Grintz in Memoriam; Tel Aviv: University of Tel Aviv, 1982), p. 38 (Hebrew).

34. *CAD*, K, p. 230, 3[1.]

35. See P.A.H. de Boer, 'The Counsellor', in *Wisdom in Israel and in the Ancient Near East: Presented to H.H. Rowley* (VTSup, 3; Leiden: Brill, 1955),

corresponding to the Mesopotamian *mēṭlūtu*.

We have seen several examples of a ten-year discrepancy between the Mesopotamian passage and *Abot*:

	Sultantepe	Abot
1. prime (כח, *lalūtum*)	40	30
2. counsel/mature age (עצה, *meṭlūtu*)	60	50
3. old age (זקְנָה, *ūmū arkū*)	70	60
4. extreme old age (שׂיבה, *sibūtu*)	80	70
5. might (גבורה, *littūtu*)	90	80

While we cannot discount the possibility that this phenomenon stems from a difference in life-expectancy between the two civilizations,[36] it is equally likely that the variance is merely literary. We have seen precise correspondence between the cultural traditions: both Sultantepe and the talmudic traditions view fifty as a short or cut-off life. The use of *šībūtu* and *littūtu* to designate the last stages of advancing age in Mesopotamia—no matter what precise years be assigned—parallels exactly the Hebrew terms שׂיבה and גבורות. On the other hand, even within the rabbinic tradition itself we have noted inconsistencies: גבורות is explicitly derived from Ps. 90.10. We would therefore expect it to be assigned consistently to the age of eighty. *Y. Bikk.*, however, apparently does not know this tradition and considers eighty the age of זקנה. While we may account for some of the other differences in the various rabbinic sources by the simple fact that the Mishnah in *Abot* deals with *life* at various stages, whereas the talmudic lists deal with *death*, others cannot be so explained, such as the difference between 'death referred to in the Torah' and 'death at the hand of God' (age 60).

In conclusion, whether or not we can argue for the direct influence of the Mesopotamian passage on the Hebrew tradition is questionable. The literary form, however, shared by all the sources are one and the same. The fact that the Sultantepe material originated earlier than the tradition of *Abot* suggests at least some indirect Mesopotamian influence upon the Jewish tradition. Both the Sultantepe list and the Israelite and Jewish traditions sprang forth from a common conceptuality of the phases of human life in the ancient Near East.

pp. 42-71; compare *b. Ḥag.* 14a (cited by R. Elijah Gaon in his commentary to *Abot*, *ad loc.*).

36. Cf. M.A. Dandamaev, 'About Life Expectancy in Babylonia in the First Millenium B.C.', in *Death in Mesopotamia* (ed. R. Alster; Copenhagen: Akademisk Forlag, 1980), pp. 183ff.

CULTS AND DEITIES WORSHIPPED
AT CAESAREA PHILIPPI–BANIAS

Vassilios Tzaferis

The establishment of the city Caesarea Philippi by the Tetrarch Philippos, the son of Herod the Great, in the year 3 BCE constituted the threshold of a new era in the history of the place, known in the Greek historical sources as Panion (Polybius, *Historiae*, XVI.18.2). The statement of Josephus Flavius, 'Philip too constructed Paneas, near the sources of the Jordan, and called it Caesarea' (*Ant.* 18.28), is explicit and leaves no doubt at all that Philip was the first to promote Panion to the status of polis, equipping it with the necessary religious, cultural and civic institutions. On the basis of the literary sources and the archaeological evidence so far discovered, we can positively declare that Philip not only founded the civic institutions, but he also erected at Paneas the first real city, which he called Caesarea in honour of his family patron Caesar. Thus, Panion, from a purely sacred locality, had now become an important city, the capital of a kingdom.

The population of the new city was mostly heathen, mainly Greeks, Ituraeans and other non-Jewish natives. In such a city, privileged by the status of being an autonomous polis, the temples dedicated to the patron gods were the most significant and indispensable establishments. The first heathen inhabitants of Caesarea did not have many alternatives in choosing their own gods. The place already had its patron god, Pan, as well as its official politico-religious cult, that of Augustus, long before the city was founded.

The impressive natural cave hanging over the springs of the Jordan had been dedicated to Pan and had become a well-accepted cult site as early as the beginning of the second century BCE. Later on, probably in 19 BCE, Herod the Great erected a magnificient temple of white marble to Augustus, known as Augustaeum. Both cults, of Pan and

Augustus, continued to function well after the foundation of Caesarea. Moreover, there are good reasons to believe that both cults were accepted by the heathen inhabitants as the official worship of their newly founded city. One can even suggest that, at least up to the years of King Agrippa II's reign (54–93 CE), these two cults remained the principal worship practised in the city.

Pan, the Lord of Caesarea Philippi

The cult of Pan preceded, by almost two centuries, the establishment of Caesarea Philippi which, as stated above, occurred in the year 3 BCE.

Apparently, the general landscape, composed of spring-waters, precipitous cliffs, forests and animals, constituted the indispensable rural background for the establishment of the cult of Pan at the cave. In addition certain historical factors and events played a decisive part in this initiative, namely, the battle between the Ptolemaic and the Seleucid armies which, according to Polybius, took place in the vicinity of the cave around 200 BCE. According to the story told by Polybius, the elephants of Antiochus's army caused a sort of confusion or panic among the Ptolemaic soldiers.

It is very probable that the victorious Seleucids interpreted this accident of confusion and panic among the Ptolemiac armies as the divine interference of Pan.[1] Consequently they established a Panion (sanctuary of Pan) at the site of the battle in gratitude to the god who rewarded them with the victory over the Ptolemies.

Whatever may have been the reasons, environmental or historical, it is an almost undisputed historical fact that, at least from the start of the second century BCE, the cave at the southern foot of Mount Hermon and above the springs of the Jordan had become a known sanctuary (Hieron) for Pan, and that from that time onward the site

---

1.   The southwestern foot of mount Hermon where one of the main springs of the Jordan river gushes out from the bottom of a natural cave was from the Hellenistic period (third to first century BCE) a well-known sacred place dedicated to the god Pan. The second century BCE Greek historian Polybius calls the site Panion, that is, the sanctuary of Pan. The same writer also tells the story of the famous battle between the Seleucids and the Ptolemies in 200–198 BCE. (*Historiae* XVI.18-19).

There is no historical or archaeological evidence to indicate the existence of a settlement or of any other sort of habitation in the area except the sanctuary of Pan in the periods which preceded the early Roman times, that is, the late first century BCE.

was called Panion, that is, the cave-sanctuary of Pan.

Natural grottos, springs, forests and rural landscape were not the external characteristics of Pan's cult alone, but also of other gods associated with the pastoral religious thought of the Greeks, such as Apollo, Dionysius, Hermes and all kinds of Nymphs. Usually, by joint association, all the pastoral or rural gods shared with Pan, either as a group or as individuals, one and the same cave.

There is sufficient epigraphic evidence to testify clearly that in the Panion at Caesarea Philippi this was the case and other gods, apart from Pan, were also worshipped. In one of the Greek inscriptions preserved under a niche carved in the cliff along the cave, the Nymphs and Hermes are clearly mentioned as associate gods to the sanctuary of Pan. The inscription reads:

Πανί τε καί Νύμφαις, Μαίης γόνον, ἔνθ᾽ ἀνέθηκεν Ἑρμείαν, Διὸς υἱόν, Οὐίκτωρ, Λυσιμάχου παῖς.

To Pan, the Offsprings of Maia, and to Nymphs, Victor, the son of Lysimachos, dedicated here to Hermes, the son of Zeus.[2]

The content of the inscription is very implicit: the Nymphs shared the sanctuary of Pan on almost equal terms. The same inscription also says clearly that Hermes too had a part in the same sanctuary. Apparently one of the ritual niches of the sanctuary was dedicated to Hermes. The date of the inscription and consequently the time of Victor's dedication, is probably in the second to third centuries CE. We may assume, however, that such a joint association (Pan, Nymphs and Hermes) within one and the same sanctuary started much earlier, probably from the beginning of the cult of Pan in the second century BCE.

The list of the associate gods in the sanctuary of Pan at Caesarea Philippi included other deities. For instance, in another inscription from the same cliff the Nymph Echo is mentioned as having her own ritual site there. The inscription reads:

---

2.   The Greek inscriptions carved under or above the niches along the cliff of Panion have been seen and copied by almost all the scholars and travellers who have visited the site in the nineteenth and twentieth centuries. One of the best publications is that of W.H. Waddington, *Inscriptions grecque at latine, de la Syrie* (repr. Rome, 1968), No. 1891.

Ἀγρίππας Μάρκου, ἄρχων,
ἔτους 223, ὀνείρω χρησμοδοτηθείς,
τὴν Κυρίαν Ἠχὼ ἀνέθηκεν ἅμα
Ἀγριππιάδι συμβίῳ καὶ
Ἀγριππίνῳ καί Μάρκῳ καὶ
Ἀγρίππᾳ, βουλευταῖς, καὶ
Ἀγρειππίνῃ καὶ Δόμνῃ,
τέκνοις αὐτῶν.

Agrippas, the son of Markos, archon, in the year 223, after having been informed by a dream, dedicated the Lady Echo together with Agrippiada his wife and Agrippinos and Markos and Agrippas, members of the Council and together with Agrippina and Domna their children.[3]

The date 223 mentioned in the inscription is equivalent to 220 CE. But again, we can certainly conclude that the Nymph Echo shared a room with Pan in his shrine from the time of the establishment of the sanctuary.

Another deity probably worshipped in the same sanctuary was the Nymph Maia. The evidence for such an assumption comes entirely from numismatic finds. On certain coins minted at Caesarea Philippi, the Nymph Maia is depicted as a female figure standing near a tree.[4] According to mythology, Maia was a beautiful Nymph, though very shy, spending all her time with her maidens in a remote cave. The myths also say that she was the daughter of Atlas and that she was born from a tree.

Another interesting and most attractive female deity who had a place of her own in the sanctuary was Nemesis, the goddess of justice. Her presence at the Panion of Caesarea is attested by a Greek inscription preserved, almost intact, above a large niche cut along the cliff. The inscription reads:

Ὑπὲρ σωτηρίας τῶν Κυρίων Αὐτοκρατόρων,
Οὐαλέριος (Τιτι)ανός, ἱερεὺς Θεοῦ Πανὸς τὴν
Κυρία(ν Νέμ)εσιν καὶ τὸν (σ)ὺν τῇ ὑπ' αὐτοῦ κοιλαν-
θείσῃ πέ(τ)ρᾳ (τ)ελεσιουργ(ηθέ)ντα (σηκ)ὸν αὐτῆς
(σὺν κ)ανκέλλῳ σιδηρῷ,
(ἔτους) π . . . Ἀπε(λλαίου).

---

3   Waddington, *Inscriptions*, No. 1894.
4.   Y. Meshorer, 'The Coins of Caesarea-Philippi', *Israel Numismatic Journal* 8 (1984–1985), pp. 43-44.

For the salvation of the Emperors, the Lords,
Valerius Titianus, the priest of god Pan, (dedicated)
the Lady Nemesis, together with the niche,
her prayer-hall with the iron parapet.
In the year. . .(month) Apellaios.[5]

The date of the inscription is missing, but without going into further historical discussion we may assume that Valerius's dedication to Nemesis was made in the beginning of the fourth century CE.

The Greek word σηκός means precinct, or enclosure, and this is exactly what was allotted to the goddess in the sanctuary: a yard, fenced by an iron parapet, and a niche where her statue stood.

The deities, Hermes, Echo, Maia and the Nymphs who shared the cave-sanctuary with Pan, constituted a company of associated gods, with either genetic lineage or common religious concepts.

Thus, according to the myths, Hermes was not only the father of Pan, but also the god of shepherds and the protector of herds and pastures. Very often he is called Hermes Nomios which means Hermes of the pastures or Hermes the rural. Maia was the mother of Hermes and also a spring-Nymph. As such, what could be more appropriate for her than to have a place of worship next to her son within the shrine of Pan. The Nymph Echo, on the other hand, was closely connected to the infatuations of Pan and originally belonged to the panaic circles. According to the myths, at Pan's command she was butchered by the shepherds for refusing his lustful invitation. The only thing which survived from that beautiful Nymph was her voice, the echo. According to another myth, Echo was not killed but paired off with Pan and gave birth to a girl, the Iyx.

In general, the Nymphs, as the daemons of Nature, dwelled in the springs, caves, mountains, forests and groves. As the spirits of the vegetation, which feed on animals and people alike, the Nymphs bore resemblance to Pan's attributes. Thus, in a most natural way, they would legitimately share with him the same places of dwelling as well as his shrine.

The only deity which, *prima facie*, did not fit the group was Nemesis the goddess of justice. Nemesis was commissioned by Zeus to distribute to individuals what each one deserved, to impose justice and determine the penalties. In the Greek classical world Nemesis was highly venerated not only as the goddess of justice but as the personification

5.   Waddington, *Inscriptions*, No. 1893.

of moral standards and common decency as well. In that capacity she demanded her own cult and statues. However, from the fourth century BCE onwards her religious ideology was integrated with various other conceptions, resulting in her fusion with other personified notions, deities and Nymphs. As a Nymph she was very often identified either as the personification of Adrasteia (Unavoidable) or of Anange (Necessity). Thus, in the Hellenistic and Roman world, she was usually worshipped as an intruder deity within *temenoi* and other major sanctuaries of team gods, though of course she always retained her right to have her own statues. In the final analysis, Nemesis, as the daughter of Night and the sister of the Fates (all of them born by the same mother) and as a deity fused with various personified ideas, was considered a member of the Nymphs' and Pan's circles. Her shrine, therefore, in the Panion of Caesarea did not constitute an anomaly but a normal and well-understood phenomenon.

The worship of Pan was the major cult at Paneas. It remained so even after the establishment of Caesarea-Philippi and the introduction of other cults which functioned at one and the same time throughout the history of the city. The fact that the city retained its original name Paneas or Panias, besides its official name Caesarea (and the fact that it was the only name which survived after the Roman period), can be considered proof that Pan was the real patron-god of the place and of the city as well. The attendant gods and deities associated with his sanctuary were of minor importance. Some of these associated gods were probably established there from the beginning of the cult, while others were added later on. However, whatever the ideological or historical reasons for their admittance to the sanctuary, their presence never marred Pan's undisputed patronage.

The incorporation of the sanctuary into the urban area of Caesarea Philippi eventually brought about certain modifications in the ritual process, in the timetable of the worship, as well as in the nature of celebrations. In the course of time (more precisely during the second century CE), under the influence of the general tendency towards religious syncretism, the cult of Pan was exposed to other influences, which affected not only the character or the process of the worship but the religious perception of the god. In one of the inscriptions, dated probably to the second century CE, engraved on the rock cliff under a carved niche, Pan is fused with Zeus and he is called Διό-Παν. The inscription reads:

Τήν δε θεὰν ἀνέθηκε
Φιλευήχῳ Διοπανί,
Οὐίκτωρ (ἀ)ρητὴρ Λυσι-
μάχοιο γόνος.

The present goddess was dedicated to DioPan the sound-lover, by the priest Victor, the son of Lysimachos.[6]

The fusion of Pan with the supreme god Zeus certainly weakened the ideological conception of Pan but in no case caused his cult or his religious status to disappear from the city of Caesarea Philippi. The demise of the cult started much later as a result of the general oppression of paganism until it was entirely suppressed in the course of the fourth century CE by the Christian Roman Empire.[7]

The Augustaeum and the Roman Imperial Cult

The erection of the Augustaeum and the consequent introduction of the Roman imperial cult at Paneas, as we have seen above, is attested by Josephus Flavius (*War* 1.404-406; *Ant.* 15.363-64). Numismatic evidence is also available.[8] Josephus's testimony is very clear and assertive concerning Herod's initiative:

> And when he returned home after escorting Caesar to the sea, he erected to him a very beautiful temple of white stone in the territory of Zenodorus, near the place called Paneion. In the mountains here there is a beautiful cave, and below it the earth slopes steeply to a precipitous and inaccessible depth, which is filled with still water, while above it there is a very high mountain. Below the cave rise the sources of the river Jordan. It was this most celebrated place that Herod further adorned with the temple which he consecrated to Caesar (*Ant.* 15.363-64).

The consecration of the temple to Augustus at Paneas by Herod was not an unusual act or an unprecedented phenomenon. The cult of kings

6. Waddington, *Inscriptions*, No. 1892.
7. In the fourth century CE, the cult of Pan as well as his sanctuary at Caesarea Philippi were active but their heydays belonged to the past. A legend narrated by the fourth-century church father Eusebius, about a certain festival taking place at the springs of Paneas and of its abolition by the Christian Asterius, clearly indicates the decline of the cult and its final suppression by the new, ascending religion, Christianity. See, Eusebius, *Ecclesiastical History*, 7, 17.
8. Concerning the numismatic evidence about the temple, see Meshorer, 'The Coins of Caesarea Philippi', p. 46.

and rulers was regularly practised in the Hellenistic period. It was first established by the various Greek cities to reciprocate political benefactions or as an attempt to come to terms with a new type of power. Whatever the reasons, the Greeks modelled the ruler's cult on religious sentiments, binding it with certain rituals.

The concept of the ruler's divinity as conceived and put into practice by the Greek cities during the Hellenistic period passed over into the Roman period. The Romans not only welcomed the idea, they elaborated upon it on a wider politico-religious base and conveyed it first to those they had subjugated and later to the Romans themselves. Herod's initiative was not therefore an eccentric act. Although his action was instigated by motives of gratitude, honour and flattery, his real intention was to establish at Paneas the cult of his patron and benefactor Augustus. In doing so, he both followed the example of other tributary cities and kings of the late Hellenistic age and carried out a Roman demand consistent with the official policy of the Roman regime.[9]

The erection of the Augustaeum at Paneas required some kind of ritual instituted there, such as festivals, feasts and sacrifices to the divine emperor. Though we lack any information, literary or archaeological, we may assume that rituals were actually established there in addition to those regularly held in the sanctuary of Pan.

Later on, with the founding of Caesarea, when the Augustaeum had become one of the official places of cult worship in the city, gladiatorial games and animal fights in honour of the emperor were probably also organized on a regular basis. The cult of Augustus continued in practice at Caesarea well after the emperor's death, at least to the middle of the first century CE. The first interruption in the cult's worship probably occurred during the reign of Agrippa II in 67 CE. According to Josephus, in that year King Agrippa II 'enlarged Caesarea Philippi... and renamed it Neronias in honour of Nero' (*Ant.* 20.211; *Life* 13). In other words, King Agrippa II, in 67 CE,

9.   Within the confines of the Roman Empire, kings and princes who owed their power to the recognition of Rome named cities for Augustus and created temples in his honour. Most significant was the activity of Herod the Great in building shrines (Augustaea) and cities (Sebasteia, Caesarea). See, Josephus, *War*, 1.403-14.

Concerning the practice of the roman Imperial cult in general see L.R. Taylor, *The Divinity of the Roman Emperor: Augustus' Deification* (Middletown, CT, 1931), pp. 224-37.

rededicated the city by adding new public buildings and institutions and changed its name from Caesarea Philippi to Neronias. Such an act was, no doubt, accompanied by certain formalities of both a religious and a civic character. The conversion of the temple of Augustus (by whose name the city was originally called by the Tetrarch Philip) to one meant for the worship of Nero (whose name the city was now given) was apparently the most appropriate decision taken by Agrippa. Even though the new name Neronias did not last for many years (it never actually replaced that of Caesarea or Paneas), the activity of the cult of Augustus, established by Herod the Great, was seriously interrupted and probably never resumed. Instead, the regular Roman imperial cult, based on whichever emperor was ruling at the time, was introduced. Such a practice did not oppose or offend the official Roman attitude as long as the Roman political and religious interests were present. If we consider both Roman policy and the fact that the Imperial cult was neither static nor monolithic, we may assume that the temple of Augustus at Caesarea Philippi was, throughout the Roman period, constantly rededicated to the currently living emperor.

The Cult of Tyche

There is as yet no literary or archaeological evidence which attests to the Tetrarch Philip having established the cult of Tyche-Fortuna at Caesarea. We can only assume that he might have done so guided by the vogue of the time. Tyche, the goddess in whose hands lay the destinies of people, cities and kingdoms was from the Hellenistic period onwards a popular deity, actually the greatest of those in human matters. Every new city founded had a temple dedicated to her. Tyche's temples were usually very imposing buildings set up in the agora or the acropolis. The goddess was reckoned as the 'fortune of the city' and often as the patron goddess, whom the citizens had to honour in order that she may become the ἀγαθή Τύχη (the beneficient Fortuna) of their city. The belief in Tyche was bolstered much more in Roman times when every Greek city had its own Fortuna or Tyche goddess, depicted as a woman majestically dressed and adorned with a wall-shaped crown loaded with fruits or local symbols. It sounds reasonable, therefore, that Caesarea Philippi should have its own Tyche adored in her own sanctuary, the Tychaeon, as all other Greek and Roman cities had.

The establishment of Tyche's cult was not always accompanied by the erection of temples or with any official civic procedure; nor did it need any official royal approval. In most cases a statue of the goddess, accompanied by an altar and some sort of open courtyard on the agora, on the acropolis or on any other prominent place was sufficient. There is a probability that such an improvised Tychaeon existed in Caesarea Philippi throughout the reigns of Philip and Agrippa II, up to the end of the first century CE. The representation of Tyche on coins struck by Agrippa II—without any architectural elements—is not only evidence that the cult of Tyche was active at Caesarea Philippi from its establishment but also suggests that no temple was dedicated to this goddess before the second century CE. Tyche acquired her first temple at Caesarea Philippi only during the second or at the beginning of the third century. The numismatic evidence for this is conclusive. On coins issued at Caesarea from the end of the second century onwards, Tyche is usually presented within structures of different styles, undoubtedly representing her temples.[10] On coins dated from the first half of the third century the goddess is shown within a tetrastyle temple with a central arch (Syrian gable) or within a distyle one. The different structures accompanying Tyche on the coins may indicate the existence of more than one temple dedicated to her in Caesarea Philippi. The numismatic evidence thus far discovered supports our understanding of the ritual practices and religious concepts attached to Tyche during the period of late antiquity. In the course of the second to fourth centuries CE she was worshipped under various guises at one and the same place.

The Cult of Zeus

The cult of Zeus-Jupiter, god and father of gods and men alike, held a predominant position throughout the Roman era, continuing the popularity it gained among the Greeks in the classical and Hellenistic periods. Temples to Zeus were commonplace throughout the Roman empire. Greek and Roman cities competed for the honour of erecting the most magnificient temple or earning the favour of the supreme god. Caesarea Philippi was no exception. The numismatic and epigraphic evidence makes very clear the prominent place occupied by the cult of Zeus alongside the worship of many other deities. We have

10. Meshorer, 'The Coins of Caesarea Philippi', p. 43.

already seen that in the course of the second century CE Pan was, in some way, fused with Zeus and worshipped within the sanctuary as Διό-Παν.[11] Apparently, the same ideological or religious reasons which brought about the fusion of Pan with Zeus also fostered the establishment of the worship of Zeus as a distinct and independent cult in the city. The establishment of the cult, or at least the date of the erection of the first temple to Zeus at Caesarea Philippi, probably occurred during the reign of the emperor Marcus Aurelius (161–180 CE).

The second century CE was exceptionally propitious for the cult of Zeus among Romans and Greeks alike. Roman policy, steered in part by the religious arrogance of the emperors, intentionally bolstered the cult of Jupiter, considering it as one of the main ways to promote the political interests of Rome. Thus, throughout the reigns of Trajan and Hadrian there was an emphasis on Jupiter, who alone could empower and protect the emperors. For the first time, in the first half of the second century, the Capitoline Triad, Jupiter, Juno and Minerva, are seen on the coinage, while Jupiter is honoured under the titles of Victor, Protector and Guardian.

The Stoics of the 'New Stoa' on the other hand, helped to foster the exalted position of Zeus-Jupiter. Zeus was the principal god of the Stoics or at least the most common among the gods they were ready to accept. The devotion to Jupiter continued under Antonius Pius (138–161 CE) and Marcus Aurelius (161–180 CE). Under Marcus Aurelius, a philosopher closely associated with the Stoic ideology, the exaltation of Jupiter reached its climax. It was probably during his reign that the first temple to Zeus was erected at Caesarea Philippi, a fact which is positively attested by the numismatic evidence.[12]

Thus far I have dealt with the pagan deities worshipped at Caesarea Philippi during the Hellenistic and Roman periods, that is, from the beginning of the second century BCE until the dominance of Christianity in the first half of the fourth century CE. The evidence available comes solely from literary, epigraphic and numismatic sources. Archaeology has as yet provided nothing concrete, but the interesting discoveries of the last three years, resulting from the two separate archaeological expeditions working at the site, allude to the splendour of the various public and civic structures of Caesarea Philippi in the Roman period. No doubt, the temples of the city which were

11. See Waddington, *Inscriptions*, No. 1892.
12. Meshorer, 'The Coins of Caesarea Philippi', p. 42.

considered as the most prominent edifices and the most venerated religious institutions, were constructed with equal, if not superior, magnificence. We can only hope that the coming archaeological seasons will provide the missing architectural evidence and the topographical setting of the temples and sanctuaries of the deities which I have dealt with above.[13]

13. Systematic archaeological excavations were started at the site of ancient Caesarea Philippi in 1987 by the Israel Antiquities Authority, the Nature Reserves Authority and five American Institutions: Pepperdine University, California; Averett College, Virginia; Hardin–Simmons University, Texas; Christian Church University, Texas; and Southwest Missouri State University.

At the present time two archaeological expeditions are in process: the Joint Expedition mentioned above, headed by the writer, and the expedition of the Israel Antiquities Authority, headed by Dr Zvi Maoz, the district archaeologist of Golan. The latter is carried out in the area of the Sanctuary of Pan, within and outside the cave. The first expedition is concentrated into two areas at the centre of ancient Caesarea. The excavations on both areas have brought to light, so far, most of the premises of Pan's sanctuary along the cliff and rich remnants from the various public buildings of the ancient city of Caesarea Philippi.

Part IV

THE THEOLOGY OF THE HEBREW BIBLE

SOME REFLECTIONS ON CREATION AS A TOPIC OF OLD TESTAMENT THEOLOGY

Rolf Rendtorff

I

The Hebrew Bible begins with creation. Old Testament Theologies usually do not. How is that? The answer is obvious: because of the theology of the respective authors of Old Testament Theologies. The preliminary decision of those authors that creation is not to be seen as a central topic in the Hebrew Bible includes not giving prominence to it in a description of Old Testament theology.

The reasons for those decisions are manyfold. In the late nineteenth century we find the last Old Testament Theology that begins with creation, written by Gustav Friedrich Oehler and published after his death in 1872.[1] He was a representative of *heilsgeschichtlich* theology who wanted to explain the history of the 'economy of revelation'. This divine economy definitely begins with creation. Almost at the same time the most well-known Old Testament Theology of the second half of the nineteenth century appeared, written by Hermann Schultz, who wanted to describe Israel's religion in its development.[2] For him the history of Israel's religion began at the level of primitive Semitic tribes which, of course, had no idea of creation.

Since then an interesting development has taken place. A lot of ancient Near Eastern material has been brought to the attention of Old Testament scholars providing evidence of the existence of creation

---

1. G.F. Oehler, *Theologie des Alten Testaments* (ed. H. Oehler; 2 vols.; Tübingen, 1873–74); ET: *Theology of the Old Testament* (2 vols.; Edinburgh, 1874–75).

2. H. Schultz, *Alttestamentliche Theologie: Die Offenbarungsreligion auf ihrer vorchristlichen Entwicklungsstufe* (Frankfurt, 5th rev. edn, 1896 [1869]); ET of the 4th edition: *Old Testament Theology: The Religion of Revelation in its Pre-Christian Stage of Development* (2 vols.; Edinburgh, 1892).

myths in other religions much earlier than the beginning of Israel's history. Old Testament theologians, however, followed other tracks, influenced by 'Dialectic Theology', putting God's salvific interventions in Israel's history in the first place. Walther Eichrodt's Old Testament Theology was the first and most famous example of this theological approach dealing with creation only in the second of the three volumes of his Old Testament Theology.[3]

In Gerhard von Rad's work we find first of all a concurrence of two different arguments in favour of setting aside the topic of creation. He explains that in Old Testament texts creation theology generally is subordinate to salvation theology and so never became an independent subject of theological thought.[4] In addition, he developed his well-known hypothesis of a 'historical creed' (Deut. 26.5-9 and elsewhere) that begins with the exodus from Egypt and formed the original basic unit of the Pentateuch (or Hexateuch). Therefore the primaeval history was only the latest *Vorbau* in the literary development of the Hexateuch.[5] But it is significant that von Rad, in spite of these two arguments against a priority position of creation, began his book on Old Testament theology with the primaeval history, and that because of canonical reasons (see below). Later in his book on wisdom in the Old Testament he gave certain creation texts a prominent role in biblical thought.[6]

Nevertheless, creation to this day has been one of the 'proverbial step-children' in the recent discipline of Old Testament theology.[7]

3. W. Eichrodt, *Theologie des Alten Testaments* (3 vols.; Leipzig: Hinrichs, 1933–39); ET: *Theology of the Old Testament* (2 vols.; Philadelphia: Westminster Press, 1961–67); creation is dealt with in vol. II.

4. G. von Rad, 'Das theologische Problem des alttestamentlichen Schöpfungsglaubens' (*BZAW*, 66; Berlin: de Gruyter, 1936), pp. 138-47.

5. G. von Rad, *The Problem of the Hexateuch and Other Essays* (trans. E. Trueman Dicken; Edinburgh: Oliver & Boyd, 1966).

6. G. von Rad, *Weisheit in Israel* (Neukirchen–Vluyn: Neukirchener Verlag, 1970). Cf. also R. Rendtorff, '"Wo warst du, als ich die Erde gründete?"': Schöpfung und Heilsgeschichte', in G. Rau *et al.* (eds.), *Frieden in der Schöpfung: Das Naturverständnis protestantischer Theologie* (Gütersloh: Gütersloher Verlagshaus, 1987) = R. Rendtorff, *Kanon und Theologie: Vorarbeiten zu einer Theologie des Alten Testaments* (Neukirchen–Vluyn: Neukirchener Verlag, 1991), pp. 96-112.

7. J.H. Hayes and F. Prussner, *Old Testament Theology: Its History and Development* (London: SCM Press, 1985), p. 274.

Most recently, Horst Dietrich Preuss, referring to von Rad's statement from 1936, declared: 'Therefore "creation" has no theological weight of its own within the Old Testament world of belief, and cannot have it within an "Old Testament Theology"'.[8] In Preuss's Old Testament Theology the leading topic[9] is 'election', and creation is dealt with in one paragraph in his chapter on 'The Electing God' (§4.6).

There are some exceptions. First of all Yehezkel Kaufmann. In the English abridged edition of his voluminous work the chapter on Israelite religion begins: 'The basic idea of Israelite religion is that God is supreme over all. There is no realm above or beside him to limit his absolute sovereignty.'[10] Recently Jon D. Levenson has discussed Kaufmann's position.[11] He agrees that it has its basis in a text such as Genesis 1, but he argues that creation thought in the Hebrew Bible is much more complex. With regard to Psalm 82, for example, Levenson argues rightly that Kaufmann has mistakenly taken the hope of the psalm that God will rule the world and take possession of all peoples (v.8) as a current reality.

Rolf Knierim, discussing 'The Task of Old Testament Theology' by systematizing Old Testament topics, finally came to the following conclusion: 'Yahweh's relationship to universal reality as expressed in the theology of creation can be discerned in the final analysis as what is at issue in the Old Testament'.[12] He wants to combine this insight with the other one that 'the notions of justice and righteousness... represent the most fundamental of the modes in which the universality of Yahweh's relationship with reality is perceived'. Therefore, according to Knierim, 'the universal dominion of Yahweh in justice and righteousness' is 'the ultimate vantage point from which to coordinate its [i.e. the Old Testament's] theologies'.

Another exception is von Rad who, because of the canonical concept

---

8.　H.D. Preuss, *Theologie des Alten Testaments*. I. *JHWHS erwählendes und verpflichtendes Handeln* (Stuttgart: Kohlhammer, 1991), I, p. 271.

9.　Preuss, in the context of an ongoing debate among German Old Testament scholars, declares election to be the 'center' (*Mitte*) of the Old Testament.

10.　Y. Kaufmann, *The Religion of Israel: From Its Beginnings to the Babylonian Exile* (trans. and abridged M. Greenberg; Chicago: University of Chicago Press, 1960), p. 60.

11.　J.D. Levenson, *Creation and the Persistence of Evil: The Jewish Drama of Divine Omnipotence* (San Francisco: Harper & Row, 1988), pp. 3-13.

12.　R. Knierim, 'The Task of Old Testament Theology', *HBT* 6 (1984), pp. 25-57 (43).

of his Old Testament theology, begins with the primaeval history in Genesis. Unlike Knierim, who came to his proposal by his own analysis of Old Testament issues, von Rad simply followed the decision reached by the Old Testament authors by starting with the 'beginning' (ראשית), that is, with creation. This seems to me to be a good decision. The final authors of the Hebrew Bible understood creation not as one topic among others or even one of lower significance. For them creation was the starting point, because everything human beings can think and say about God and his relation to the world and to humankind depends on the fact that he created all this. Therefore not only does he rule the whole of creation, but he is also finally responsible for what happens within the world he created. The so-called Deutero-Isaiah expressed this in a stringent way:

> I am the LORD and there is no other,
> I form light and create darkness,
> I make weal and create woe,
> I am the LORD, who does all these things (Isa. 45.6-7).

II

Reading Old Testament creation texts in their given (canonical) context leads to a view quite different from the usual one. The context of Genesis 1 and 2 makes it impossible to read these chapters only as texts about creation as such. They are telling a story whose continuation is far beyond themselves. Joseph Blenkinsopp in his forthcoming Anchor Bible Reference Book on the Pentateuch,[13] whose manuscript I had the privilege to read, begins the chapter on 'Human Origins (Gen. 1.1–11.26)' with a paragraph on 'the historiographical pattern'. He shows that these first eleven chapters are related to the following stories in Genesis by a carefully structured genealogical scheme. At the same time he explains the relationship of the biblical primaeval history to Ancient Mesopotamian texts, in particular to the *Atrahasis* text, that makes it evident that the creation story (or stories) are to be read in conjunction with their following text leading through the deluge to the reconstruction of the creation in God's covenant with Noah (Genesis 9). This means that these stories

---

13. J. Blenkinsopp, *The Pentateuch: Structure, Origins, Formation: The Present State of Inquiry* (Anchor Bible Reference Library; Garden City, NY: Doubleday, 1992).

are to be read retrospectively from the point of view of those living after the deluge. They are looking back to the creation in its original perfection and beauty, being conscious of the human sin that endangered the very existence of the creation, but trusting in God's graciously established covenant with humankind and all living beings, promising that, in spite of the continuing human sinfulness, creation in its post-deluge order (Gen 9.1-7) will persist.[14]

Thus, creation is part of the first chapter of human history. One might assume that the readers of the following chapters of the Pentateuch, and even beyond that, would take it for granted that the God who speaks and acts is the creator of the world, even if it is not mentioned all the time. It could be questioned whether this was the case with every story in its original form and context. But today the problems of dating the texts as well as the problem of the age of creation traditions in Israel are more controversial then ever.[15] In any case, the reader of the given context understands that Abraham has been singled out from the whole of humanity by God, the creator of the world. The genealogy at the end of the primaeval history leads to Abraham (Gen. 11.27), and in God's first speech to Abraham as the ancestor of Israel 'all families of the earth' are mentioned as being somehow included in or, at least, affected by this new story (Gen. 12.1-3). The God who calls or 'elects' Abraham is the God of all humankind.

In the following chapters this is only mentioned from time to time, sometimes without specific emphasis: in Gen 24.3, for example, Abraham makes his slave swear 'by the LORD, the God of heaven and earth' (cf. v.7). Some scholars see that as a proof of a rather late date for the chapter, but the question is controversial. In Gen. 18.25 Abraham calls YHWH 'the Judge of all the earth', which can only mean that he is the one who has the capacity to judge all people on the earth because, in the given context, he created them. Again, this discussion between Abraham and God, on the way from Mamre to Sodom, is seen by some scholars as a rather 'late' text. With much more emphasis God is called 'עליון אל, creator of heaven and earth' in Gen. 14.19, and this title is identified with YHWH in v.22. The origin

14. Cf. R. Rendtorff, '"Covenant" as a Structuring Concept in Genesis and Exodus', *JBL* 108 (1989), pp. 385-93.

15. These problems are unfolded in an illuminating way in J. Blenkinsopp's forthcoming book (see n. 13).

and age of this text is even more controversial.

One could thus argue that only in some rather marginal places in the patriarchal stories is God called the creator. But one could also argue inversely that in the given context it is self-evident that the God who is here speaking and acting is the same as the creator in the primaeval history. The question is of particular interest because it could be linked up with the other question of whether the text of the book of Genesis, like those of other Old Testament books, had on its earlier 'original' level a more limited idea of God. This would involve questions of the origin of Israelite monotheism as well as of the 'sources' of the Pentateuch, their age and redaction or composition and the like. It would go beyond the scope of this paper to discuss this kind of problem, but I wanted to show the interrelations of these different groups of questions. I believe that in the framework of an Old Testament Theology one will have to decide on what level to argue or how to relate the different levels to each other.

III

Let us turn to the last book of the Pentateuch. Seemingly, Deuteronomy has no theology of creation. But that God is the creator of the world is obviously a basic element in the theological convictions of the author(s). It is significant that this notion appears several times in order to support and to strengthen certain arguments: 'For ask now about former ages, long before your own, ever since the day that God created human beings on the earth...' (Deut. 4.32). To think as far back as possible inevitably leads to the time when God acted as creator of human beings. This seems to be self-evident for the author as well as for his readers. But then the argument is inverted: remembering all the things mentioned in this section Israel shall 'acknowledge that the LORD is God; there is no other besides him' (v. 35). The preceding knowledge that God is the creator of the world, and the acknowledgment of his creatorship following the experience of his deeds, are two sides of the same coin. In the following section the issue is Israel's election, and again it leads to the acknowledgment 'that the LORD is God in heaven above and on the earth beneath; there is no other' (v. 39). And again, there is a consequence of this acknowledgment: to 'keep the statutes and commandments, which I am commanding you today' (v. 40). To remember the creator at the beginnings of human history, and to acknowledge the creator as the presently electing and commanding God, both these aspects belong to each other.

The interrelation between election, commandments and God the creator is also to be found at some more places in Deuteronomy: in 7.6-11 the acknowledgment formula reads: 'Know therefore that the LORD, your God is *the* God (כי־יהוה אלהיך הוא האלהים)' (v. 9). In 10.12-22 it reads: 'The heaven and the heavens of heaven belong to the LORD your God, the earth and all that is in it' (v.14), and: 'The LORD your God, he is the God of gods and the LORD of lords, the great, the mighty and the awesome God' (v.17). From the variations in terminology we learn, among other things, that the formula 'YHWH is *the* God' (יהוה הוא האלהים) means exactly that: he is the one and only God who created the world and rules it. I think the formula has to be understood that way also in places like 1 Kgs 8.60, 18.39 and others. We also understand the exact meaning of the introductory divine speech at Mount Sinai in Exod. 19.4-6 where we find the same combination of election and commandments (covenant), and the declaration: 'Indeed, all the earth is mine' (v.5b).[16]

These observations show that the belief in God the creator is present throughout the Pentateuch, being mentioned from time to time in different contexts. It is explicitly unfolded only in the first chapters, but there is no reason to doubt that authors and readers are always conscious of this fundamental element of the Israelite religion.

IV

One of the badly neglected Old Testament texts is the great 'confessional prayer' in Neh. 9.6-37. Joseph Blenkinsopp, whose commentary is one of the very few detailed treatments of this text,[17] puts it rightly next to Psalm 136, the only one of the 'historical' psalms that begins with creation. Yet the difference may be more significant. Psalm 136 jumps in a dramatic shift of scenes from the creation of heaven, earth and the heavenly lights to Israel's exodus from Egypt (vv. 9-10). Nehemiah 9, however, follows the sequence

16. Cf. R. Rendtorff, 'Die Erwählung Israels als Thema der deuteronomische Theologie', in J. Jeremias *et al.* (eds.), *Die Botschaft und die Boten* (Festschrift H.W. Wolff; Neukirchen–Vluyn: Neukirchener Verlag, 1981), pp. 75-86.

17. J. Blenkinsopp, *Ezra–Nehemiah: A Commentary* (OTL; London: SCM Press, 1989).

of Genesis from creation to the election of Abraham (vv. 6-7). Both of these two events open with the identical introductory formula 'You are the LORD' (אתה־הוא יהוה) which does not appear anywhere else in this long prayer. This parallelism shows the close connection between these two great deeds of God in early history. In addition, they are bound together by the closing formula 'for you are just' (כי צדיק אתה v. 8). This formula is repeated near the end of the prayer in v. 33 (ואתה צדיק) confirming that God is 'free of blame for what had happened' (Blenkinsopp) while Israel has done wrong.

This prayer is a very interesting text. On the one hand it seems to be rather isolated, according to its genre as well as in its immediate context, while on the other hand it is very familiar with the Pentateuchal and Deuteronomic traditions which it quotes throughout. Hence it shows an inner-biblical development which might be characteristic for a certain kind of use of the traditions in postexilic Israel. In the context of this paper the close connection, and even parallelism, between creation and the election of Abraham is of specific interest. After saying that 'the host of heaven worships you' (v.6) the prayer immediately continues with Abraham. This appears to be the most important event after creation.

In this section on Abraham the use of different traditions is significant. First it is said that God did 'elect' Abraham. Here the word בחר is used, which is a term from Deuteronomic theological language, there used for the election of Israel.[18] In Deuteronomy we also find a relation between creation and election (see above). But Nehemiah 9 is the only place in the Hebrew Bible where the term בחר is used concerning Abraham. By that use Israel's election is placed in close proximity to creation. The next point is that God brought Abraham out of Ur Kasdim. This sounds like a quotation from Gen. 15.7. Also the following remark, that God found Abraham's heart faithful (נאמן), is reminiscent of Gen. 15.6: Abraham 'trusted (והאמן) in the Lord'. Finally, the mentioning of the covenant which God made with Abraham is worded in the same way as in Genesis 15 where ברית is immediately followed by the promise to give the land to Abraham's descendants; only the list of nations is different. The remaining point, the change of the name from Abram to Abraham, is related to Gen. 17.5, a chapter close to Genesis 15; and only in these

18. See Rendtorff, 'Die Erwählung Israels'.

two chapters in Genesis is God's covenant with Abraham mentioned. All this speaks of 'a new role and destiny' (Blenkinsopp) given to Abraham in this first act of God after the creation. It is important, as Blenkinsopp points out, that the term ברית in the whole prayer is only used in relation to Abraham. Like the use of בחר, this shows that Abraham stands here for Israel as a whole. God's covenant with Israel, represented by the faithful Abraham, is God's first and fundamental act after creation. What follows shows that Israel did not follow the ways of Abraham. But nevertheless it can always pray to the God who established his relationship to Israel through Abraham and who will be faithful to his promises, because he is צדיק.

Let us turn back to Psalm 136. At first glance these two texts are totally different (see above). In Psalm 136 God is praised as the victorious one who in his power as creator leads Israel through all imperilments into the land he gave to his people as נחלה. But if we look at the end of the psalm we realize that Israel is now in a state of degradation caused by enemies (vv. 23-24), and also in a state of hunger (v.25). This does not seem to be too far from Neh. 9.36: 'Today we are slaves (in) the land that you gave our fathers to enjoy its fruit and its good gifts'. Here, like in Nehemiah 9, the praying community reminds God of his deeds in the past. Thereby the two texts start from different points in Israel's history, the covenant with Abraham and the exodus; but both of them link this beginning back to an earlier one, the beginning, creation, where God's history with his people really began.

Thus these two texts show an interesting and important way in which in postexilic Israel, creation could be made to be the most important point from where to start reflecting upon one's own present situation and God's ability to change it. If the God who elected Abraham and led Israel out of Egypt is really God, the creator, then he can and will lead Israel out of the present situation of degradation and distress.

These reflections are only a small excerpt from my present studies, offered to Joseph Blenkinsopp as a token of warm friendship and esteem.

'THOU ART THE CHERUB':
EZEKIEL 28.14 AND THE POST-EZEKIEL
UNDERSTANDING OF GENESIS 2–3

James Barr

In his valuable *History of Prophecy in Israel*, Joseph Blenkinsopp rightly emphasizes the gateway position of Ezekiel 'between the Old Order and the New'.[1] Ezekiel completes some of the patterns that prophecy had taken during the First Temple and certainly initiates many tendencies that became normal or regulative in the Second Temple period. In some cases it may be difficult to determine on which side the stress should lie.

One relevant aspect is the re-emergence of the Eden myth.[2] My interest lies in the two oracles against the king of Tyre, Ezek. 28.1-10 and 28.11-19, especially the latter. For my purposes, the first of these is fairly clear: it depicts the king of Tyre as a human who has come to think he is a god. He has wisdom like Daniel and enormous wealth. But God will bring 'strangers' upon him who will defile his splendor, and he will be cast down into the Pit. The second oracle is set in 'Eden, the garden of God' (v. 13) or on 'the mountain of God' (v. 16), a place adorned with gold and precious stones. Here again a person is to be castigated and expelled: 'You were blameless in your ways from the day you were created till iniquity was found in you' (v. 15), but 'your heart was proud because of your beauty' (v. 17). And so, this person came to a dreadful end.

But who was this person? Was it the first human, Adam, as he is

---

1. As he entitles chapter 5. Cf. J. Blenkinsopp, *History of Prophecy in Israel* (Philadelphia: Westminster Press, 1983), p. 177.

2. Mentioned briefly in Blenkinsopp, *History*, p. 202. Since the matter is complicated and obscure, Blenkinsopp naturally had no space to discuss its details within his volume. Cf. also his remarks in his *Wisdom and Law in the Old Testament* (Oxford: Oxford University Press, 1983), p. 6.

called in Genesis? Or was it a superhuman being, one of the divinely appointed agents who guarded the garden? The question, as we will see, is important for understanding Genesis, the history of prophecy, and aspects of religion in the Second Temple period. But I shall not have space enough to follow out these aspects in full: I shall concentrate on one linguistic-textual question which, though in itself a small detail, appears to exercise a disproportionate degree of influence on the general interpretation of the passage.

At Ezek. 28.14 in the MT, the verse begins with the phrase את־כרוב. If it means, 'You are the [or, a] cherub [plus various, somewhat obscure, attributes]', this gives a distinct identity to the person addressed. It means that the whole oracle is addressed to one who did the service that cherubim were supposed to undertake, whatever that might be. If, however, it means something else, it might suggest that the main person addressed in the whole oracle is not the cherub, but someone else, a person who is only juxtaposed or associated with the cherub. Such a person in the Garden of Eden is likely to have been the first man, known in Genesis as Adam.

Now the MT has been regarded with scepticism by scholars at this point. 'Nothing can be made of *M "thou (art) the cherub anointing (?) that covers and I will place thee,"* ', wrote G.A. Cooke, '...*G* points to a better reading'.[3]

What is this better reading? The LXX here has the phrase, μετὰ τοῦ χερούβ, 'with the cherub'; to quote the phrase at more length: μετὰ τοῦ χερούβ ἔθηκά σε 'with the cherub I placed you'. Something similar lies in the Syriac *whwyt mkrwb*, 'and you were with the cherub'.

A very large number of commentators have followed the Greek text. R.R. Wilson lists many of them in an interesting article, mentioning the numerous difficulties that are thought to arise if the text is not emended after the Greek version.[4] Among these scholars the most

---

3. G.A. Cooke, *A Critical and Exegetical Commentary on the Book of Ezekiel* (ICC, 18; Edinburgh: T. & T. Clark, 1936), p. 317.
4. For a bibliography of commentators who have taken this path, see R.R. Wilson's article, 'The Death of the King of Tyre: The Editorial History of Ezekiel 28', in J.H. Marks and R.M. Good (eds.), *Love and Death in the Ancient Near East* (Guilford, CT: Four Quarters, 1987), pp. 211-18, especially n. 21 on p. 215. See, e.g., H.G. May, 'The King in the Garden of Eden: A Study of Ezekiel 28:12-19', in B.W. Anderson and W. Harrelson (eds.), *Israel's Prophetic Heritage*

important in recent times is doubtless Zimmerli with his monumental study in the *Biblischer Kommentar*.[5] He translates the passage, 'I associated you with [the]...guardian cherub'.

The apparatus of *BHS* commends a similar course as 'probable', citing the Greek and Syriac as mentioned above. In other words, the Hebrew form את is taken as *'et*. It then produces either a sense such as 'with', the way which the LXX took it, or, making a further excursion on the basis of the same evidence, the direct object particle.[6] Thus the RSV understands 'with': 'With the anointed guardian cherub I placed you', which the NSRV slightly alters to 'With an anointed cherub as guardian I placed you'. Similarly NEB reads, 'I set you with a towering cherub as guardian',[7] but the REB appears to follow the track of the object particle: 'I appointed a towering cherub as your guardian'. Readers of such modern translations will probably have no means of knowing that the phrase can be taken in any other way.

What was the Hebrew form of the MT? The Masoretic vocalization shows that the first word is taken to be the second person masculine singular personal pronoun. This is normally אַתָּה as everyone knows, but here (and very rarely elsewhere) it has the form *att*, normally the corresponding feminine. This exceptional usage is not well known; perhaps some commentators did not know it, but it is a recognized phenomenon. It is annotated as such in the Masora, which writes, ג בשׁון זכר, 'three cases [in the Bible] with masculine meaning', and it is registered in standard dictionaries. The form, as a masculine, is extremely rare: out of some 740 to 750 cases of the second person masculine singular pronoun, there are only three examples: this one and two others, Num. 11.15 and Deut. 5.24.[8] We may add that there

---

(Muilenburg Festschrift; London, SCM Press, 1962), pp. 166-76, especially p. 168.

5.   *Ezechiel* (BKAT, 13; Neukirchen–Vluyn: Neukirchener Verlag, 1962), pp. 672 and 675; English Edition, *Ezekiel: A Commentary on the Book of the Prophet Ezekiel* (trans. R.E. Clements; Hermenia; Philadelphia: Fortress Press, 1982), II, p. 85.

6.   Each of these solutions involves other adjustments of the text, in particular, probably, the deletion of the *waw*, 'and', that in MT goes with the following verb 'I gave'; this will be mentioned below.

7.   For the textual reasoning followed by NEB, see L.H. Brockington, *The Hebrew Text of the Old Testament* (Oxford: Oxford and Cambridge University Presses, 1973), p. 230.

8.   As stated correctly in BDB, p. 61b.

are five places where the *kethib* אֹת was written but the *qere* restates it as the normal אַתָּה.[9]

These facts, I submit, immediately alter the text-critical probabilities of the passage. The form as written in the MT is extremely rare and contradicts the grammatical expectations of the reader. This readily explains why the LXX and the Peshitto had what appears to be a 'variant reading'. Not at all to their discredit, they failed to recognize the written form.[10] The form אֹת might, by mere statistical probability, be the direct object particle, but no verb was obviously in sight to govern this object. Failing that, it was familiar as the preposition 'with'. Both Greek and Syriac translated it so. In both cases it is by far most easily explained as a misidentification of the extremely unusual form of the MT. Therefore no Greek and Syriac 'variant reading' may serve as a basis for an emendation of the MT. On the contrary, their readings, properly analysed, indirectly confirm the MT.

As all are agreed, the passage is very obscure. In both of the other places which have the form אֹת, and no *qere*, the context probably made it clear what the word was, and the LXX understood it as the pronoun. Again all of the cases with *qere* are correctly diagnosed by the LXX. But in the very difficult and obscure text of Ezek. 28.14 it was otherwise. Seeing the two letters אֹת, the translator opted for the common equivalence 'with'. Whatever the obscurities and possible errors of the MT at other points in Ezekiel 28, at this particular point it is much easier to suppose that the LXX failed to recognize אֹת as the pronoun than to suppose that it really was the preposition or particle, later wrongly vocalized by the Masoretic tradition as the extremely rare form meaning 'thou'. To put it in the other way, if the Masoretic tradition had seen the form אֹת and there was some doubt what it was, it is understandable that they would have thought of diagnosing it as 'with' or as the direct object particle, but it is frankly unbelievable that they would have identified it as the very rare form of 'thou'. The

9. The list of five is given in BDB, p. 61b, except that the 1 Sam. 24.18 reference should be corrected to 24.19.

10. On the processes of semantic scanning involved in the reading of unpointed text, see my articles 'Vocalization and the Analysis of Hebrew among the Ancient Translators', *VTSup* 16 (1967), pp. 1-11, and '"Guessing" in the Septuagint', in *Studien zur Septuaginta: Robert Hanhart zu Ehren* (Abhandlungen der Akademie der Wissenschaften in Göttingen; Mitteilungen des Septuaginta-Unternehmens, 20; Göttingen: Vandenhoeck & Ruprecht, 1990), pp. 19-34.

Masoretic vocalization is credible only if it rested on a *phonic* tradition of the word as *att*. Thus there may be good reasons, in terms of the general content of the passage, for emending the passage as many scholars have done, but it is doubtful whether there is a good *textual* reason for it. While it is easy to explain the LXX and the Syriac renderings as a misreading of the extremely unusual Hebrew represented by the MT, the opposite does not hold true.

What happens in v. 14 has an effect two verses later in v. 16, where there is an additional reference to the 'cherub' in similar words. The phrase is אָבַדְךָ כְּרוּב הַסֹּכֵךְ מִתּוֹךְ אַבְנֵי אֵשׁ. Here again there is a major obscurity: what exactly is the verb, the first word in this series? It looks like the root meaning 'perish, destroy, cause to vanish', but what form of that verb is it? Many commentators have felt it necessary to propose alterations, at least in the vowels.[11] BDB, retaining the MT and following several older grammarians, explains the form as an imperfect first person singular in which the *aleph* of the prefix has merged with the *aleph* of the root.[12] This might well be right. If it is right, it is once again a very unusual form which could easily mystify any reader of average competence, especially so if we think of a reader working from an unpointed text. Given some possible variations, whether in form or in semantic interpretation, the verb could be first person or third, and could refer to past or future. In essence we have the same situation: the verb form of the MT may be very rare, exceptional or obscure.

Where the interpretations of v. 14 listed above have been followed, the effect has been that the 'cherub' of v. 16 is the subject of this clause: the cherub expels or destroys 'you' (the central person of the oracle) from among the stones of fire. The LXX again leads this way: καὶ ἤγαγέν σε τὸ χεροὺβ ἐκ μέσου λίθων πυρίνων 'And the cherub led you out from among the fiery stones'. Some modern translations take the same line. Thus the RSV and NRSV translate 'and the guardian cherub drove you out', while the NEB and REB read 'and the guardian cherub banished you'.

In another tradition of understanding, however, it was the guardian cherub who was banished or to be banished. Linguistically, this was done by taking the noun phrase 'guardian cherub' in v. 16 as a vocative expression in apposition to the object 'you' of the verb plus

11. See again *BHS* apparatus, v. 16 note d; Brockington, *Text*, p. 230.
12. BDB, p. 2a.

suffix ואבדך. Thus for example, the KJV translates, 'I will destroy thee, O covering cherub'; the JPSV, 'and I have destroyed you, O shielding cherub'. My study proceeds mainly from the text of v. 14, but will have to note the connections with v. 16.

Considerable ancient evidence supports the MT. Its text is, of course, what Jerome understood and expressed in the Vulgate, which the KJV largely followed with its 'Thou art the anointed cherub that covereth'. 'Iuxta hebraicum', he wrote in his commentary,[13] the text meant: 'Tu cherub extentus et protegens' in v. 14, and 'Et perdidi te, O cherub protegens' in v. 16. In other words, God addresses the cherub; in v. 16 that word is in a vocative construction. Jerome's testimony is significant, for he certainly knew the LXX text and treated it as an alternative (and must have known that of Symmachus, who also understood את as the particle 'with').[14] But Jerome also knew that the syntax of the Hebrew was 'you are the cherub' in v. 14 and, even more striking, 'you, o cherub' in v. 16. These readings presuppose not only a text like that of the MT, but also a corresponding syntactical analysis. Moreover, they imply that Jerome had the benefit of Jewish opinion in his translation, though he does not explicitly say so.[15]

Though Jerome translated with 'tu cherub'... at v. 14, he said nothing expressly about the form of the Hebrew pronoun. Nevertheless his commentary indicates that he was aware of its peculiarity. Discussing the word *cherub*, he mentions the word in itself and its plural *cherubim*.[16] He begins by saying that *cherub* is the form

13. *S. Hieronymi Presbyteri Opera* (CChr, 75; Turnhout: Brepols, 1964), I.4, pp. 395-97, lines 327-30, 383ff.

14. See F. Field, *Origenis Hexapla* (Oxford: E Typographeo Clarendoniano, 1875), II, p. 847.

15. This is not surprising, when the *Targum Jonathan* also sees it so. This Targum is highly paraphrastic in respect of the general sense, but it preserves the syntactic patterns essential to the interpretation furnished by the MT. Where the Hebrew has words about the cherub, the Targum makes it into the king [of Tyre]: v. 14 begins: 'You are a king (את מלך) anointed for the kingdom'; v. 16 contains: 'and I destroyed you, O noble king (ואבדינך מלכא), because you planned to exercise domination over the holy people' (Translation as in S.H. Levey, *The Aramaic Bible* [Wilmington, DE: Michael Glazier, 1987], XIII, p. 84. Aramaic words are cited from Sperber's edition). It is very probably good evidence for the ancient date of the form and syntax of the MT, at least in these two phrases. This again is serious evidence in favor of the MT.

16. *S. Hieronymi Presbyteri Opera*, p. 395, ll. 336-37.

'genere masculino numero singulari'. To mention the singular number is relevant at a point where he wants to distinguish the singular from the plural. But to mention the masculine gender is not relevant to this comparison, nor is it likely that Jerome would have included this piece of irrelevant information as a matter of course. Our discussion has furnished an obvious reason why it came into his mind at this point. To all who know Hebrew, the form of the pronoun *att* is familiar as the feminine form. Except for those who have the esoteric knowledge of its rare masculine function, its collocation with 'cherub' would be puzzling. Does it mean, someone might have asked—the most obvious possibility—that 'cherub' was feminine? Jerome had, in the corner of his mind, a need to obviate that suggestion. He may not have known the full and correct explanation, or if he knew, he may not have thought it necessary to deploy it at this point. In any case, the note he wrote tends to confirm that he knew that the form was *att*.

Another smaller textual point confirms our explanation of the Greek and Syriac readings here. The LXX text furnishes a pleasant and smooth clause, 'with the cherub I placed you'. There are additional textual problems, however. After the 'cherub' the MT has two other words which the Greek does not have; about these we have nothing to say. But another difference creates the smoothness of the Greek phrase—it does not represent, or ignores, the 'and' which the MT attaches to the verb 'I gave (placed)', וֹנְתַתִּיךָ. The absence of this 'and' has attracted the minds of scholars, as the *BHS* apparatus indicates. But here again we can explain this omission. The syntax of the MT implies two clauses: the nominal clause 'you are the cherub' and the verbal clause 'and I put you'. Once the אַת at the beginning of the sentence was understood as 'with', only one clause remained, the verbal clause, 'with the cherub I put you'. The omission of 'and' resulted from the identification of אֵת already made. The translators often felt free to disregard *waws* and such elements for the sake of syntactic and semantic requirements. The LXX therefore provides no evidence that it had before it a text in which this *waw* was not present.

I should assure readers that these pages are not written with that animus against the preference of any other text to the MT which has become even more strident than before in recent times. I simply think that certain types of cases can be explained along the lines here followed, as in this case. How it is elsewhere is another matter. My argument has shown how a reading of great rarity or obscurity can generate variants, both in ancient texts and more modern scholarship. As Albrektson has powerfully argued, the idea 'difficilior lectio potior' is not an adequate general principle or a valid heuristic device.[17] It merely means that in those cases where the more difficult reading has been original, the more difficult reading has been original. It generalizes from a number of instances where this can be seen to have happened. Our passage in Ezekiel seems to be one of these instances.

If this is convincing, then it gives us one very important phrase, 'Thou art the cherub', along with the corresponding vocative syntax in v. 16. If this is so, it has a decisive effect on the understanding of the chapter, even if many other aspects remain obscure. It is not a 'mere' textual matter for it means that the person addressed in the second oracle, the one who was full of wisdom and perfect in beauty, who walked among the precious stones until finally iniquity was found in him, was a semi-divine being or a divinely placed agent, not the first man, Adam. This does indeed relate to the story of Genesis 2–3, where cherubs guarded the garden after Adam and Eve were expelled, but here it is a cherub—doubtless a different one!—who is in disgrace. This being was perfect (something never said of Adam in Genesis, though it has often been said on his behalf—sometimes, perhaps, by persons who have taken the idea from Ezekiel 28). It walked among the precious stones. It was one of the cherubs but it forsook its work of guardianship, fell into sin and evil, and was expelled. It is suggestive to consider Pope's view that the story derives from an older (Canaanite and Ugaritic) myth of the god El, who was deprived of his pre-eminence and consigned to the underworld.[18] In other words, the story does not so much parallel Adam's disobedience, but the 'angelic' fall, of 'Lucifer, son of the morning' in Isa. 14.12 (RSV: 'Day Star, son of Dawn'), who is 'fallen from heaven'. He had aspired to ascend to heaven, to set his throne on high, but now he was cast down to Sheol—a comparison which Jerome himself rightly and naturally made.[19] Ezekiel stresses the 'wisdom' of this being, a feature which makes him rather more similar to the snake of Genesis 2, and

17. B. Albrektson, 'Difficilior lectio potior', *OTS* 21 (1981), pp. 5-18.

18. M.H. Pope, *El in the Ugaritic Texts* (VTSup, 2; Leiden: Brill, 1955), pp. 97-103; cf. discussion and bibliography in R.R. Wilson, 'The Death of the King of Tyre' (n. 2 above).

19. *S. Hieronymi Presbyteri Opera*, p. 397, ll. 391-93.

less like the humans of that story, who conspicuously lacked that quality. He stresses also its 'beauty', another feature of which Genesis says nothing. One final note about Jerome. As has been said, he knew that the Hebrew text was 'You are the cherub'. But a post-Ezekiel exegete, like the rest of us, he did not mind if it was also taken with the LXX as 'with the cherub'. If a serious doctrinal question had been at stake, he would doubtless have insisted on following the Hebrew and opposed the LXX approach. But for him it did not matter: a human fall and an angelic fall came together and amounted to very much the same story just as it did later for Milton. Thus he can say 'iste autem Cherub, sive creatus cum Cherub': 'this cherub, or a created being with a Cherub'.[20] Doctrinally, either understanding came to very much the same thing.

One possible objection may be mentioned: the double reference (vv. 13, 15) to the 'creation' of the addressee of the oracle. Creation would, of course, fit very well for Adam. Although there is little direct material on the subject in the Hebrew Bible, it is not impossible for superhuman beings. Even of gods it was possible to speak of their 'being fashioned' (Isa. 43.10 [נוֹצַר])—especially when one was speaking polemically of a deity in process of being demoted, demolished or denied.[21]

I may now suggest that Ezekiel 28 has exercised a considerable influence on the understanding of Genesis 2–3. First, although I have distinguished between the two oracles against the king of Tyre in Ezekiel 28, it is likely that the two were lumped together in their general theological impact. If so, the setting of the second oracle in Eden, the garden of God (not mentioned in the first oracle where the setting is 'in the seat of the gods, in the heart of the seas') was nevertheless taken to apply to the first oracle. Thus since Ezekiel, interpreters have often applied the essential idea, that a person who was a man wanted to be counted as a god, to Adam and Eve, whose story in Genesis says nothing explicit about their desire to be counted as gods or equivalent to God. Conversely, the ideas of revolt and violence, explicit in the second oracle, were also applied to the first humans. In other words, the traditional picture of Genesis 2–3 as a story of human 'revolt' against God, inflamed by 'hubris' and the desire to take over God's position as governor of the world, may in considerable

---

20. *S. Hieronymi Presbyteri Opera,* p. 395, ll. 341-42.
21. Note the citation of this verse by Blenkinsopp, *History,* p. 213.

measure come from the combination of Ezekiel 28 with the Genesis passage.

It would be possible—though speculative—that the same interests may have influenced the LXX readings which we have examined. The passage was difficult, but the translator knew it was about the Garden of Eden. From Genesis it was known that *a man* was placed in the garden, no doubt with a cherub nearby as a guard. Later the humans were expelled and cherubim were left in charge, itself not so very distant from saying that the cherub led the man out. Memories of Genesis may have guided the Greek text in saying exactly this. Genesis did not, however, suggest that the cherub itself might be the being about whom the oracle was written. Consciously or unconsciously, perhaps accidentally, perhaps not, the LXX wrote a text that avoided this suggestion. It is difficult to be sure about this; these thoughts, though suggestive, are hardly demonstrable.

The same, however, may be thought about modern scholarship with greater probability. Scholars find the passage obscure but they know it is about the story of Eden. In finding their way through the complexities of the text, they, too, think of the story in Genesis 2–3. Equally, they have hypotheses of the first man as a king or a divine being coming from Genesis, which the Ezekiel text might support. Surely it would be simple if the cherub led the man out? Surely it makes sense if the person central to the oracle was put in Eden *along with* the cherub? If there are text traditions that support these thoughts, are they not likely to represent the genuine ancient text? But we pass back to Ezekiel himself.

If, on the one hand, Ezekiel 28 looks back to a version of the Eden myth—certainly one considerably different from that of our present Genesis 2–3—on the other hand, it looks forward to an aspect that was to be greatly developed in Second Temple times: the emphasis on the angelic 'Fall' as an event that accompanied the 'Fall of Humanity' and was possibly even more important and catastrophic. Concurrently evil and guilt were increasingly considered to be quasi-metaphysical, world-controlling forces, forces derived from events back in the beginnings of the world. As is well known, in the Second Temple period, the snake of Genesis 2–3 became the Satan or devil; in the same period the brief and obscure notice about the marriages of the sons of God with the daughters of men in Genesis 6.1-4 came to be expanded and built up into a gigantic scheme of apocalyptic revolt and destruction. Ezekiel's oracles are a pointer in these directions, an early one if they really come from his time.

This article has concentrated on a very narrow band of data and has made no attempt to approach the many other problems of the chapter and the many interesting insights in other directions that it offers. For example, R.R. Wilson's stimulating suggestions about connections with the Jerusalem priesthood and temple have had to be left aside. It is hoped that the single detailed point made here may leave room for the incorporation of these ideas also. And it is hoped that this essay will fittingly mark and honour Joseph Blenkinsopp's long scholarly interest in the integration of Second Temple religion with earlier precedents.

REMEMBER THAT YOU WERE ALIENS:
A TRADITIO-HISTORICAL STUDY

Christiana de Groot van Houten

Introduction

Study of the tradition history of the Old Testament has brought to the fore the dynamic way in which Israel used its past. Remembering events of long ago was a means of interpreting the present. It was especially significant in proclaiming what God was doing in the present, and how the Israelites were to respond. The traditions had revelatory power; they illumined the here and now, and opened up new possibilities.[1] Not only was the present understood in terms of the past, but the past was understood in terms of the present. There is a dialogue going on between tradition and present experience, and both parties to the conversation emerge changed.[2]

The process of remembering and appealing to the past is crucial to the formation and maintenance of community. There is no community without tradition as there is no tradition without community.[3] The relationship between tradition and community, if the community is to

1. W.E. Rast, *Tradition History and the Old Testament* (Philadelphia: Fortress Press, 1972), p. 73.
2. P. Trible describes the Bible as a pilgrim. It journeys through time engaging the complexities of life by means of traditions which themselves become transformed through the encounters. See her example of the journey of a portrait of God in *God and the Rhetoric of Sexuality* (Overtures to Biblical Theology; Philadelphia: Fortress Press, 1978), pp. 1-5.
3. See S. Hauerwas, 'The Moral Authority of Scripture: The Politics and Ethics of Remembering', in *A Community of Character* (Notre Dame: University of Notre Dame Press, 1981), p. 53. This is further demonstrated in his analysis of Cowslip's warren in Richard Adams' novel, *Watership Down* (New York: Macmillan, 1972), as a warren that was no longer a community because it no longer recalled the founding stories. See his 'A Story-Formed Community: Reflections on Watership Down', in *A Community of Characters*, p. 18.

survive, must be living and dialogical. The community is shaped by the story it tells, at the same time that it remolds and reshapes the story.

It is incumbent on a faithful community to face the future in terms of its traditions. Practical decisions regarding how a community is to be organized, how it is to relate to other communities, what the boundaries will be and how the members ought to relate to each other, are addressed by recalling their narrative. To do this is not to be a static, or even a conservative, community. Tradition need not prevent change, although there are limits to how much a community can change without losing its identity.[4]

It is the connection between Israel's tradition and its social ethic—in particular, the ethics regarding the treatment of strangers—that will concern us in this study. In the Pentateuch the relationship between tradition history and the treatment of the stranger (alien) can be examined by studying those laws dealing with strangers which are motivated by an appeal to the Exodus tradition.[5] This is only one among several ways in which these laws are motivated. For example, the laws in the Pentateuch dealing with the alien (Heb. גר) could be motivated by appealing to humanitarian instincts (Exod. 23.12); promising the blessing of God (Deut. 14.29); or threatening disfavor with God (Deut. 24.15); reminding the Israelites of their calling as a holy people (Deut. 14.21); connecting the law with a goal (Deut. 14.29); or appealing to authority (Lev. 19.10).

This study of the relationship of Israel's tradition to its treatment of aliens will focus only on those motivation clauses[6] which appeal to the past, to the Exodus tradition.[7] Fortuitously, there are laws dealing

---

4.   The rabbits of Hazel's warren appropriated and applied their tradition in a way which promoted change and flexibility, within limits. See 'A Story-Formed Community', p. 26.

5.   The motivation clauses attached to biblical laws are one of the features which sets them apart from other ancient Near Eastern laws. See the study by R. Sonsino, *Motive Clauses in Hebrew Law: Biblical Forms and Near Eastern Parallels* (SBLDS, 45; Chico, CA: Scholars Press, 1980).

6.   A motivation clause is a grammatically subordinate sentence in which the motivation for the commandment is given. See the article by B. Gemser, 'The Importance of the Motive Clause in Old Testament Law', in *Congress Volume* (VTSup, 1; Leiden: Brill, 1953), pp. 50-66, for a catalogue of the various ways motivation clauses are introduced and the forms they take.

7.   This includes: Exod. 22.20 (ET v. 21); 23.9; Deut. 5.15; 16.12; 24.17, 18,

with aliens and backed by such a motivation clause in each legal collection in the Pentateuch. This allows us to trace how the tradition functioned over a long period of time in Israel's history. The laws in the Book of the Covenant will be dealt with first, then the Deuteronomic laws and finally the Priestly laws.[8]

This study in tradition history will illuminate the relationship between Israel's founding narrative and its social ethic. I want to study the way in which a community is shaped by its narrative, and the way a community shapes its narrative. In addition, studying how the tradition is appealed to in order to deal with strangers reveals how Israel drew and maintained the boundaries between itself and others. Noticing who is inside and who is outside is one way to discern what Israel's self-understanding was. Hence, this exercise in tradition history is also an examination of the developing self-identification of the Israelites.

The Covenant Code

There are two laws dealing with the alien and motivated by appealing to the Exodus tradition in the Covenant Code. Exod. 22.20 (ET v. 21) and Exod. 23.9 are both apodictic in form, and contain almost identical prohibitions.

> You shall not wrong (תונה) or oppress (תלחצנו) a resident alien (Exod. 22.20).

> You shall not oppress (תלחץ) a resident alien (Exod. 23.9).[9]

These laws are addressed to the patriarch, who in the Book of the Covenant is the legally responsible member of society. The laws presume that the patriarch is in a position in which he could abuse and oppress the alien.

21, 22; Lev. 19.33, 34; 25.39-46. Studying the relationship between biblical laws and salvation history is a typically Protestant enterprise, and in this paper I do not mean to suggest that this is the superior or only valid way of backing biblical laws. See the analysis of J.D. Levenson ('The Theologies of Commandment in Biblical Israel', *HTR* 73 [1980], pp. 17-34) for a critique of the understanding of law promulgated by nineteenth and twentieth century scholars.

8. For a thorough discussion of the introductory issues involved with each of these legal collections, see Dale Patrick's *Old Testament Law* (Atlanta: John Knox Press, 1985).

9. All translations are from the NRSV unless otherwise noted.

The social situation which is envisioned in these laws is illustrated in the narratives of Genesis 19 and Judges 19.[10] Israelites are living in towns or villages which are small enough that a stranger is recognized. Because there are no inns, the wayfarer passing through goes to the square and waits there for an offer of hospitality. In addition to there being no inn, there is also no police force. If none of the residents offer hospitality, the travellers will spend the night in the square, at the mercy of any local gang. Even when strangers are provided with lodging, they can still be at risk. Both narratives graphically portray how vulnerable strangers, both women and men, were in ancient Israel.[11]

These laws do not require hospitality, although the virtue of hospitality was clearly known. Rather, they put certain actions off limits. The sort of oppression referred to in Exod. 22.20 and 23.9 is violent oppression. It is not neglect that is being prohibited, but rape, beating, robbery and murder.[12] These commandments are motivated by appealing to their past:

for you were aliens in the land of Egypt (Exod. 22.20).

you know the heart of an alien, for you were aliens in the land of Egypt (Exod. 23.9).[13]

10. See A.D.H. Mayes, *Judges* (OTG; Sheffield: JSOT Press, 1985), pp. 72-73 for a description of tribal society and his conclusion that the Book of the Covenant would be an appropriate legal code for it.

11. The identification of aliens with strangers needing hospitality is based on their always being referred to in the singular, and because the Sabbath command in the Covenant Code (Exod. 23.12) presumes that the alien is taken into the patriarch's household. J. Pederson (*Israel: Its Life and Culture* [London: Oxford University Press, 1973 (1927)], I, pp. 39-46) argued that the aliens in the Book of the Covenant were the defeated Israelites, and this thesis is still current. M. Mauch's article on 'Sojourner', in *IDB* (Nashville: Abingdon Press, 1962), IV, pp. 397-99 perpetuates this. However, the laws in the Book of the Covenant are not dealing with large numbers of defeated residents, but with some small groups of strangers.

12. The verb ינה is most often used to describe the oppression of weak Israelites by the powerful. See Lev. 19.33; 25.14-17; Deut. 23.17; Jer. 22.3; Ezek. 18.7, 12, 16; 22.7, 29; 45.8. The second verb, לחץ, is used to refer to foreigners oppressing Israel. See Exod. 3.9; Judg. 2.18; 4.3; 6.9; 10.12; 1 Sam. 10.18; 2 Kgs 13.4; Jer. 30.20; Amos 6.14; Ps. 106.42.

13. B.S. Childs, *The Book of Exodus: A Critical, Theological Commentary* (OTL; Philadelphia: Westminster Press, 1962), p. 454 describes both of these clauses as Deuteronomistic glosses. However, he does not argue the case. Although

Their foundation narrative[14] is being recalled in order to encourage morally upright action. The motivation clause assumes that, given this founding story, certain actions are appropriate and others are inappropriate.

This motivation clause is addressed to Israelites who are no longer aliens but are economically and socially stable and permanent. They have become landholders and home owners. They now hold positions of power. The appeal to tradition reminds them that they were not always so secure. Although this motivation clause does not spell out how the Israelites changed from being aliens to being permanent residents, it does remind them of the contingent nature of their present status. They were once in the vulnerable spot the alien is now in. Remembering their past as aliens is intended to create empathy. The residents of Gibeah who see a Levite with his servant and concubine waiting in the square for an offer of lodging, are to look and see themselves as they once were.

The motivation clause seeks to bridge the gap separating those we know from those we do not know. That gap often results in a dualistic morality. There is one set of rules for those included in the in-group, and another for those in the out-group. If, when we see a stranger, we are moved to see ourselves, then the stranger becomes a member of the in-group, and will be treated with kindness. The Israelites' tradition is encouraging them to be open to newcomers and to take the risk of including an unexpected guest. Far from being conservative, it reminds them that the present is contingent, and on that basis to be open to change.

In these laws Israel's foundation narrative does indeed shape its social ethic. They call for human solidarity and prohibit ethnocentrism on a very local scale, and back this requirement by recalling their

---

they are the only two in the Covenant Code which refer to the Exodus, and although this appeal is much more common in Deuteronomy, there are also differences. In Deuteronomy the motivating clause reminds them that they were *slaves* in Egypt, not *aliens*.

14. F.A. Spina ('Israelites as *gerim*: Sojourners in Social and Historical Context', in C.L. Meyers and M. O'Connor [eds.], *The Word of the Lord Shall Go Forth: Essays in Honor of David Noel Freedman in Celebration of his Sixtieth Birthday* [Winona Lake, IN: Eisenbrauns, 1983], pp. 321-35) argues for the authenticity of this tradition. By that he means that the tradition that a group of proto-Israelites were aliens in Egypt is reliable. In time this tradition came to be applied to all Israel.

story. Actions are deemed inappropriate because they do not fit with a people whose past is the same as the alien who is now in their midst.

Deuteronomic Law

There are four stipulations in the Deuteronomic legal collection which regulate how Israelites are to treat aliens, and which are motivated by appealing to the Exodus tradition.[15] Two cultic laws, the Sabbath law (Deut. 5.15) and the legislation for the Feast of Weeks (Deut. 16.12), both of which include the alien among the participants, are motivated by referring to the Exodus tradition. Laws more clearly in continuity with the two studied in the Book of the Covenant require that the alien and orphan be treated justly (Deut. 24.17, 18) and that the alien, along with the widow and orphan, be allowed to glean (Deut. 24.21, 22). Both of these also are motivated by an appeal to their past in Egypt. In this legal corpus, both cultic and civil laws pertain to the alien, and both are rationalized by referring to their foundation narrative.

Before investigating in detail how these laws are motivated, the identity of the alien needs to be clarified. Aliens in Deuteronomy have a different status than aliens in the Book of the Covenant. They need more than lodging for the night. Aliens are often classed with widows and orphans, and the Deuteronomic laws dealing with all three groups seek to give them a stable place in society.[16] By extending to them gleaning rights (Deut. 24.21, 22), participation in feasts (Deut. 16.11, 14), and a portion of the tithe (Deut. 26.12), the laws seek to prevent all three groups (widows, orphans and aliens) from becoming impoverished. Aliens are not classed with the poor in Deuteronomy, because if these laws are obeyed, they will not be poor.[17] The aliens dealt with in these laws are long-term, vulnerable residents of the community.

---

15. Deut. 10.19 is not included in this study because the injunction is in the context of a sermon and not part of the legal collection.

16. See Deut. 14.29; 16.11, 14; 24.19, 20, 21; 26.12.

17. N. Lohfink, in a paper, 'The Option for the Poor: Views of an Old Testament Scholar', presented at the 1990 Annual Meeting of the CBA, demonstrates that the laws for the widow, orphan and alien create a support system which could sustain these marginal groups. The semantic range of the term 'poor' has changed to include only those Israelites who have fallen on hard times and need some temporary help to climb out of their poverty.

Furthermore, aliens in this legal corpus are non-Israelites. For example, in Deut. 14.21 both the alien and the foreigner are allowed to eat the meat of an animal found dead, but the Israelite may not eat it. As non-Israelites, the dietary laws do not apply to either of them. In addition to distinguishing aliens and Israelites, Deuteronomy also distinguishes between aliens and foreigners, and the distinction is economic. The alien is given the meat from a carcass, whereas the foreigner can be sold it (Deut. 24.21). Similarly, the law regulating loans prohibits Israelites from charging their fellow Israelites interest, but allows them to charge the foreigner interest (Deut. 23.20). The poor non-Israelite is designated an alien, and is accorded the same generous treatment as marginal Israelites, but the foreigner is able to pay, and is not granted these privileges. The alien dealt with in these four Deuteronomic laws is a non-Israelite, vulnerable, long-term resident; someone similar, but not identical to the alien encountered in the Book of the Covenant.

The motivation clauses attached to these four laws are almost identical. The Israelite is told, 'remember that you were slaves in the land of Egypt'.[18] Interestingly, all of these motivation clauses describe their status in Egypt as slaves, rather than as aliens. This description is typical in Deuteronomy. Deuteronomy consistently connects their time in Egypt with slavery. Egypt itself is designated as the 'house of slavery' (בית עבדים).[19] So strong is the association between Egypt and slavery in Deuteronomy, that motivation clauses attached to laws dealing with aliens, widows and orphans are backed by reminding them that they were slaves in Egypt.

Furthermore, God in Deuteronomy is known primarily as their liberator. The prologue to the Decalogue is typical, 'I am the LORD your God, who brought you out of the land of Egypt, out of the house of slavery'. (Deut. 5.6). This identification of God as the one who liberated them from Egypt occurs nine times.[20] God is the mighty deity who with a strong hand and an outstretched arm, with signs and wonders, redeemed them from the house of slavery, from the iron

---

18. It occurs in this form in Deut. 5.15 and 24.21, 22. Deut. 16.12 and Deut. 24.17, 18 omit the words, 'the land'. The law regulating the release of slaves (Deut. 15.15) is the only other law in Deuteronomy which is backed in this way.

19. References to their being slaves in Egypt, in addition to the five occurrences already mentioned are: Deut. 6.12, 21; 8.14; 13.6, 11.

20. Deut. 5.15; 6.12, 21; 7.8; 8.14; 13.6 (ET v. 5), 11 (ET v. 10); 15.15; 24.28.

furnace.[21] This portrait is enhanced if Egypt is a place of bondage, and their status there slaves, rather than it being described as their host country, and their status there strangers. The oppression connected with Egypt in Deuteronomy functions as a foil which highlights the power and benevolence of their God.

This new portrayal of their past is also tied to Deuteronomy's humanitarian concern. Its description of their own past as an oppressed people serves to make them sympathetic to the marginalized elements in their own towns. Deuteronomy strives to relieve the burden of those who suffer from economic injustice in a time when the gap between rich and poor was very wide.[22] It is the economic oppression of the peasant class at the time that the Deuteronomic laws were formulated which sheds light on their founding narrative. From its vantage point, the tradition is remolded. Their status in Egypt is now characterized as slave, rather than as alien.

The motivation clauses examined in the Book of the Covenant reminded the Israelites that they were aliens, and left it at that. They did not make explicit that they were to identify with the plight of aliens, feel empathy and act accordingly, however, because the Israelites were referred to as aliens, that was clear. Because the terminology has changed, the logic of these motivation clauses is not as clear as those in the Covenant Code. Why should the Israelite vineyard owner leave what is left after the first harvest of the widow, orphan and alien because he was a slave in Egypt? The call to identify with the alien which was implicit in the Covenant Code is obscured here. It seems that the author is lumping all those groups (widows, orphans, aliens and slaves) together as vulnerable, dependent, oppressed members of society.[23] A person who has been in one of these groups,

21. See the article by B.S. Childs, 'Deuteronomic Formulae of the Exodus Traditions' (VTSup, 16; Leiden: Brill, 1967), pp. 30-39, which traces the development of the expressions, 'Yahweh brought you out of Egypt', and 'your eyes have seen the signs and wonders'.

22. See F.S. Frick, *The City in Ancient Israel* (SBLDS, 36; Missoula, MT: Scholars Press, 1977), pp. 77-114 for a description of the urban, stratified society presupposed by the laws in Deuteronomy. They are dated to the time of the monarchy, and testify to the disintegration of community which occurred because of the economic burden of supporting royalty.

23. This is also the case in the Decalogue of Deuteronomy. The Sabbath command is backed by being connected to a goal: 'so that your male and female slave may rest as well as you' (Deut. 5.14b). Here the slaves are representative of the long

understands well the plight of the others. By reminding the Israelites that they were once slaves, the call to identify and empathize with the unfortunates, although differently formulated, is still the heart of the motivation clause.

In addition to characterizing Israelites as slaves rather than as aliens, other changes have occurred in the Deuteronomic formulation of the motivation clause referring to the Exodus. In typical expansive Deuteronomic style, two of the Deuteronomic motivation clauses remind the Israelite that they were slaves in Egypt, and then make explicit that this is the reason that they are to obey a law dealing with the alien. The injunction to invite all and sundry, including the alien, to the Feast of Weeks, is backed by the clause: 'Remember that you were slaves in Egypt and diligently observe these statutes' (Deut. 16.12). The law regulating gleaning is motivated similarly: 'Remember that you were a slave in the land of Egypt; therefore I am commanding you to do this' (Deut. 24.22).

Another new element is introduced in the motivation clause backing the Sabbath rest. The commandment to allow the entire household to rest is motivated as follows:

> Remember that you were a slave in the land of Egypt, and the LORD your God brought you out from there with a mighty hand and an outstretched arm; therefore the LORD your God commanded you to keep the Sabbath day (Deut. 5.15).

The prohibition against depriving the alien or orphan of justice, or taking a widow's garment in pledge, is also backed in this way:

> Remember that you were a slave in Egypt and the LORD your God redeemed you from there; therefore I command you to do this (Deut. 24.18).

This longer motivation clause introduces God's response to their being slaves in Egypt. It reminds the Israelites that when they were oppressed and weak, God acted on their behalf. His power and might benefitted them. The significance of this new element becomes clear when the social location of the addressee is remembered.

The commands in Deuteronomy are addressed to Israelites who have extensive households (indicated by the commands for the Sabbath and Feast of Weeks), they have vineyards (indicated by the law of

---

list of people and animals who must rest. See E. Nielsen, *The Ten Commandments in New Perspective: A Tradition-Historical Approach* (SBT, 2.7; Naperville, IL: Allenson, 1968), p. 39.

gleaning) and enough excess income that they can lend money (indicated by the command not to take a widow's garment in pledge), and they are among the elders who adjudicate legal disputes (indicated by the command not to deprive the alien or orphan of justice). These are patriarchs who have high social status and great economic strength. From being slaves, they have become wealthy enough to be slave owners.

The new element in the motivation clause reminds them that their deliverance from slavery was not due to their own efforts, but to God's. Their present security is a gift. Drawing attention both to their past status as slaves and how that was changed by being liberated by God, is an effective way to encourage generosity. Laws requiring liberality are backed by reminding them of God's graciousness towards them. They are forced to recall that they are now in a position analogous to God, and that the alien, widow and orphan are in the same oppressive position they once occupied. As God used his might for them, they are now to use their strength for the weak. The expanded reference to the Exodus tradition encourages them to imitate God.

These motivation clauses, although differently formulated to bring them in harmony with the particular theology of Deuteronomy, have functioned in much the same way that the motivation clauses referring to the Exodus tradition operated in the Covenant Code. In both cases their founding narrative is used to back laws requiring established, land-owning Israelites to be generous to those in society who are in dependent positions. It is encouraging them to recognize their present status as contingent, and on that basis identify with those in need. They are not to look at their property as something they deserved, or earned, and which they can dispose of as they wish, but as a gift which equips them to be generous. This application is consistent with their founding narrative—the story of the liberation of a group of slaves by a mighty, gracious God.

Priestly Laws[24]

Up to now the relationship between the Israelites' story and their social ethic has been quite consistent. The changes that have occurred

24. The 'Holiness Code' is not treated separately from the Priestly legal corpus because the case that it was at one time an independent law collection is not convincing. See the arguments of R. Rendtorff, *The Old Testament: An Introduction* (trans. J. Bowden; Philadelphia: Fortress Press, 1986), p. 145.

234

have resulted in a more complete inclusion of the alien. Lev. 25.45
puts this tidy relationship to the test. Unlike the previous laws, it is not
brief, but stands in the middle of two paragraphs which are closely
related, and which are both backed in their entirety by referring to
the Exodus tradition (Lev. 25.39-55). Because they are of a piece,
they will be studied as a unit.

This group of laws instructs that Israelites who go into debt-servitude to fellow Israelites are not to be considered slaves, but hired
workers. Slaves, however, may be acquired from foreigners and aliens.
Furthermore, if Israelites go into debt-servitude to aliens or temporary residents, they retain the right of redemption. If they are not
redeemed by a relative, they will be released in the year of jubilee.
These regulations are backed twice by recalling that God delivered
them from Egypt, and they are his servants (Lev. 25.42, 55).

The status of the aliens referred to in these laws is quite different
from the marginal members of society encountered in the Book of the
Covenant and the Deuteronomic law. These aliens have extended
families in the land, and are wealthy enough that they can lend money
and acquire Israelites as debt-slaves (Lev. 25.47). The Israelites
addressed also occupy a different social position. Although some are
well off and can lend money to their fellow Israelites (Lev. 25.39,
40), there are others who are impoverished and who have gone into
debt-servitude (Lev. 25.39, 40). It is these Israelites that the law seeks
to protect by instituting the year of jubilee which allows them to
return to their ancestral property (Lev. 25.39-41) or to be redeemed
at any time by their kin (Lev. 25.47-49).[25]

The situation envisioned here is understandable in light of the
changes which occurred in Judah at the time of the Babylonian deportation and the subsequent repatriation of some Babylonian Jews. The
Babylonians exiled the upper classes and allowed the peasantry, the
'poor of the land' (2 Kgs 24.14; 25.12), to remain. Those left in the

25. The proposal of R. North in *Sociology of the Biblical Jubilee* (Rome:
Pontifical Biblical Institute, 1954) that these laws are ancient is not convincing. He
decides that they could stem from either the time of occupation or Ezra's time, and
concludes the former is more likely. However, more recent study of the language
used in this chapter indicates that it contains phraseology such as 'a Sabbath to the
LORD', which is late. See the paper presented by Henry T.C. Sun at the November
1990 Annual Meeting of the SBL, 'The Structure, Composition and Date of
Lev. 25.1-55'.

land were allowed to take over the property of those who had been deported (Jer. 39.11). In Ezek. 11.14, 15 we read the sort of argument which was used to justify the expropriation of the property of those in exile. When the returnees came back to Judah following Cyrus's Edict of Restoration (538 BC), conflict arose over property ownership.[26] In addition there was an influx of outsiders during the time of Babylonian supremacy. In no wise did the land lie fallow, enjoying its Sabbaths, as envisioned in 2 Chron. 36.20-21.

There were clearly religious differences between the returning Jews and those who had remained in the land.[27] However, these were compounded by the political and economic disputes between the two groups of Jews and the Gentiles now residing in Judah. The narratives in Nehemiah illustrate the tension between the peasants and their Jewish brethren (Neh. 5). The people of the land cannot feed their families because they are going into debt servitude, they cannot pay their taxes, they have no grain stored in case of famine, and their sons and daughters are indentured to other Jews (Neh. 5.1-5).

It is this sort of situation that the laws of jubilee are addressing. They are allowing Jews who have lost their ancestral estates to return, as well as granting amnesty for those in debt. The series of reforms instituted by Nehemiah (Neh. 5.6-19), B. Levine argues, are based on the laws of Leviticus 25.[28] Although the reform of Nehemiah is limited to seeking justice for the Jews, according to the biblical text, Gentiles are also involved, and are clearly well-established in the land (Neh. 5.6-8). The socioeconomic status of these Gentiles fits with the

26. See the reconstruction of the social and political situation in Judah in the Persian period in J. Blenkinsopp's *Ezra–Nehemiah: A Commentary* (OTL; Philadelphia: Westminster Press, 1988), pp. 60-70.

27. Daniel L. Smith analyzes the conflict of these two groups sociologically as the conflict between a group which has learned new strategies for survival in a minority context and which maintains these new customs and traditions when it returns to its homeland and clashes with those who had not experienced the same uprooting and new self-identification, and had not developed the same customs (*The Religion of the Landless* [Bloomington, IN: Meyer-Stone Books, 1989], pp. 63-69, 179-201).

28. In addition to examining the measures involved in the reform, he also points to the affinity of language between the two. The phrase 'fear of the LORD', which is the motivating force behind the reform of Nehemiah (Neh. 5.15), is a typical motivating clause in the Priestly law. See p. 273 of his commentary, *Leviticus* (JPS Torah Commentary; Philadelphia: Jewish Publication Society, 1989).

status of the alien spoken of in Leviticus 25.

Given this historical situation, the differing regulations concerning the aliens and Israelites are illuminated. The Israelite is protected from enslavement due to debt servitude, however, the alien receives no such protection. Israelites may take aliens as slaves, and they may become the property of the Israelite (Lev. 25.45). This unequal treatment of Israelites and aliens is backed by the motivation clause in v. 42:

> For they are my servants (עבדי), whom I brought out of the land of Egypt;
> they shall not be sold as slaves are sold.

The Exodus tradition is appealed to in order to back the requirement that Israelites be a free people. God's liberation of them from Egypt made freedom an essential part of their identity. Because they are God's servants, they may not be enslaved. This same Exodus tradition also backs the flip side of this law. It rationalizes a law which both protects Israelites and endangers aliens and foreigners. The preferred status of the Israelites is connected to regulations allowing aliens and foreigners to be a source of slaves.

That the Israelites may not be enslaved because they are a people who have been liberated is a new application, but one that quite clearly fits the narrative. Throughout their history, they have recited their founding story and reminded themselves that God worked to free them and to bring them to their own land. However, the further stipulation that others may be enslaved is a new, and seemingly inappropriate application. Up to now, in this survey, the Exodus tradition has not functioned to create an oppressive hierarchy between Israelites and aliens, or to encourage dualistic morality.

It is well to note that Israel's election as a people and its deliverance from slavery imply both preference and separateness. It was the Israelites who were freed, not another people. They were the chosen people, not the Egyptians. They, according to the Exodus tradition, have a preferred status in God's eyes. Although the whole world belongs to God, only Israel is called to be a holy nation and a priestly kingdom (Exod. 19.5, 6). The laws in the Covenant Code and the Deuteronomic laws softened their separateness and their preferred status by allowing the outsider, in varying degrees, to be included. However, this openness to the stranger does not abrogate the exclusiveness of Israel's status.[29]

29. For example, we noted that the alien, although treated with generosity in the

In the previous examples the Exodus tradition was used to motivate inclusion of the alien, in part because of the high social status of the Israelite compared with the alien. Because Israelites were permanent residents and economically stable, it was appropriate to consider those who were on the fringe of society not as the enemy, but as themselves in times past. The laws of jubilee address a strikingly different situation. Some Israelites have lost their land and some are in debt-servitude, a status akin to being slaves in Egypt. In this new setting their identity as a people is threatened because some have no stake in the promised land. To these Jews their tradition proclaims that they are slaves of God alone. It reminds them of their preferred status and their identity as a free people.

The laws of jubilee illustrate how dynamic Israel's founding tradition is. It is not only appealed to by a community that is well off in order to encourage generosity to those in need, but also by a community whose existence is threatened by a widening gap between the rich and poor among them. It equips the latter to build an equitable community through land reform and debt amnesty, and also encourages their solidarity over against wealthy aliens by emphasizing their preferred status.

The progression from laws in the Book of the Covenant which prohibited oppression to laws requiring partial social and cultic inclusion and economic support in the Deuteronomic corpus reaches its zenith in the laws enumerated in Lev. 19.33, 34. They are the most inclusive and expansive yet:

> When an alien resides with you in your land, you shall not oppress the alien. The alien who resides with you shall be to you as the citizen among you; you shall love the alien as yourself, for you were aliens in the land of Egypt. I am the LORD your God.

There are three laws here in rapid succession. The alien is not to be oppressed; the alien is to receive the same status as the citizen (אזרח), and the Israelite is to love the alien as himself. The last command is especially remarkable. It balances a similar law in Lev. 19.18.

> You shall not take vengeance or bear a grudge against one of your people, but you shall love your neighbor as yourself: I am the LORD.

Deuteronomic laws, is not considered an Israelite (Deut. 14.21) and that the foreigner is treated as a second-class citizen (Deut. 23.20).

The parallelism between these two laws strengthens the content of the laws dealing with the stranger. Not only does it call for them to love the stranger, but does so using the same formula which required them to love the neighbor. What was implicit in previous laws is here made explicit and taken to its logical conclusion. There is no longer any in-group versus out-group morality. Aliens have become insiders, and there are no privileges to which they are not entitled.

Significant for understanding this law is the designation of the Israelite as a citizen (often translated as native-born or native to the land). This designation is typical in the Priestly laws, and is almost unique to it.[30] The strong preference for this term indicates its significance. The importance of their land, as a land promised to the Israelites,[31] and set apart for them leads to the designation of Israelites as 'natives'. This term draws attention to their identity as a people of this land. Furthermore, the Priestly laws emphasize that the land is holy and it must be kept holy by right behavior.[32] If the inhabitants do not live pure lives, the land will vomit them out (Lev. 18.24-28). For this reason all who live in the land, both natives and aliens, must abide by the laws.

The command to love the alien is too brief to contain many clues as to its social setting. It is clear that the Israelites are living in their land, and aliens are living among them, not as temporary residents, but as permanent members. The historical context is made clearer when we consider the other Priestly laws which require that the Israelite and alien be treated as equals.[33] This group of laws belongs to the last layer of redaction in the Pentateuch.[34] They derive from the late restoration community and have the intent of unifying the

30. It occurs 17 times in the Old Testament, and of these, only three are not part of the Priestly legislation—Josh. 8.33; Ezek. 47.22; Ps. 37.35.

31. For example, in Lev. 26.42 God remembers the covenant made with the patriarchs and the land.

32. G.J. Wenham's *The Book of Leviticus* (NICOT; Grand Rapids: Eerdmans, 1979), pp. 18-25 contains an excellent discussion of 'holiness' in the theology of the Priestly laws.

33. This requirement is found in Exod. 12.19, 49; Lev. 16.29; 17.8, 10, 12, 13, 15; 18.26; 19.33, 34; 20.2; 22.18; 24.16, 22; Num. 15.14, 15, 16, 26, 29, 30; 19.10.

34. H. Cazelles, 'La mission d'Esdras', *VT* 4 (1954), pp. 113-40 argues that these laws belong to the last level of redaction, and fit with the mission of Ezra (dated to the reign of Artaxerxes II: 404–358 BC).

permanent residents in the land.[35] This was a concern of the Persian government which is reflected in the missions of Ezra and Nehemiah and enacted in these Priestly laws.[36] They accomplish the goal of creating stability among diverse groups in the population of Judah by allowing the alien to become ritually pure and cross the boundary separating Israelite from alien. The Passover legislation in Exod. 12.43-49 allows the alien, who is distinguished from the bound or hired servant and the foreigner, to celebrate the Passover if he and his household become circumcised. Once circumcised, the alien is regarded as a citizen (native). Henceforth all the duties and privileges of being a member of the 'congregation' belong equally to both.[37] This surprisingly egalitarian law is backed by appealing to their past, to the time when they were aliens in Egypt. Their characterization as aliens rather than slaves makes sense in terms of the situation being addressed. The concern of the laws is not to make an elite upper class sympathetic to the plight of the poor. Rather, it is to create a stable community composed of two distinct sub-groups who live in the same land. Characterizing their status in Egypt as such a sub-group fits with that goal.

Here again sacred story is being used to include the outsider. This is consistent with its functioning in both the Deuteronomic laws and the Book of the Covenant. Their narrative is again backing a social ethic which embraces the alien.[38] In both the Book of the Covenant and the Deuteronomic law, that inclusion was only partial; here it has become complete. What was initiated in laws protecting the traveller has progressed to the point that the distinction between an Israelite and alien no longer exists, because the alien has become an Israelite.

This last example again illustrates the dialogical relationship

---

35. P. Grelot discusses the theology and literary features of this last level of redaction in 'La dernière étape de la rédaction sacerdotale', *VT* 6 (1956), pp. 174-89.

36. The sequence, dating and precise missions of these two leaders is greatly disputed, and for the purposes of this paper need not be resolved. See the discussion of these issues in J. Blenkinsopp, *Ezra–Nehemiah*, pp. 139-44.

37. Exod. 19.21 makes it clear that the congregation is composed of these two elements.

38. There is implicit in this generous law a power play, in that the aliens are considered the outsiders by the Israelites. The aliens, as permanent, well-established residents in the land may not consider themselves aliens at all. The identity of the alien in the restoration community has been disputed. See my *The Alien and Israelite Law* (JSOTSup, 107; Sheffield: JSOT Press, 1991), pp. 151-55.

between the tradition and the community. The tradition shapes the community, and the community shapes the tradition. Differing depictions of this tradition have been appealed to at various points in their history in order to meet the new challenges. In the interchange between tradition and community that tradition remained intact and revelatory, and the community, although changing over time, remained true to its founding narrative. For Israel to be faithful to its story, it must be free, and it must have preferred status and to recognize this as a gift from God. This gift is not to be hoarded, but is to equip them to be generous and open—a blessing to the world. The Exodus tradition, in the laws dealing with the alien, encouraged the Israelites to remain true to their identity and to their calling. Because the Israelites were faithful to this tradition, they survived as Israelites.

THE GOD OF HOSEA*

Niels Peter Lemche

When I originally planned to elaborate on the theme the God of Hosea, my intention was, on the basis of Hos. 6.2-3, to present this god as a Yahweh who did not know what his own future would be like, but who was, in Hosea's days, only one god among many other gods belonging to the pantheon of western Asia.[1] Although Hosea may have reacted against this interpretation of Yahweh, he was, when speaking about the God of Israel, hardly able to give up the religious language and ideas current in his own age. Thus it was originally my intention to show that Hosea was not the creator of a new monotheistic faith of Israel, that is, the monotheistic or monolatrous belief in Yahweh as the sole God of Israel. Rather he should have been presented as the spokesman of some local shrine in the Northern Kingdom (although he seems to castigate almost every possible sanctuary of his own country). According to this view the prophecies of Hosea were at a later date adopted by a strictly monotheistic environment, but this fate Hosea had to share with many of his prophetic colleagues.

Although many scholars may consider this view of Hosea fairly modern it is, however, difficult to maintain in the light of the present crisis in prophetical studies (not to speak of Old Testament studies in general). Thus we are entitled to ask: Who really were Hosea and his colleagues? And how are we going to evaluate the writings that carry

---

* The revised version of a paper read at the SBL Meeting in Rome, July 17 1991.

1. More or less based on a view of Israelite religion like that given in my lecture at the IOSOT Congress in Leuven, now published as 'The Development of the Israelite Religion in Light of Recent Studies of the Early History of Israel', in (J.A. Emerton [ed.], *Congress Volume Leuven 1989* (VTSup, 43; Leiden: Brill, 1991), pp. 97-115.

their names? Just to mention some of the more obvious alternatives: Was Hosea a fortune-teller? Or was he the spokesman of some evangelical part of the Yahwistic religious movement, as maintained by a number of German and Scandinavian Lutheran scholars? Did the prophets of the eighth century try to reform the religious community, or did they create a new religion, as some scholars have recently maintained? Or do we have to abandon such ideas as being nothing more than misinterpretations of the biblical genre of prophetical literature nourished by modern scholars, which may only be the creation of much later editors and collectors?

And what about the genre? How are we to evaluate the genre of prophetical literature, which has no parallel in other parts of the ancient Near East? As far as we know, no prophet from Mari or elsewhere ever collected his prophecies into books or tried to provide them with a literary framework like other literary products as psalms, hymns, prose narratives, and so on. Only modern collectors have created books of Mari prophecies! Although this is certainly an argument from silence, we may still say that it is a strange fact that not even the Babylonian world possessed anything which can be even remotely compared to the prophetic books of the Old Testament, although it is obvious that the Mesopotamians were never without prophets of their own. In short, the whole genre of prophetic books seems to be artificial. Prophets did not write books, they prophesied.

Will it therefore be meaningful to continue the quest for the prophetic message, that is, for the prophet's *ipsissima verba*, or would it be better, in the path of scholars like Otto Kaiser, Robert Carroll or Knud Jeppesen[2] to consider the prophetic books to be exclusively—or almost exclusively—the products of their editors?

The problems connected with the study of the prophets of the Old Testament do not end here. We cannot separate the study of prophet-

2.   Whereas the contributions of Otto Kaiser and Robert Carroll are well-known and easily available (we need only refer to their commentaries of Isaiah and Jeremiah, respectively), it can only be regretted that the volume on Micah by Knud Jeppesen, *'Græder ikke saa saare': Studier i Mikabogens sigte I-II* (Aarhus: Aarhus Universitetsforlag, 1987) ('Don't Cry so Bitterly': Studies in the Scope of the Book of Micah) is so far only available to readers of the Scandinavian languages. In his book, Jeppesen tries to demonstrate that the book of Micah cannot be considered the work of an eighth century prophet, but it represents a much later collection or 'patchwork' of prophetic material.

ism from the more general issue of the history of 'Israelite' religion, and—as I have maintained in several publications—neither can we separate the issue of Israelite religion from Israel's general history (although there need not be absolute identity or parallelism between general history and religious history). However, in societies like the ancient Palestinian ones,[3] general and religious history must be considered one and the same thing; we may speak of a general history, but the members of ancient societies always understood general and religious history to be identical.

In principle a reconstruction of 'Israelite' religious history may follow two different courses.

1. One may choose to keep the essentials of the Old Testament 'history of Israel', and to consider the belief in Yahweh to be a truly monotheistic faith from its very beginning. Supposedly a great number of scholars will prefer to retain this picture of the old Israelite religion, irrespective of whatever reconstruction of the general course of history they decide for. According to such a view

3. It is one of the more intricate issues of present developments in the study of 'Israelite' history, that terminology has to change. We cannot, any more, simply speak about 'Israelite history' (or 'Judaean', for that matter), as it is becoming more and more obvious that the notion of 'Israel' in almost every textbook is only another example of paraphrasing the Old Testament. It would take too long to discuss this problem here. However, it should be noted that (1) Israel is in the Old Testament an *ideological concept*, not a historical one, and (2) the state of Israel (Samaria/ Samarina) was not in the Iron Age a religious community but a political society (although religion of course played a major part in the life of its citizens), not very different from other states of western Asia. The 'Israel' of the Old Testament is obviously already a Jewish society that hardly predates the emergence of Judaism in the middle and second part of the first millennium BCE. For a discussion of some of these issues, I can refer to the preliminary contributions by E.A. Knauf, 'From History to Interpretation', in D.V. Edelman (ed.), *The Fabric of History* (Sheffield: JSOT Press, 1991), pp. 26-64, and T.L. Thompson, 'Text, Context and Referent in Israelite Historiography', in *The Fabric of History*, pp. 65-92, as well as to the pioneering and penetrating study by the late G.W. Ahlström, *Who Were the Israelites* (Winona Lake, IN: Eisenbrauns, 1986). It is also one of the by-products of my own elimination of the Canaanites (N.P. Lemche, *The Canaanites and their Land* [JSOTSup, 110; Sheffield: JSOT Press, 1991]), that their antipodes, the Israelites, must belong in the same category as the Canaanites, among the legendary 'peoples and nations of the remote past'. In this paper, written in the intermediate period between an old pattern and its successor, the terminology has been updated, although remnants of obsolete ideas and opinions may survive here and there.

Yahweh may have been the only immigrant in Palestine at the beginning of the Iron Age, accompanied by a very limited number of believers (the so-called 'group of Moses'). Moreover, the personality of Yahweh was already in those early days the one that appears in Old Testament writings. In Palestine his small community of supporters were at first received by a small number of converts, later on the gods of 'Canaan' became more popular, and the adherents of the monotheistic Yahwistic faith more or less succumbed to the temptations of the Canaanite religious practices. This is very much the concept of Israelite religious history as maintained by scholars like George Mendenhall and Norman Gottwald as well as many scholars who may not even be prepared to accept their historical reconstructions. In the light of this reconstruction it would be correct to consider the prophets of the Old Testament to be religious *reformers*.

2. However, I suppose that some scholars may decide more seriously to pay attention to the modern reconstructions of the history of Palestinian society in the Iron Age, according to which historical Israel arose as one Palestinian state among a number of other newly founded political aggregations of the Iron Age. According to such a view it would be more likely that Yahweh was in fact only one among a comprehensive number of gods belonging to the Palestinian world. An unbiased and positivistic review of the extant material pertinent to the religious situation in Palestine in the first half of the first millennium BCE would undoubtedly support this view of the status of Yahweh in early times.[4]

This second understanding of the development of Yahwistic religion opens up an avenue leading to two different views of the prophets. It is on one hand possible—following Bernhard Lang—to consider the prophets to be spokesmen of a new religion, the 'Yahweh-Alone-Movement'.[5] If so, prophets like Hosea and his contemporaries, Isaiah,

---

4. Cf. Lemche, 'The Development of the Israelite Religion', also W.G. Dever, *Recent Archaeological Discoveries and Biblical Research* (Seattle: University of Washington Press, 1990), pp. 121-66. Cf. also the inspired work by H. Niehr, *Der höchste Gott: Alttestamentliche JHWH-Glaube im Kontext syrisch-kanaanäischer Religion des 1. Jahrtausends v. Chr.* (BZAW, 190; Berlin: de Gruyter, 1990).

5. B. Lang, *Monotheism and the Prophetic Minority* (Sheffied: Almond Press, 1983). I have formerly advocated a point of view very much the same as the one entertained by Lang, thus in my *Ancient Israel* (Sheffield: JSOT Press, 1988), pp. 240-48, or in 'The Transformation of the Israelite Religion', in A.W. Geertz and

Micah and Amos, are not advocating a return to the genuine and old Israelite religion from times past, but they should be considered real religious innovators.

It is, however, a precondition of this view of the prophets that the monotheistic Yahwistic religion was called into existence already in pre-exilic times. Another precondition is, of course, that the prophetic books contain genuine material going back to, say, the eighth century BCE. Only then will we have a chance to obtain a faithful picture of the religious conditions prevailing in Hosea's times.

On the other hand it is possible to formulate a variant of the hypothesis of prophets as religious innovators. If the amount of genuine material[6] in the prophetic books is only slight or impossible to distinguish from secondary or redactional material or the books themselves were written not by the prophets and their disciples but by late editors and writers, then the true religious innovators were not the prophets themselves, but the people who collected the prophetic books. In this case we may never know what role a prophet like Hosea really played.

In the second case we should ask: What was the primary objective of such editors when they formulated their own religious message under the pseudonyms of prophets of ancient times? Three possibilities may be mentioned: (1) it is possible that tradition simply 'told' them that the prophets of ancient times were—irrespectively of who they really were—advocates of the religious opinions just like the editors themselves; (2) they may have wanted to stress that Yahweh himself initiated the religious reformation that introduced monotheism; or (3) they may just have chosen to attach names of old religious authorities belonging to tradition to their own books in order to make their own writings legitimate and acceptable.

To illustrate my point, we may refer to the fact that there is a certain harmony between the view of prophets in the prophetic books and in the historical literature, especially in the Deuteronomistic history. In the Deuteronomistic history prophets often appear as the

J.S. Jensen (eds.), *Religion, Tradition, and Renewal* (Aarhus: Aarhus University Press, 1991), pp. 119-35.

6. 'Genuine material'—although a term quite often found in discussions of biblical texts—is of course nonsense, except according to the romantic notion of originality, making old more important than young, just because it is old.

central figures in the plot. Thus the prophets normally get the upper
hand when they are confronting the kings of Israel and Judah, whereas
the kings—also David—behave more or less like witless fools. It is
also the intention of the Deuteronomistic writer(s) to stress that
Yahweh in a very direct way and from the very beginning communi-
cated his warnings to Israel through this medium, the prophets.[7]

The display of Deuteronomistic interest in the prophets is of course
underlined by their editing of the book of Jeremiah.[8] However, other
parts of the prophetic literature may also be mentioned in this connection. The behaviour of the prophets in such passages also seems to
accord well with the exilic or postexilic Deuteronomistic idea of how
a prophet should act. Scholars may of course disagree on the extent of
Deuteronomistic reworking and editing in different prophetic books.
We only know for certain that they produced the book considered
to be Jeremiah's. Some Deuteronomistic parts are obvious in
Amos,[9] and of course the headings to such books as Isaiah,[10] Amos,
Hosea,[11] Micah[12] and Zephaniah may, perhaps, also be considered

7. There is no reason to elaborate on the claim of the 'Smend-school' of
Göttingen, that the prophetic narratives in the Deuteronomistic History represent a
certain stratum, the DtrP. Cf. especially W. Dietrich, *Prophetie und Geschichte*
(Göttingen, 1972). Such redactional theories are of little consequence here.

8. Cf. on this the two volumes by W. Thiel, *Die deuteronomistische Redaktion
von Jeremia 1–25* (Neukirchen–Vluyn: Neukirchener Verlag 1973) and *Die
deuteronomistische Redaktion von Jeremia 26–45* (Neukirchen–Vluyn: Neukirchener
Verlag 1981). Cf. also the introduction in R.P. Carroll *Jeremiah* (London, 1986),
pp. 38-46. In contrast to Thiel, he discusses the possibility of post-Deuteronomistic
material to Jeremiah, incorporating Deuteronomistic ideas. Although seemingly at
variance with the traditional German 'approach', Carroll, is, inadvertently,
displaying some sort of German methodology, as a post-Deuteronomistic editor with
Deuteronomistic traits would sound very much a DtrR[2] in contrast to Thiel's
Deuteronomistic writer (whom we may name DtrR[1], thus opening for the possiblity
of also DtrR[3], DtrR[4], etc.).

9. W.H. Schmidt, 'Die deuteronomistische Redaktion des Amosbuches: Zu dem
theologischen Unterschied zwischen dem Prophetenwort und seinem Sammler',
ZAW 77 (1965), pp. 168-92.

10. On this see O. Kaiser, *Isaiah 1-12: A Commentary* (OTL; London: SCM
Press, 2nd edn, 1983), pp. 1-10.

11. O. Kaiser (*Einleitung in das Alte Testament* [Gütersloh: Gerd Mohn, 5th edn,
1984], p. 226), however, only says that Hos. 1.1 shows that the book was edited
in Judah.

12. Jeppesen, *'Græder ikke saa saare'*, pp. 115-18, concentrates on an exilic date.

Deuteronomistic imprints on these books. In this light it should not be a surprise to anybody that already Amos refers to the fact that the Israelites forbade the prophets to prophesy (Amos 2.11-12). When the book of Amos was composed or edited, the evidence of this passage exactly paralleled a concept of prophetism which it shared with the historical books of the Old Testament.

In this way it is possible to point to an interaction between historical and prophetic literature. If so, the prophetic books already mentioned may be considered first-hand testimonies relating to the more general prophetic legends in the books of Kings, or the depiction of prophetism in the Deuteronomistic preaching.[13] Or, put another way the historical books present practical and historical locations for the preaching of the prophets as expressed in the prophetic literature. We may certainly say that so far the Deuteronomistic History and the prophetic books are mutually in accordance. The historical books are supported by the prophetic books and *vice-versa*, and that makes it highly questionable, from a historian's point of view, to base the analysis of prophetic behaviour in the prophetic books on the legendary material in Kings (not to speak of Samuel or other parts of the Deuteronomistic History).

In this case it becomes increasingly difficult to understand personalities such as Amos, Hosea, Isaiah and the like. The textual basis for the traditional view of the prophets has simply evaporated. The impression we get of the acts and behaviour of the prophets was created, not by the prophets themselves, but by the editors of the prophetic and historical books and not according to a historical tradition but in an artificial way; this is, as a matter of fact, but a further example of how the editors recreated the past of their own nation.

I am unable in such a short space to solve the problems posed so far in this study. However, as soon as a problem has been diagnosed, it is necessary to take account of it. Although some may entertain the idea that we should carry on with prophetic studies in the old-fashioned and honourable way, this is hardly a legitimate procedure any more.

---

13. 'Still the LORD solemnly charged Israel and Judah by every prophet and seer, saying, "Give up your evil ways; keep my commandments and statues given in all the law which I enjoined on your forefathers and delivered to you through my servants the prophets." They would not listen, however, but were as stubborn and rebellious as their forefathers had been. . .' (2 Kgs 17.13-14; REB).

Somehow the acquisition of new knowledge can be compared to a kind of fall of humankind. We cannot escape the consequences of new knowledge whether we like it or not. To continue with old-fashioned prophetic studies would be either to blindly ignore the insights of present-day biblical scholarship—hardly a commendable procedure—or to introduce new arguments in order to oppose the modern ideas.

Let us return to the God of Hosea and I will try to present some of the issues that may turn up as a result of different approaches to this prophetic book. It will of course be impossible to say that Hosea's notion of God was such and such and that the book of Hosea should be viewed in the context of the eighth century BCE if it only represents a collection of various sources, most of them more than 200 years later than Hosea's own time. My main witness will be the passage in Hos. 6.2-3:[14]

> After two days he will revive us,
>   on the third day he will raise us,
>   to live in his presence.
> Let us strive to know the Lord,
>   whose coming is as sure as the sunrise.
> He will come to us like that rain,
>   like spring rains that water the earth.

There is no room here for detailed exegesis of this passage. However, it is obvious that Hosea is employing mythological language which is rich in metaphors. It is also obvious that his employment of such language must lead his audience in a distinct direction. The saying in v. 2 mentioning the resurrection after two or three days is certainly important, however, perhaps mainly because of the later interpretations of this text. I do not suppose that this expression is anything but a metaphor saying that the god mentioned by Hosea is the one who grants life to mankind. The two or three days carry no specific meaning, and the stress is placed on the god's ability to create life where only death prevails.[15] No doubt Hosea is speaking about Yahweh.

---

14. Quotation according to the Revised English Bible.

15. Cf. the comprehensive discussion in H.W. Wolff, *Hosea* (BKAT, 14.1; Neukirchen–Vluyn: Neukirchener Verlag, 3rd edn, 1976), pp. 149-51; also J. Jeremias, *Der Prophet Hosea* (ATD, 24.1; Göttingen: Vandenhoeck & Ruprecht 1983), p. 85.

However, we may ask whether the metaphors are genuinely Yahwistic or whether Hosea has borrowed the ideas expressed in this verse from metaphors belonging to some other god.[16] Or, are Yahweh and the god whose religious language he has borrowed virtually—in the eyes of Hosea—one and the same god? The language used in the following verse may indicate who the second god was, and the references to fertility, to the dawn, to the spring rain and the early rain in the autumn compare well with the idea of reviving in v. 2. We are more or less confronted with metaphors and ideas normally considered to belong to the god Baal.[17]

The God of Hosea—according to this passage—is certainly Yahweh. We may therefore conclude that the god described in Hos. 6.2-3 is Yahweh, however a Yahweh who did not despise the attributes otherwise attached to the god Baal (or to any other god who fulfilled the same functions as Baal). So far this text compares well with a number of Old Testament passages which also contain the same 'Baalistic' traits. I only need to refer to Ps. 65.10-14.

Does the book of Hosea say where we should look for this god Yahweh? The book of Hosea contains a lot of religious polemics directed against various sanctuaries and shrines of the Northern Kingdom. Some of these are mentioned by name, other sanctuaries are just summarized in general accusations directed against the religious practices of the people of Samaria or Ephraim (as in Hos. 4.13). Among the sanctuaries mentioned by name we find Gilgal and Beth-Aven (Bethel), but most likely also the sanctuaries of Adam, Shechem, Mispah, Tabor and Shittim (if we follow the emendation of Hos. 5.2 as indicated by *BHS*).[18] The sanctuary at Shechem may not itself be

---

16. Although summarily rejected by Wolff and Jeremias (*loc. cit.*), the comments by scholars of the past such as H. von Baudissin and others, which are more open to arguments drawn from the general history of religion that indicate connections with Adonis and Osiris, should not be left totally out of consideration here.

17. As is clearly expressed by Jeremias (*Hosea*, p. 86): 'Das durch und durch kanaanisierte Israel kann in seiner Antwort auf die prophetische Botschaft nicht anders von Jahwe reden als von einem Naturgott, dessen Heil sicher und berechenbar ist', although I will certainly question Jeremias's general interpretation of the passage, seeing it as an introduction to the following condemnation: the Israelites possess no other idea of Yahweh than this false 'Baalistic one'!

18. As proposed by the editor of *Dodekapropheton* in *BHS*, K. Elliger, in *ZAW* 69 (1957), pp. 156-57, MT וְשַׁחֲטָה שֵׂטִים should be read וְשַׁחַת הַשִּׁטִּים or וְשִׁחֵת בַּשִׁטִּים.

mentioned by name, but the priesthood belonging to Shechem is certainly the goal of the accusations in Hos. 6.9, where the priests are accused of behaving like highwaymen on the road that leads to Shechem. I see little reason to doubt that the priests mentioned in this passage must come from Shechem.[19] Virtually all important shrines of the Northern Kingdom are mentioned in the book of Hosea as places where you are asked not to worship the God of Israel.

The book of Hosea also contains accusations of false worship. First and foremost, the book of Hosea rejects all kinds of bull worship. The bull, or rather the young bull, is rejected as the עגל שמרון (8.6). which is evidently the same as the God of Bethel (cf. Hos. 10.5 where the inhabitants of Samaria are accused of worshipping the young bull of Beth-Aven). The metaphorical language, which is connected with the worship of the young bull, also reappears in a passage such as Hos. 12.12, including warnings against bull sacrifices at Gilgal, or in the general accusation against Ephraim of 'kissing young bulls' (13.2). The metaphor comparing Israel, or rather Ephraim, to a heifer (Hos. 10.11) is certainly appropriate, the heifer being the natural consort of the young bull.[20]

Another image of God appears in the sections in the book of Hosea where Yahweh is described as the God of Israel because of his historical acts of liberation. Most of these actions precede Israel's existence in her land, and we may especially refer to a number of allusions to the liberation from Egypt and to the desert. Recently a number of investigations of the exodus tradition in Hosea have appeared; however, although I question the historical foundation of these studies, there is hardly any reason to discuss them here.[21]

19. Against Wolff (*Hosea*, p. 156), who speaks of a Levitical group in opposition to the shrine of Shechem which tries to prevent the believer from reaching this sacred spot.

20. That this is not properly recognized by two relatively modern commentaries like Jeremias (*Hosea*, pp. 134-35) or Wolff (*Hosea*, pp. 239-40) says pretty much about the inability of modern scholars to comprehend the real impact of Baal religion in a so-called Yahwistic environment. Many scholars seem mentally (theologically) incapable of grasping the true pre-exilic (or even postexilic) religious reality in Palestine.

21. Notably D.R. Daniels, *Hosea and Salvation History: The Early Traditions of Israel in the Prophecy of Hosea* (BZAW, 191; Berlin: de Gruyter, 1990), and H.-D. Neef, *Die Heilstraditionen Israels in der Verkündung des Propheten Hosea* (BZAW,

It is, however, characteristic of Hosea that the breakdown of relations between Israel and Yahweh is referred back to events in Israel's past. We may especially take note of the Baal–Peor incident (cf. Hos. 9.10), but we may also note events that happened when Israel lived in its land, such as in Hos. 1.4 where the revolution of Jehu seems to be rejected, or Hos. 2.17 where the valley of Achor is called the future gate of hope (although this is certainly based on a tradition which says the opposite) and finally in the mentioning of Gibea in Hos. 10.9, which may refer to the gruesome events of Judges 19. In spite of these seemingly concrete examples, the accusations against the people of Samaria are mostly general without references to special events and crimes, although the population of the Northern Kingdom seems to have been guilty of every imaginable abuse.

References in Hosea to political events in the time of the prophet mostly appear in the form of general accusations against Israel because of its departure from Yahweh. Thus, for example, in 7.10-16 Israel and Ephraim are accused of travelling to Egypt and Assur in order to obtain help. The phrasing of this passage is imprecise and the historical content evasive. As a matter of fact, it may be totally wrong to find evidence of any historical event of the late eighth century in such a passage, which may or may not refer to concrete events. This passage may be no more than a general and paradigmatic admonition against misbehaviour, including the habit of forsaking the land of Israel in order to travel to foreign countries.[22]

This can only be an extremely simplified presentation of the images

169; Berlin: de Gruyter, 1987). Both studies are basically written under the supervision of members of what we may call the traditional German school, ignoring the general debate on the early history of Israel, although this debate is certainly extraordinarily important for the evaluation of Hosea's interpretation of salvation history.

22. Cf. the language found in the preceding phrase (Hos. 7.8-9): 'Ephraim is mixed up with aliens; he is like a calf half done. Foreigners feed on his strength, but he is unaware.' According to Jeremias (*Hosea*, pp. 97-98), this reflects the situation in 733, when Assur removed a greater part of the Northern Kingdom from Israelite control. Wolff (*Hosea*, pp. 160-61) likewise thinks that allusions to the Syro-Ephraimite wars can be found here. Presumably these commentators would never have nourished such ideas without the information contained in the books of Kings, and even now they act like the priests of Delphi trying to interpret the mumbling of Pythia.

of God in the book of Hosea, and several problems and topics have not been considered, such as the relationship (if any) between the religious language of 6.2-3 and the warnings against the worship of bulls, or religious meaning of the marriage metaphors in Hosea.[23]

In the final part of this article I shall try to present two different ways of interpreting the notion of God in the book of Hosea, on the basis of two different approaches to the prophetic literature: (1) on the basis of Hosea's own time, and (2) on the basis of the time of the editors or collectors. Only a sketch of the problem can, of course, be included.

According to the first and generally accepted approach most of the already mentioned religious comments of Hosea go back to the eighth century BCE. If this is true, the question must be: Was Hosea a religious reformer or the spokesman of a new monotheistic religion? It should be emphasized that the question can only be answered on the basis of the text of the book of Hosea itself. It is not recommended that we rely on opinions expressed by other parts of the Old Testament, and we certainly have to disregard the opinions expressed in the Deuteronomistic History.[24]

Most of the religious polemics in Hosea are directed against bull worship, whether this be the royal cult at Bethel or private religious enterprise at other northern shrines. The image of the young bull is rejected as the work of an artisan. We may, however, ask whether other parts of the rituals of the Northern Kingdom are rejected as well. We may refer to the rejection of the priesthood of Shechem (and elsewhere) in this connection. However, such passages only indicate that the priests are unworthy fellows, not that the sanctuary at Shechem is an unholy place.[25] To be brief, the book of Hosea does not indicate where Israelites are allowed to worship Yahweh. It also lacks proper monotheistic characterizations of the God of Israel.

More general rejections of the ritual practices of the Israelites can also be found. In this connection I should especially mention the

23. Cf. on this the inspired article by W.D. Whitt, 'The Divorce of Yahweh and Asherah in Hos. 2.4–7.12ff.', *SJOT* 6 (1992), pp. 31-67, who argues that the real conflict is not the one between Yahweh and Israel symbolized by the marriage of Hosea to Gomer, but the one between Yahweh and his own wife, Asherah.

24. The reason being, simply, that this literature postdates Hosea's eighth century by at least 100 to 200 years. It can only be considered a secondary source of information as far as Hosea's time is concerned.

25. So far Wolff's commentary makes some sense, cf. n. 20 above.

rejection of the sexual (fertility) part of the worship. Robert Carroll has, on the other hand, quite convincingly described such passages, which abound in Hosea, as 'religious pornography', not to be taken at their face value.[26] Such criticism was most likely directed against the worshippers of the Bull of Samaria and it is used in addition to the other sections abusing this worship in order to further incriminate the followers of the bull. As a matter of fact we have very little—if any—knowledge of a sexual religion in ancient Palestine of the kind imagined by all too many biblical scholars.[27]

The next problem centres on Hosea's being a true monotheistic prophet because of his religious polemics. In a number of passages he accuses his compatriots of having forsaken Yahweh for Baal or the 'Baalim'. We should combine this criticism with the rejection of bull worship. The background of this criticism is the fact that a statue of a bull was located at the shrine at Bethel, and that in Hosea's days the God of Bethel was considered to be the most popular one by people living in the Northern Kingdom. The young bull in west Asiatic religious tradition seems to be the image of Baal, who is at the same time the provider of fertility. As a consequence the religion as found in the Northern Kingdom may have mainly focused on fertility worship, more than on other parts of human life such as justice or general ethical questions. Hosea seemingly rejects this worship, but when he tries to formulate his image of Yahweh, it is a Yahweh who carries with him most of the traits associated with bull worship. In his choice

26. Carroll, *Jeremiah*, p. 134: 'Since Hosea, religious pornography has become a standard form of abusing opponents'.

27. I imagine that the age-old story of sexualism in biblical studies is a subject which should be taken up by a psychiatrist rather than a biblical scholar and that the question must be whether the interest in such subjects is really aroused by the biblical material or by some followers of Sigmund Freud. The interest in fertility religion that was extremely conspicuous a generation ago has happily diminished by now, as it turned the ancient inhabitants of Palestine and Western Asia into something more likely to be found in the more dark and remote parts of modern western cities. On the other hand, it contributed to the notion of the 'Canaanites' as an *anti-people*, condemned to be exterminated as it is piously expressed by some—mainly Deuteronomistic—passages in the Old Testament. In this way, the traditional scholarly concept of fertility religion may (presumably unknowingly) have reflected the more sinister attitudes of the earlier part of this century and it thus testifies to the twisted nature of the European mind in modern times.

of religious metaphors, Hosea is unable to free himself from the language of his opponents.

In this way Hosea was placed in a dilemma which was associated with Yahwism whenever it tried to free itself from the influence of fertility worship. As the supreme god, Yahweh had to perform also the duties that normally—in a polytheistic milieu—belonged to Baal and the Baalim. At the end of the day Yahweh himself changed his name, and became Adonai, a name or title which was, however, more or less synonymous with Baal, and if we are to believe the Graeco-Roman sources, Adonai—or Adonis—carried the features of Baal also down to Hellenistic and Roman times.[28]

However, the Deuteronomistic historian correctly claimed the God of Bethel to be Yahweh, although, in Hosea's eyes, this worship of bull-Yahweh was no longer legitimate. On the other hand, in spite of the fact that Hosea's notion of God differed from the official religious beliefs of the Northern Kingdom, he was in accordance with his audience when he announced that Yahweh was the God of Israel. This was common knowledge in Israel in the eighth century. It is therefore highly questionable that Hosea should have been the spokesman of a new religious movement like the 'Yahweh-Alone-Movement'.

If this is correct it would be possible to introduce other material from the eighth century BCE, for example the onomastic material collected and evaluated by J. Tigay.[29] Tigay's main argument is that Yahweh was the all-important god when kings ruled Israel. We may even speak of a kind of monotheism, or at least a practical mono-latrous cult. However, Tigay's book is, as indicated by a number of reviewers, based on a very problematic procedure, and has to be left out of consideration in this context. It would not have been unwelcome if Yahweh's position as the supreme god in the Northern Kingdom could be proven on the basis of contemporary onomastic material.[30]

---

28. Some years ago I expressed the idea—partly as a joke—that the reason for the idea of an aniconic God in early Judaism was the lack of an iconography which was peculiar to Yahweh ('"Fædrenes" Gud' ['The God of the Fathers'], in S. Pedersen, *Gudsbegrebet* [Copenhagen: Gad, 1985), pp. 46-59, p. 58). I see no 'traces' of a belief in an aniconic god in Palestine in pre-exilic times.

29. See J. Tigay's important but problematic monograph, *You Shall Have No Other Gods* (Atlanta: Scholars Press, 1986).

30. One of the sharpest criticisms of Tigay's book I know of is the one published

I have now to leave this first option and turn to the period of the editors. The time lapse between Hosea and the editors of the book of Hosea must for practical reasons be left out of account.[31]

The alternative will be to study the message of the book of Hosea in the context of its redaction. In this connection the question of the original context of old 'Hoseanic' material is inconsequential. It seems certain, because of the headline to the book, that the final redaction of Hosea presupposes the existence of Deuteronomism. This does not necessarily make the Deuteronomists the authors of the book, although its religious message is not far removed from Deuteronomistic theology. A number of parallels can be found between the book of Hosea and Deuteronomism,[32] but certainly also dissimilarities. This, however, indicates that, while the book may not in its final shape predate the Deuteronomistic movement, it could just as well postdate Deuteronomism, in spite of the fact that it is not in total disagreement with Deuteronomistic thinking and beliefs.[33] In this case it would be

by W.D. Whitt, in *SJOT* 6 (1992), pp. 49-50. In spite of its seductive nature, this book must evidently be left out of consideration in a serious reconstruction of the pre-exilic religion in the two states of Israel and Judah.

31. Although it should be maintained that every single moment of the so-called period of tradition from the prophet Hosea down to the final edition of his book may have been just as decisive for the religious message of the book as is the time of the prophet himself. It is, however, almost hopeless to rediscover the diachronic imprint of tradition on the many layers of the book of Hosea (this being the reason that we are normally met by only one comparison, between the prophet's *ipsissima verba* and the editors' redactional reformulations). This is not to show disrespect to serious efforts of redactional history, for example in the recent books by G.I. Emmerson, *Hosea: An Israelite Prophet in Judaean Perspective* (JSOTSup, 28: Sheffield: JSOT Press, 1984), or M. Nissinen, *Prophetie, Redaktion und Fortschreibung im Hoseabuch: Studien zum Werdegang eines Prophetenbuches im Lichte vom Hos 4 und 11* (AOAT, 231; Neukirchen–Vluyn: Neukirchener Verlag, 1991).

32. Normally explained as proto-Deuteronomistic traits in the message of Hosea. Cf. for example Else Kragelund Holt, 'רעת אלהים and חסד im Buche Hosea', *SJOT* 1.1 (1987), pp. 87-103, who argues that although a proper 'Deuteronomistic' covenant theology cannot be found in Hosea, the Hoseanic message prepares the way for this part of Deuteronomistic thought.

33. To counter the accusation of 'pan-Deuteronomism', I would argue that much scholarly literature emphasizing the exilic nature of large parts of the Old Testament has too readily fallen into the trap set up by the Deuteronomists themselves, that everybody after having been dragged to Babylon turned into Deuteronomists. In this way the Deuteronomists successfully tried to gloss the religious differences of their

interesting to compare the book of Hosea with other literature belonging not in the eighth and seventh centuries, but rather in the sixth to fifth centuries (that is the exilic or even the Persian period), reconsidering the fact that a growing number of modern authors now believe parts of the Old Testament such as Exodus 15 or Deuteronomy 32—although formerly thought to be very old—to be no earlier than the exile.[34]

If a passage like Hos. 6.2-3 could be placed in a new setting, in the sixth or fifth centuries instead of the eighth century, this will not affect its message in any conspicuous way. In this case, however, the passage in question cannot be a proof of emergent mono-Yahwism in the pre-exilic period; to the contrary it says that the struggle between various religious parties did not end when the Babylonians conquered Jerusalem and destroyed its temple. When a passage like Hos. 6.2-3 was included in the redactor's final edition of the book of Hosea, this redactor evidently thought that the message was pertinent also to his own situation, and it may thus be used as proof of a continuing battle between different sections of the exilic/postexilic Jewish societies. It is also interesting to note that in this context the 'Baalistic' characterizations of Yahweh were understood to be relevant expressions of God—at least by some parts of the early Jewish community. We may also assume that religious beliefs and practices, which were considered unwelcome by the members of the reform movement in the exilic and postexilic periods, were able to survive when monotheistic Yahwistic faith was formulated.

The evaluation of the religious polemic in the book of Hosea does not change much even if we assume that it belonged not in the eighth century, but more likely in the sixth or fifth centuries. The new element would be that polemics were in this case directed against bull worship and Baalistic religious traits in the sixth or fifth century, not in the eighth century. We only have to acknowledge that the religious problems which were formerly considered to be a matter of the

own time (the exilic/postexilic period) and to monopolize the religious expression of early Judaism.

34. Cf., for example, Niehr, *Der höchste Gott*, p. 66, or—on Exod. 15—M.A. Brenner, *The Song of the Sea: Ex 15:1-21* (BZAW, 195; Berlin: de Gruyter, 1991). In my *Early Israel* (VTSup, 37; Leiden: Brill, 1985), pp. 334-36, I spoke in favour of a date for Exod. 15, no earlier than the seventh century. Dr Brenner's study, however, shows that also this date may be too early.

pre-exilic period, in fact belonged to or were left unsolved in the exilic and postexilic periods, and it proves that the conversion of the Palestinian population in this period from members of a polytheistic community into a monotheistic Yahwistic congregation was in no way unproblematic.[35]

I have to stop here. This can only be a first presentation of a new project, if it should ever materialize. I have presented a number of options and I still consider the question of how to evaluate the religious polemics in the book of Hosea an open one. However, if we give up the quest for Hosea's *ipsissima verba*, the prophecies contained in the book carrying his name (and, by analogy, in all so-called pre-exilic prophetic books) may be a fruitful contribution to the study of the emergence of the Jewish religion, not in the eighth century BCE, but in the sixth to fourth centuries.

35. On the cover of the second edition of Morton Smith's book, *Palestinian Parties and Politics that Shaped the Old Testament* (London 1987), it is maintained that the book was not readily available to non-American readers before its reappearance. Sometimes it looks as though it has not been available to the American public either. However, Morton Smith's idea of an ongoing battle between various factions of the exilic and postexilic Jewish society is brilliantly promulgated, but the neglect of his book is a sad example of what happens to a scholarly work which is published ahead of its time. Not even in 1990, when Herbert Niehr published his *Der höchste Gott*, was attention paid to Morton Smith's volume, although Niehr may have used it in support of his own thesis.

BIBLIOGRAPHY OF JOSEPH BLENKINSOPP

Compiled by John W. Wright

Books

The Corinthian Mirror (London: Sheed & Ward, 1964).

The Promise to David: The Anointed King in God's Plan (London: Darton, Longman & Todd; Glen Rock, NJ: Paulist Press, 1964).

From Adam to Abraham: Introduction to Sacred History (London: Darton, Longman & Todd, 1964; Glen Rock, NJ: Paulist Press, 1966).

Paul's Life in Christ: A New Creation (London: Darton, Longman, and Todd, 1965) = *Jesus is Lord: Paul's Life in Christ* (New York: Paulist Press, 1967); *L'apôtre Paul: Sa vie dans le Christ* (Mulhouse: Editions Salvator, 1968).

A Sketchbook of Biblical Theology (London: Burns and Oates, 1968).

Deuteronomy: The Book of the Covenant (Milwaukee: Bruce Publishing Company, 1968).

Genesis 1–11: A Scripture Discussion Outline (Milwaukee: Bruce Publishing Company, 1968).

The Men who Spoke out: The Old Testament Prophets (London: Darton, Longman & Todd, 1969).

Celibacy, Ministry, Church: An Enquiry into the Possibility of Reform in the Present Self-Understanding of the Roman Catholic Church and its Practice of Ministry (New York: Herder & Herder, 1968; London: Burns and Oates, 1969); *Celibatio, Sacerdozio, Chiesa: Un Nuovo Modelle per dopo la Crisi* (trans. P.C. Bori; Rome: Herder, 1970).

Sexuality and the Christian Tradition (Dayton: Pflaum Press, 1969; London: Sheed and Ward, 1970).

Pentateuch (London: Sheed & Ward, 1971; Chicago: ACTA Foundation, 1971).

Gibeon and Israel: The Role of Gibeon and the Gibeonites in the Political and Religious History of Early Israel (SOTSMS, 2; Cambridge: Cambridge University Press, 1972).

Prophecy and Canon: A Contribution to the Study of Jewish Origins (Center for the Study of Judaism and Christianity in Antiquity, 3; Notre Dame: University of Notre Dame Press, 1977).

Wisdom and Law in the Old Testament: The Ordering of Life in Israel and early Judaism. (London and New York: Oxford University Press, 1983).

Ezra–Nehemiah: A Commentary (OTL; Philadelphia: Westminster Press, 1988).

Ezekiel (Interpretation; Louisville: John Knox Press, 1990).

A History of Prophecy in Israel from the Settlement in the Land to the Hellenistic Period (Philadelphia: Westminster Press, 1983); *Une histoire de la prophetie en Israël* (trans. M. Desjardins; Montreal: Fides, 1992).

The Pentateuch: An Introduction to the First Five Books of the Bible (Anchor Bible Reference Library; New York: Doubleday, 1992).

Priest, Prophet, Sage: Leadership Roles in Ancient Israel (The Library of Ancient Israel series; ed. D. Knight; in progress).

Articles

'Some Notes on the Samson Saga and the Heroic Milieu', *Scr* 11 (1959), pp. 81-89.

'John vii. 37-39: Another Note on a Notorious Crux', *NTS* 6 (1959–1960), pp. 95-98.

'The Quenching of Thirst: Reflections on the Utterance in the Temple, Jn. 7:37-9', *Scr* 12 (1960), pp. 39-48 = *Contemporary New Testament Studies* (ed. Sr. M. Rosalie Ryan, CSJ; Collegeville, MN: Liturgical Press, 1965), pp. 304-11.

'Anagni and St. Thomas Becket', *Month* 24 NS (1960), pp. 99-106.

'Ballad Style and Psalm Style in the Song of Deborah: A Discussion', *Bib* 42 (1961), pp. 61-76.

'The Oracle of Judah and the Messianic Entry', *JBL* 80 (1961), pp. 55-64.

'The Hidden Messiah and his Entry into Jerusalem', *Scr* 13 (1961), pp. 51-56, 81-88.

'The Frustrated Pilgrim: Afterthoughts on Simone Weil', *Wiseman Review* 489 (1961), pp. 277-85.

'The Lincoln Myth', *Month* 26 NS (1961), pp. 230-35.

'The Unknown Prophet of the Exile', *Scr* 14 (1962), pp. 81-90, 109-18.

'Apropos of the Lord's Prayer', *HeyJ* 3 (1962), pp. 51-60.

'The Lord's Prayer and the Hill of Olives', *HeyJ* 3 (1962), pp. 169-71.

'Liturgy and the Incarnation', *Life of the Spirit* 17 (1962), pp. 51-65.

'Structure and Style in Judges 13–16', *JBL* 82 (1963), pp. 65-76.

'Stylistics of Old Testament Poetry', *Bib* 44 (1963), pp. 352-58.

'On Saving One's Soul', *Life of the Spirit* 17 (1963), pp. 355-68.

'Jonathan's Sacrilege: 1 Sm 14,1-46: A Study in Literary History', *CBQ* 26 (1964), pp. 423-49.

'Biblical and Dogmatic Theology: The Present Situation', *CBQ* 26 (1964), pp. 70-85.

'The Ascension as Mystery of Salvation', *Clergy Review* 50 (1965), pp. 369-74.

'Mary, the Church and the Kerygma', *Clergy Review* 50 (1965), pp. 629-33.

'The Church's Mission in St. Luke', *Clergy Review* 50 (1965), pp. 698-704.

'The Lamb of God', *Clergy Review* 50 (1965), pp. 868-72.

'The Coming of Christ', *Clergy Review* 50 (1965), pp. 940-945.

'On Clericalism', *New Blackfriars* 46 (1965), pp. 562-70 = *Cross Currents* 17 (1967), pp. 15-23. = in *Readings in Social Theology* (ed. E.J. Morgan; Dayton: Pflaum Press), pp. 30-41.

'The Church Among the Nations', *Tablet* 219 (1965), pp. 624-25.

'Old Testament Studies at Geneva', *Month* 34 (1965), pp. 352-59.

'Renewal of Religious Life: A Return to the Gospel', *Tablet* 219 (1965), pp. 1261-62.

'Are there Taces of the Gibeonite Covenant in Deuteronomy?', *CBQ* 28 (1966), pp. 207-19.

'Theme and Motif in the Succession History and the Yahwist Corpus', in *Volume du Congrès, Genève 1965* (VTSup, 15; Leiden: Brill, 1966), pp. 44-57.

'Faith or Fact? Review Article on J. Peter, *Finding the Historical Jesus* and R.D. Smith, *Comparative Miracles*', *New Blackfriars* 47 (1966), pp. 380-6.

'Rethinking Biblical Inerrancy', *Clergy Review* 51 (1966), pp. 40-46.

'A New Kind of Priesthood', *Clergy Review* 51 (1966), pp. 285-90.

'A Changing Church', *Tablet* 220 (1966), pp. 209-10.

'Where Have All the Prophets Gone?', *Ave Maria* 104.16 (1966), pp. 10-11.

'Type and Antitype', in *New Catholic Encyclopaedia* (New York: McGraw–Hill, 1967), XIV, pp. 351-52.

'We Rejoice in our Sufferings', *Way* 7 (1967), pp. 36-44 = *The Mystery of Suffering and Death* (ed. M.J. Taylor; New York: Alba House, 1973), pp. 45-56.

'Presbyter to Priest: Ministry in the Early Church', *Worship* 41 (1967), pp. 428-38.

'The Original Meaning of Original Sin', *Bible Today* 31 (1967), pp. 2183-90.

'Deuteronomy', in *Jerome Biblical Commentary* (eds. R. Brown *et al.*; Englewood Cliffs, NJ: Prentice–Hall, 1968), pp. 101-22.

'Towards a Scriptural Understanding of the Role of Women Religious in the Church', in *Proceedings of the Institute for Local Superiors* (ed. A.L. Schlitzer; Notre Dame: University of Notre Dame Press, 1968), pp. 87-137.

'A Place for the Erotic?', *Homiletic and Pastoral Review* 69 (1968), pp. 203-209 (= *Celibacy, Ministry, Church*, pp. 72-90).

'Sex and the Christian: The Erotic and the Scriptures', *Commonweal* 87 (1968), pp. 435-59.

'The Political Drama of Holy Week', *Ave Maria* 101.14 (1968), pp. 13-15.

'Revolutionary Christianity?', *The Guardian* (Jan. 11, 1968), p. 6.

'Christianity as a Revolutionary Movement', *Newman* 3 (1968), pp. 33-40.

'Kiriath-Jearim and the Ark', *JBL* 88 (1969), pp. 143-56.

Introduction to U.K. edition of *The Underground Church* (ed. M. Boyd; London: Sheed & Ward, 1969), pp. vii-xiv.

'To Purify the Language of the Tribe', *Newman* 4 (1969), pp. 58-66.

'The Language of the Tribe: Corrupting the Word', *Commonweal* 90 (1969), pp. 505-508.

'Leaving a Private World', in *Why Priests Leave: The Intimate Stories of Twelve who Did* (ed. J.A. O'Brien; New York: Hawthorne Books, 1969), pp. 99-111.

'Theological Synthesis and Hermeneutical Conclusions', in *Immortality and Resurrection* (ed. P. Benoit and R. Murphy; Concilium, 60; New York: Herder & Herder, 1970), pp. 115-26.

'The Prophetic Reproach', *JBL* 90 (1971), pp. 267-78.

'My Entire Soul is a Cry: The Religious Passion of Nikos Kazantzakis', *Commonweal* 93 (1971), pp. 514-18.

'Why Keep on Celebrating Christmas?', *Commonweal* 95 (1971), pp. 302-303.

'Parrhesia: Free Speaking and Free Being in the Church', *Living Light* 8 (1971), pp. 91-98.

'Sexuality and the Christian Tradition: Law or Love?', in *Sex: Thoughts for Contemporary Christians* (ed. M.J. Taylor; Garden City, NY: Doubleday, 1972), pp. 29-47.

'Some Reflections on Teaching Old Testament', *Living Light* 10 (1973), pp. 223-34.

'Prophecy and Priesthood in Josephus', *JJS* 25 (1974), pp. 239-62.

'Did Saul Attempt to Make Gibeon his Capital?', *VT* 24 (1974), pp. 1-7.

'The Quest of the Historical Saul', in *No Famine in the Land: Studies in Honor of John L. McKenzie* (ed. J.W. Flanagan and A.W. Robinson; Missoula, MT: Scholars Press, 1975), pp. 75-99.

'Search for the Prickly Plant: Structure and Function in the Gilgamesh Epic', *Soundings* 58 (1975), pp. 200-20.

'The Structure of P', *CBQ* 38 (1976), pp. 275-92.

'Judaism and Teaching the Old Testament', *Living Light* 13 (1976), pp. 360-71.

'Sex and the Single God', in *Sex and the Social Project* (ed. J.H. Grace; Pittsburg: Edwin Mellen, 1978), pp. 3-20.

'Macavity and Moriarity', *Baker Street Journal* 28 (1978), pp. 103-104.

'Sexual Morality (in the Bible)', in *New Catholic Encyclopaedia* (New York: Publishers Guild and McGraw-Hill, 1979), XVII, pp. 605-6.

'Sexuality Human (in the Bible)', in *New Catholic Encyclopaedia* (New York: Publishers Guild and McGraw–Hill, 1979), XVII, pp. 607-608.

'A New Kind of Introduction: Professor Child's *Introduction to the Old Testament as Scripture*', *JSOT* 16 (1980), pp. 24-27.

'Response to W. McKane's Review of *Prophecy and Canon*', *JSOT* 18 (1980), pp. 105-107.

'Tanakh and the New Testament: A Christian Perspective', in *Biblical Studies: Meeting Ground for Jews and Christians* (ed. L. Boadt *et al.*; New York: Paulist Press, 1980), pp. 96-119.

'Biographical Patterns in Biblical Narrative', *JSOT* 20 (1981), pp. 27-46.

'Fragments of Ancient Exegesis in an Isaian Poem (Jes. 2, 6-22)', *ZAW* 93 (1981), pp. 51-62.

'Interpretation and the Tendency to Sectarianism: An Aspect of Second Temple History', in *Jewish and Christian Self-Definition* (ed. E.P. Sanders; Philadelphia: Fortress Press, 1981), pp. 1-26.

'Abraham and the Righteous of Sodom', *JJS* 33 (1982), pp. 119-32.

'The "Servants of the Lord" in Third Isaiah: Profile of a Pietistic Group in the Persian Epoch', *Proceedings of the Irish Biblical Association* 7 (1983), pp. 1-23.

'Old Testament Theology and the Jewish-Christian Connection', *JSOT* 28 (1984), pp. 3-15.

'The Documentary Hypothesis in Trouble', *Bible Review* 1.4 (1985), pp. 22-32.

'Yahweh and Other Deities: Conflict and Accommodation in the Religion of Israel', *Int* 40 (1986), pp. 354-66.

'The Mission of Udjahorresnet and those of Ezra and Nehemiah', *JBL* 106 (1987), pp. 409-21.

'Second Isaiah: Prophet of Universalism?', *JSOT* 41 (1988), pp. 83-103.

'Introduction to the Prophetic Books', in *Harper Bible Commentary* (ed. J.L. Mays *et al.*; San Francisco: Harper & Row, 1988), pp. 530-41.

'Anti-Semitism in Christianity: Response to Joel Carmichael', *Midstream* 34.4 (1988), p. 37.

'The Literary Evidence', in V. Tzaferis, *Excavations at Capernaum: Volume 1978–82* (Winona Lake, IN: Eisenbrauns in Association with Pepperdine University, 1989), pp. 201-11.

'A Theological Reading of Ezra–Nehemiah', *Proceedings of the Irish Biblical Association* 12 (1989), pp. 26-36.

'Biblical Studies (OT)', in *New Catholic Encyclopaedia Supplement 1978–88* (Palatine, IL: Jack Heraty and Associates in Association with the Catholic University of America, 1989), XVIII, pp. 42-46.

'Deuteronomy', in *New Jerome Biblical Commentary* (ed. R.E. Brown *et al.*; Englewood Cliffs, NJ: Prentice–Hall, 1990), pp. 95-109.

'Theological Honesty through History', in *Hebrew Bible or Old Testament: Studying the Bible in Judaism and Christianity* (ed. R. Brooks and J.J. Collins; Notre Dame: University of Notre Dame Press, 1990), pp. 147-52.

'My View: An Agenda for the 21st Century', *Bible Review* 6.1 (1990), pp. 12-13.

'The Sage, the Scribe and Scribalism in the Chronicler's Work', in *The Sage in Israel and the Ancient Near East* (ed. J.G. Gammie and L.G. Perdue; Winona Lake, IN: Eisenbrauns, 1990), pp. 307-15.

'A Jewish Sect of the Persian Period', *CBQ* 52 (1990), pp. 5-20.

'The Judge of All the Earth: Theodicy in the Midrash on Genesis 18:22-33', *JJS* 41 (1990), pp. 1-12.

'Temple and Society in Achaemenid Judah', in *Second Temple Studies. I. Persian Period* (ed. P.R. Davies; JSOTSup, 117; Sheffield: JSOT Press, 1991), pp. 22-53.

'The Social Context of the "Outsider Woman" in Proverbs 1–9', *Bib* 72 (1991), pp. 457-73.

'We Pay no Heed to Heavenly Voices', in *Scripture and Canon* (ed. P. Machinist; Detroit: Wayne State University Press, forthcoming).

'Wisdom in the Chronicler's Work', in *In Search of Wisdom: Essays in Memory of John G. Gammie* (ed. L. Perdue; Philadelphia: Westminster Press, forthcoming).

Works Translated

'1–2 Samuel', '1–2 Kings', '1–2 Chronicles', in *The Jerusalem Bible* (London: Darton, Longman & Todd, 1966).

N. Brox, *Understanding the Message of Paul* (Notre Dame: University of Notre Dame Press, 1968).

P. Bratsiotis, *The Greek Orthodox Church* (Notre Dame: University of Notre Dame Press, 1968).

R. Schnackenburg, *Christian Existence in the New Testament*, II (Notre Dame: University of Notre Dame Press, 1969).

INDEX OF REFERENCES

HEBREW BIBLE

JOURNAL FOR THE STUDY OF THE OLD TESTAMENT

Supplement Series